John Bigelow

France and the Confederate navy

1862-1868

John Bigelow

France and the Confederate navy
1862-1868

ISBN/EAN: 9783337057053

Printed in Europe, USA, Canada, Australia, Japan

Cover: Foto ©ninafisch / pixelio.de

More available books at **www.hansebooks.com**

FRANCE

AND

THE CONFEDERATE NAVY

1862–1868

AN INTERNATIONAL EPISODE

BY

JOHN BIGELOW

NEW YORK
HARPER & BROTHERS, FRANKLIN SQUARE
1888

Copyright, 1888, by HARPER & BROTHERS.

All rights reserved.

PREFACE.

At one stage of our civil war it seemed as though its fate was to be decided less by the belligerents than by the national powers on the other side of the Atlantic. The insurgents, in their desperation, were ready to make any sacrifice to secure their independence. They offered to Spain, as the price of recognition, to guarantee to her the possession of Cuba; to France, they offered to guarantee Maximilian's sovereignty in Mexico, and for the loan of a squadron of the emperor's navy several millions of dollars in cotton; while to England they offered yet greater temptations. It was even rumored that a restoration of British supremacy in the insurgent states would not have been esteemed too high a price to pay for the overthrow of the government at Washington. It was in one of these paroxysms of desperation that the agents of the Confederate States managed to tempt the Emperor of the French to authorize the construction in the dockyards of France of several vessels of war for the Confederate navy more formidable than any then afloat.

Had these vessels reached the coast of America, the territory of the United States might possibly now be under two or more independent governments; or, if under one, a widely different one from that under which we are now living or from any which our fathers designed for us. The history of that conspiracy and of the means by which the calamities with which it was so big were averted, invite the reader's attention in these pages.

The somewhat peculiar structure of this story requires a word of explanation. It has no pretension to the dignity of a history. The order in which events are presented is not such as the Muse of History would adopt; but it is the order in which they were disclosed to the writer. If this course has no other advantage, it spares me the necessity of treating events which are still in the crucibles of controversy and criticism; it allows me to confine my testimony to events of which I am in some respects the most competent surviving witness, and to present them in the order in which they were disclosed to me and to the government I represented. As the course of history is determined as well by what is not known as by what is known, I feel that I may render quite as substantial service by testifying to those matters only that fell within the sphere of my own observation and by implication of those which were concealed from me, as by a more ambitious work, which would involve the treatment of many matters of which I had no personal knowledge; of many which are still only partially disclosed, and of which others are competent to deal with as well or better than myself. I begin my story, therefore, with the beginning of my acquaintance with the plans of the Confederate States to procure ships of war in France, instead of beginning at the beginning of their operations there a year or more before, which would have been the historical order, and I proceed to throw such light as I have upon subsequent events only as it reached me. It is by following this order of development, which reveals what was not known as well as what was known by the Federal government from time to time, that its policy can be comprehended and the acts and omissions of its agents correctly appreciated. I venture to believe, therefore, that the lack of artistic merit in its arrangement will not impair whatever value, if any, this statement would otherwise have as a contribution towards a history of one of the most critical periods of our national existence.

The writer has endeavored to so perform what has seemed to be his duty, in a way to reopen no old wounds, to awaken no slumbering animosities, nor to shorten the mantle of charity which the wise and good of both sections of our country since the war have been diligently weaving over common errors and shortcomings.

CONTENTS.

PART I.

CHAPTER I.

A Mysterious Visitor and his Revelations.—The Imperial Government Compromised.—Iron-clads Building for the Confederates at Bordeaux and Nantes.—Captain Bullock's Confessions........Page 1

CHAPTER II.

Appeal from the Government of France to the People of France.—Remonstrances of Mr. Dayton.—Berryer's Opinion.............. 16

CHAPTER III.

An Instruction from Secretary Seward.—The French Press Forbidden to Publish Berryer's Opinion.—The Emperor's Address from the Throne.—The Corps Legislatif not Permitted to Discuss the Arman Amendment.—Protest from Mr. Seward..................... 28

CHAPTER IV.

The Press and the Imperial Ministers.—The *Opinion Nationale*.—The Mexican Loan Failure.—Imperial Sympathy with the Insurgents.—Embarrassment Resulting from the Exposure of the Conspiracy.—Delivery of the Iron-clads to the Insurgents Forbidden.—The Emperor Charged with Bad Faith by the Confederates........... 37

CHAPTER V.

The Plot to Secure One of the Iron-clads by a Fictitious Sale.—The Emperor Waiting for Lee to Take Washington to Recognize the Confederacy... 48

CONTENTS.

CHAPTER VI.

A Confederate Iron-clad Escapes.—Its Arrival on the French Coast.—Takes Refuge in Spain.—Watched by the United States Frigate *Niagara*.—Double Dealing of the Imperial Government.... Page 56

CHAPTER VII.

The Spanish Government Asked to Detain the *Stonewall*.—Commodore Craven's Embarrassment.—Report of the United States *Chargé d'Affaires* at Madrid.—The Career of the *Stonewall* Described by her Captain until her Final Surrender to the United States Authorities at Havana.—Vindication of Commodore Craven......... 70

CHAPTER VIII.

Prosecution of Arman to Recover the Price of the Confederate Steamers Sold to Foreign Powers.—Berryer's Argument.—Strange Rules of Evidence in French Courts.—Arman's Balance Sheet....... 90

PART II.

CHAPTER IX.

Slidell's First Interview with the Emperor.—Thouvenel Talks "Banalties."—Slidell Submits Benjamin's Proposal to Hire the Emperor's Fleet to Break the Blockade.—Proposes to Make Common Cause with the French in Mexico............................... 107

CHAPTER X.

Slidell's Second Interview with the Emperor.—Invites him again to Break the Blockade.—Proposes to Submit the Issue between the United States and the Confederate States to the Emperor, Knowing his Views.—Asks the Emperor not to Watch too Closely what was Going on in his Ship-yards.—The Confederate Government had no Objection to his Seizing St. Domingo....................... 126

CHAPTER XI.

The Emperor's Reasons for Refusing to Recognize the Confederate States.—Slidell Offers to Pledge the Confederate States to Guarantee Cuba to Spain.—The Emperor Preferred having the Whigs in Power in England to the Tories.—Refuses to Guarantee the Exit of the

Confederate Steamers unless their Destination was Concealed.—Roebuck's Proposal to Interview the Emperor.—The Emperor Orders Slidell's Son to be Received as a Pupil at St. Cyr....Page 139

CHAPTER XII.

Slidell's First Interview with Drouyn de Lhuys.—The Minister Declines to Express any Opinion about Recognizing the Confederate States.. 142

CHAPTER XIII.

Slidell's Second Interview with Drouyn de Lhuys.—The Emperor's Silence about American Affairs in his Address to the Chambers Excused.—Slidell's Note to the Emperor Requesting him to Order the Minister of Marine not to Interfere with the Sailing of the Rams Building for the Confederates.......................... 146

CHAPTER XIV.

Slidell's Third Interview with Drouyn de Lhuys.—Referred by him to the Minister of Marine for Information about the Rams.—Rouher Gives Assurance that the Rams may Leave when Finished.—Drouyn de Lhuys Refuses Permission to Advertise the Confederate Cotton Loan in France.—His Refusal Withdrawn by Order of the Emperor... 150

CHAPTER XV.

Slidell Advises against any more Attempts to Fit out a Navy in Europe.—Concludes that "the Weak have no Rights, the Strong no Obligations."—Gwin on his Way to Mexico with an Autograph Letter from the Emperor to the French Commander.—Secretary Benjamin Reviews the Conduct of the French Government.—Slidell Directed to Maintain "a Reserved Demeanor"...................... 159

CHAPTER XVI.

The Washington Government Charged with Bribery and Employing Spies.—Letters of Slidell and Benjamin.—Mason's Offer to Corrupt the Telegraph Company.—Edwin de Leon's Mission to "Enlighten Public Opinion in Europe" and Rig the Press.—Slidell's Effort to Tempt the Emperor with a Bribe.—Mason and Slidell Bull the Confederate Cotton Loan in the London Market at an Expense of over $6,000,000 in a Single Month........................... 167

CHAPTER XVII.

Further Communications from M. X.—Message from General Prim.—His Proposal to Sell Cuba for $3,000,000.—The Infante of Spain in the Intrigue .... Page 190

CHAPTER XVIII.

Conclusion 194

APPENDIX A.

No. 1.—Mémoire à Consulter 199
No. 2.—Consultation de M. Berryer 217

APPENDIX B.

Court-Martial of Commodore Craven 232

APPENDIX C.

The Minister of Justice to the American Minister 238

Index 241

PART I.

FRANCE

AND THE

NAVY OF THE CONFEDERATE STATES.

PART FIRST.

Chapter I.

A Mysterious Visitor and his Revelations.—The Imperial Government Compromised.—Iron-clads Building for the Confederates at Bordeaux and Nantes.—Captain Bullock's Confessions.

On the 10th of September, 1863, David Fuller, the messenger of the Paris Consulate, handed me the card of a stranger, who wished, he said, to see me personally. Permission granted, a man of middle age presently entered, and after closing the door carefully behind him proceeded to say that he had a communication to make of considerable importance to my government. He was a Frenchman of the Gascon type, small of stature, with glittering black eyes, and thick, coarse, jet-black hair, which had appropriated to itself most of his forehead; he was sober and deliberate of speech, as if he had been trained to measure his words and was accustomed to be held responsible for what he said.

I was not prepossessed by his appearance, perhaps because of my rather extensive experience of people continually presenting themselves at the Consulate in quest of a market for their suspicions, rumors, and imaginings, and who usually introduced themselves, like the person before me, as bearers of information of vital importance.

I asked him to be seated, and waited for him to proceed. He asked if I was aware that the Confederates were building war vessels in France. I replied that rumors of the kind had reached me, but as they came from or through wholly irresponsible sources, usually needy Confederate refugees, and had received no confirmation from our consuls at the ship-building ports, I had ceased to attach much importance to them. He proceeded to state as facts within his own knowledge that there were then building in the ports of Bordeaux and Nantes for account of the Confederate States of America several vessels, some of which were armor plated and rams, which together were to cost from twelve to fifteen millions of francs; that the engines for some of them were built and ready to be put in, and that for the armament of these vessels artillery and shells had also been ordered. I here remarked that no vessel of war could be built in France without the authorization of the French government. He replied that the official authorization for the construction, equipment, and arming of these vessels had already been issued from the Department of the Marine. I asked him if he meant seriously to affirm that the vessels he spoke of were building under an official authorization of the government. He reaffirmed his statement, and added further that he was prepared to prove it to my entire satisfaction.

I tried not to betray my sense of the supreme importance of this communication, which was too circumstantial and precise to be wholly imaginary, if possibly exaggerated. Besides, I had attached more importance than any one else seemed to, to rumors of the same nature which had reached me previously, simply for the reason that the difficulties which the Confederates had encountered in their efforts to recruit their navy in England made it seem not only natural but almost inevitable that they should transfer their preparations to a country the government of which was supposed to be in greater sympathy with their schemes, and where, under such circumstances, the courts of justice would have less power to annoy.

I said to my visitor, "Of course what you state is of grave importance to my government if it can be substantiated, but of none at all without proofs which cannot be disputed or explained away."

"Of course not," he replied.

"What kind of proofs can you furnish?" I asked.

"Original documents," he said; "and, what is more, I will engage that with my proofs in hand, you can effectually secure the arrest of the ships."

As the contractors, according to his statement, had already received an official authorization from the Department of Marine to execute their contract for the Confederates, I asked him why he supposed any proofs he might produce could change the destiny of the ships. He replied that the official authorization appeared on its face to have been procured through false representations.

He thereupon produced a certified copy of the government authorization and some half-dozen original letters and papers, showing, beyond a doubt, the substantial truth of his statements. These papers he proposed to leave with me and to wait upon me again on the Saturday following, the interval to be employed by him in procuring some supplementary proofs which he described to me. I could no longer resist the conclusion that my visitor, whom for greater convenience I will call Mr. X, was in earnest, and that he was in possession of, or controlled, evidence of which no time should be lost in securing possession. Before he left I asked him upon what conditions I was to receive this service at his hands, for there was not much ground for presuming that his zeal for our national unity was entirely disinterested. He said that of course the papers were not obtainable without some expense and much trouble, and that when the documents he proposed to furnish me had actually defeated the naval operations of the Confederates in France, he would expect 20,000 francs. I replied to him that that was a large sum of money, but that I could not say that it was too large until I had seen what he proposed to bring me as its equivalent. If, however, I decided to use the papers, he might rely upon being properly compensated. To a question of mine which implied some curiosity to know how these proofs got into his hands, he intimated that some of the parties concerned in building these vessels were not as earnest as Captain Bullock* to have them placed at his disposal. This was all his answer. He did not name any person nor seem inclined to be more explicit.

At the hour agreed upon on Saturday, the 12th, Mr. X reappeared with his supplementary proofs. These, with those already in my possession, were conclusive; nothing could have been more conclusive. The following autograph note from M. Arman, of Bordeaux, to M. Voruz, of Nantes, would alone have answered our purpose.

Arman to Voruz.
(Translation.)

"*Dear Mr. Voruz,*—I have received your letter of the 9th, and Bullock's check for 720,000 francs enclosed. I hasten to send you a receipt, and also, in accordance with your request, the papers which you have signed, in the hand of Bullock for the first payment of two ships of four hundred horse-power which I am building for account of the Confederates, simultaneously with those you are having built with Jollet & Babin and Dubigeon fils. I beg you to arrange with Mr. Bullock to finally reimburse us for the guarantee commissions we pay to Mr. Erlanger.

"Accept, etc.

"Arman."

Arman was the builder at Bordeaux with whom Captain Bullock had contracted for the construction of the ships referred to in the foregoing note. He was also said to be "solid" with the emperor, who

---

* The agent of the Navy Department of the Confederate government in Europe.

was anxious to encourage ship-building in France, as well as to discountenance Republicanism in America; and, finally, he was a member of the Corps Legislatif. M. Voruz was a large iron-founder and machinist at Nantes, and he was also a member of the Corps Legislatif. Both were devoted imperialists.

As time was of supreme importance to the Confederates, and as M. Arman could not undertake to deliver all of the ships required within the ten months stipulated for by his contract, he had arranged with M. Voruz, of Nantes, for the construction of part of them, he undertaking the rest and being responsible to the Confederates for all. Of course these facts only came to my knowledge later. At the time of which I am speaking, I knew nothing of the relations between Arman and Voruz beyond what was revealed in the papers submitted to me. While this letter was conclusive, at least, as to one of the parties to this contract, the following letter from Captain Bullock, which was next placed in my hands, was equally conclusive as to the other:

BULLOCK TO VORUZ.

"LIVERPOOL, *August* 12, 1863.

"I have received, Mr. Voruz, your letter of the 4th instant, with memoranda of prices of rifle cannon and accessories. I am unable to give you a direct and positive order for such cannon before learning from Captain Blakeley* how his *canon cerclé* has succeeded. Nevertheless, I should be pleased to treat with you,

---

* A noted manufacturer of ordnance having an office at Montpelier Square, Rutland Gate, London.

if we can agree with you upon the conditions; we will discuss them when I am at Nantes.

"It is my intention to confide my affairs to as few hands as possible, and I hope that we may agree upon all essential points, so that our relations may be extended even in case of peace. Our government will be obliged, no doubt, to apply to France for the construction of its engines, and so far as I am personally concerned I should be enchanted if the relations we have had together should lead in the future to still more considerable orders. I will thank you to inform me how the corvettes progress, and when the second payments will be due. I shall write you a week before my arrival at Nantes."

Mr. X next showed me Erlanger's guarantee, the cost of which Arman wished Voruz to persuade Bullock to assume.

Erlanger's Guarantee to Arman.

"Paris, *June* 9, 1863.

"*Mr. Arman*,—I engage to guarantee the two first payments for the ships which you are constructing for the Confederates for a commission of five per cent., which I shall retain out of funds which I have for you. I shall reserve to myself the privilege of declining to guarantee the last three fifths; but if I consent, my commissions on the sums guaranteed will not be more than three per cent. Accept, etc.,

"E. Erlanger."

The foregoing guarantee was the financial sequence of the following note from John Slidell, the Confederate Plenipotentiary at Paris, to Arman, which was next handed to me.

Let me observe that not long after these arrangements were consummated a son and partner of the subscriber to the above guarantee married a daughter of Mr. Slidell.

Slidell to Arman.

"Paris, *June* 6, 1863.

"*Mr. Arman,*—In consequence of the ministerial authorization which you have shown me and which I deemed sufficient, the contract of the 15th of April becomes binding.

"Accept, etc.   Slidell."

The authorization which is referred to in this note, and which Slidell "deemed sufficient," was issued by the Department of the Marine on the 6th of June in response to an application from M. Arman of the 1st of that month, of the tenor following:

Ministerial Authorization.

(Translation.)

"Bordeaux, *June* 1, 1863.

"*Mr. Minister,*—I request of your Excellency authority, in accordance with the royal ordinance of July 12, 1847, to equip with an armament of from twelve to fourteen thirty-pounders four steamships, now constructing, of wood and iron:

"Two in the ship-yards at Bordeaux;
"One by Messrs. Jollet & Babin at Nantes;
"One by Dubigeon at Nantes.

"These ships are destined by a foreign shipper to ply the Chinese and Pacific seas, between China, Japan, and San Francisco.

"Their special armament contemplates their eventual sale to the governments of China and Japan.

"The guns will be furnished by Mr. Voruz, Sr., of Nantes, and the accessory pieces, according to circumstances, at Bordeaux or Nantes.

"The export of these arms will only be delayed the time necessary for the construction of the ships, which are consigned to Messrs. A. Eymand and Delphin Henry, shippers, at Bordeaux, to whom, in 1859, I sent the steamer *Cosmopolite* under the English flag.

"The construction of these ships has been in progress since

the 15th of April last. I beg your Excellency will be good enough to accord to Mr. Voruz, as early as possible, the authorization which I ask, as prescribed by the royal ordinance of July 12, 1847. ARMAN."

The minister's reply to this application ran as follows:

(Translation.)

"MINISTRY OF MARINE, *June* 6, 1863.

"*Sir*,—I hasten to advise you in reply to your letter of the 1st instant, that I cheerfully (*volontiers*) authorize you to equip with an armament of twelve thirty-pound guns the four steamships now constructing of wood and iron at Bordeaux and Nantes. I will thank you to inform me, in time, when the ships will be ready for sea, that I may give the necessary instructions to the heads of the department in these two ports.

"COMTE P. DE CHASSELOUP-LOUBAT."

That a minister of marine was stupid enough to believe, for a moment, that any foreign shipper could be found to build, equip, and arm four or five first-class vessels of war, and take his chance of marketing them on the other side of the planet, was not supposable. It would be a wild enough scheme for any one to go to France for one such vessel on such a venture; it was yet more incredible that any foreign shipper could give an order to build several vessels of war and equip them in French ports at an expense of several millions of dollars —an event in itself quite without precedent in the history of France—without the emperor and his ministers knowing who the foreign shipper was. To know who ordered these ships was to know the service for which they were designed, and also to know that the destination assigned in the application and in the license was for purposes which the government could not publicly approve or avow, and in distinct and deliberate violation of the emperor's declaration of the 10th of June previous, which forbade "any Frenchman taking a commission for the armament of vessels of war for either of the two belligerents, or accepting letters of marque, or co-operating in any way whatsoever in the equipment or arming of any vessels of war or corsair of either belligerent." *

---

* The recent publication of Captain Bullock's "Secret Service of the Confederate States" in Europe shows that the Confederate agents, in their dealings with the Imperial government, made no secret of the unlawful purpose for which the authorization to build these ships had been solicited.

"When M. Arman applied to the Ministry of Marine and the Colonies," says the captain, "for the authorization to arm the ships, he stated precisely what it was previously understood by the Imperial government that he should state, namely, that the ships were intended for a line of packets between San Francisco, Japan, China, etc.; and that the armament was required for their protection against pirates in the Eastern seas, and, moreover, to fit the vessels for a possible sale to the Japanese or Chinese governments. M. Arman had been told that he must give a plausible reason for building such formidable ships, and that the government would not interfere with their despatch from France, or permit an inquisitive inquiry into their ultimate destination and purpose.

"The foregoing was exactly in accordance with their despatch from hints given to Mr. Slidell by persons in high positions who were in close and constant intercourse with the emperor. I have no means of knowing whether M. Drouyn de Lhuys had been informed of the arrangement with M. Arman, or the intimations conveyed to Mr. Slidell, but I have the original document, signed by M. Chasseloup-Loubat, Minister of Marine and of the Colonies, authorizing M. Arman to arm the ships. It will be perceived that the battery of each corvette was to have been

The evidence before me was conclusive that, unless the emperor himself had been deceived, which was hardly credible, he was treating us with duplicity; that he was hovering over us, like the buzzards in Jerome's famous picture over the exhausted camel in the desert, only deferring his descent until we should be too feeble to defend ourselves. This view is now fully confirmed, as far as the testimony of Captain Bullock can confirm it. The nature of the arrangement between the Confederate agents and the Imperial government, of which then, of course, I knew nothing, I will give as he professes to have understood it, and which I assume to be in conformity with the version of it which he received from Slidell, the agent of the Confederacy in Paris, and of Mason, the agent of the Confederacy in London:

---

twelve or fourteen *canons de trente*, and it will hardly be thought credible that the experts at the Ministry of Marine, or the officials who inspected the guns, were deceived as to the character of the ships, or that they ever thought such powerful armaments could have been intended for defence against Chinese pirates in the year 1863.

* * * * * * * *

"It will hardly be thought by any one that if the purpose had been to conceal from the French government the true destination of ships so wholly fit for war, and so manifestly unfit for commerce, the attempt to deceive would have been made through the transparent pretence that they were designed for a line of packets between San Francisco and China.*

---

* "The Secret Service of the Confederate States, or How the Confederate Cruisers were Equipped, by James D. Bullock, Naval Representative of the Confederate States in Europe during the Civil War." 2 vols. London, 1883.

"About the middle of March, 1863, Mr. Slidell sent the business agent of a large shipbuilder to inform me what his principal could undertake, and I went immediately to Paris to put affairs in such train that the work could be begun as soon as the financial arrangements were satisfactorily settled. Mr. Slidell made an appointment for a joint consultation between himself, the builder with whom he had already conferred, and me. The class of vessels and the armament did not require much consideration; the chief, and indeed the only important, points for serious deliberation were the terms of the neutrality proclamation and the probable chance of getting the ships to sea when completed.

"The shipbuilder who thus came forward to supply our want was M. Arman. His establishment was at Bordeaux, he had done much work for the French navy, was then building two iron-cased floating batteries, and a very large troop-ship for the government, and there could be no doubt that he had the plant and all the necessary staff and commercial credit to justify his undertaking large contracts for any description of ships. M. Arman was also a deputy in the Corps Legislatif for the Gironde, he had been personally decorated in his own shipyard at Bordeaux by the Emperor, and, during the whole period of the transactions which followed, he appeared to have no difficulty in obtaining personal interviews with the Minister of State, M. Rouher, and even with his imperial majesty himself.

"M. Arman stated that he had been confidentially informed by the Minister of State that the Emperor was willing for him to undertake the construction of ships for the Confederate government, and that when the vessels were ready to be delivered he would be permitted to send them to sea under the French flag to any point which might be agreed upon between him and the representative of the Confederate States.

"I mentioned to M. Arman that, building the ships with such an assurance from the government, it would not be necessary to practise any concealment as to their mere character and equipment, as it would soon be apparent that they were vessels intended not for commerce, but for war. There was no reason to suppose, I said, that the United States would be less desirous to prevent ships leaving French than English ports, for the service of the Confederate government, nor was it likely that their representatives would be less watchful in France than they were in England, and I suggested that, as soon as it became apparent that he was building vessels suitable for war, the United States Minister would learn the fact through his spies, and he would lay his suspicions before the Minister of Foreign Affairs, and I asked how he thought the matter would then be dealt with? He replied that the probability of such an inquiry had been fully considered, and he had been informed that if he would apply to the proper department for authorization to complete, arm, and despatch the ships for a specified purpose which was in itself lawful, the government would not force him to make any further or more specific explanations, but that he would be permitted to despatch them to the destination set out in the original application, on the plea that the government could not impede a legitimate branch of French trade. He furthermore said that he had informed the emperor that he purposed building the ships for trading between San Francisco, China, and Japan; that they would be clippers, having great speed both under canvas and steam, and would be armed for defence against pirates in the Eastern seas, and with the view to possible sale either to the Chinese or Japanese government. M. Arman assured us that the emperor fully understood the matter, and so did M. Rouher, and that there would be no difficulty in arranging all details with the several executive departments under whose supervision it would be necessary for him to act. He should simply state, without the slightest hesitation, the purpose for which he was building the ships, and ask for the necessary authorization in the usual formal matter-of-course way.

"I had no means of testing M. Arman in regard to his personal communications with the emperor and M. Rouher, but they confirmed the intimations that had been so confirmed to Mr. Slidell through persons of position who were in close relations with the imperial court, and who had inspired him with confidence by having communicated other information of approaching events which proved to be correct, and could not have been foreseen or obtained by clandestine means. Mr. Slidell was very confident that the policy of the Imperial government, and the purposes the emperor then had in view, were such as to render it very desirable that the Confederate States should be able to maintain their position, and he had reason to believe that the Confederate States would be able to maintain their position, and he had also reason to believe that the hesitation of England alone prevented their recognition by France.

"My course under the circumstances was clear. My instructions were to keep as many cruisers at sea as possible, and I could only use my own judgment to the extent of determining the best class of vessel, the places where they could be built with the least fear of seizure or detention, and the mode of putting them in commission as Confederate ships-of-war afterwards. The result of the consultation with Mr. Slidell was, that I proceeded to Bordeaux, inspected M. Arman's premises, and finally arranged with him all the particulars for four clipper corvettes of about fifteen hundred tons, and four hundred horse-power, to be armed with twelve or fourteen 6-inch rifled guns—the *canon rayé de trente* of the French navy, that gun being adopted because of the facility of having the batteries constructed in France from the official patterns." *

I was next handed a paper purporting to be a copy of the contract between Bullock and Arman.

As the plans and specifications for the ships underwent some modifications, it is not worth while to recite the original contract here.

The plan finally decided upon is thus set forth by Captain Bullock: †

"The design finally selected was for a vessel of the following dimensions and steam-power, the measurements reduced to English standards. Length between perpendiculars, 171 feet 10 inches; breadth outside of armor, 32 feet 8 inches; mean draught with 220 tons of coal, battery and all stores on board, 14 feet and 4 inches. Engine three hundred horse-power nominal, twin screws, working separately so as to be capable of a counter motion at the same time. The armor-plating was 4¾ inches amidships, tapering gradually to 3½ at the extremities, in single plates, manufactured by Messrs. Petin-Gaudet & Co., at Rive de Gier. The details of specification for ship and engines provided for

---

* Bullock's "Secret Service of the Confederate States," vol. ii., pp. 25-28.   † Ibid., vol. ii., pp. 33-34.

THE SHIPS.

everything to be of the best quality, conforming in dimensions and material to the types of the Imperial navy, and the guaranteed speed was not less than twelve knots in smooth sea with 220 to 290 tons of coal. In calculating the displacement, 100 tons was allowed for guns and ordnance stores, and the arrangement was to have one heavy gun forward, to be mounted in a fixed armor turret so as to be fired in the line of the keel or on either bow, and two 6-inch rifled guns in an after turret or casemate. The bow-guns were to be 300-pounders of the Armstrong pattern, and they were made to M. Arman's order by Sir William Armstrong, at Elswick. The lighter guns were to be made in France."*

---

* Two 70-pounder Armstrong guns were afterwards substituted.

Chapter II.

Appeal from the Government of France to the People of France.—Remonstrances of Mr. Dayton.—Berryer's Opinion.

I FELT that I now held in my hands all the proofs that could be of any use in changing the destination of these ships, four of which at least threatened to be more formidable on the high seas than any ships in our navy, and each of which, I supposed, to be capable of entering the harbor of New York and of laying the vast wealth of our commercial metropolis under contribution with comparative impunity.

I had, *First*, the letters of the ship-builders at Bordeaux and Nantes, acknowledging that they were building together four vessels-of-war, of the most formidable description, "for the Confederate States."

Second. A copy of their application for a license to build these ships, which was based entirely on false representations.

Third. An official copy of the license, which showed, beyond any reasonable doubt, that the emperor and his Minister of Marine, if no other members of his ministry, were presumptively accomplices in the fraud.

Fourth. I had a letter from the agent of the

Confederates, stating that these ships were building for them under his directions; and,

Finally, I had the official letter of the diplomatic representative of the Confederate States, approving of the contract and guaranteeing the price of them.

Thus the whole ground was covered, and covered too by testimony which required no supplementation; testimony before which, at sight, the Minister of Foreign Affairs must bow or take an attitude of unequivocal hostility to the United States.

The documents furnished me by Mr. X, first and last, reached to twenty-one in number, some original and some authentic copies, all of which I promptly transmitted to Mr. Dayton, then at the head of our legation in Paris, by whom they were submitted to the French Minister of Foreign Affairs.

M. Drouyn de Lhuys was surprised and vexed, but cautious. He saw in these papers new evidence of what he had enough already—that he had but a limited share of the emperor's confidence. He knew that Chasseloup, the Minister of Marine, was the most unlikely of men to have signed the "authorization" exhibited to him by Mr. Dayton, except at the instance of some power superior to his own. He asked time to look into it, and, of course, showered protestations that the neutrality of the Imperial government should not be compromised. He dared not promise the obvious and only just and lawful relief which the situation called for, for he was not sure that such a promise could be kept; he, therefore, did all and the best a minister could do, who was not ready to resign his portfolio rather than be made a party to a shabby conspiracy against a power to which he was daily making professions of friendship.

We did not have to await the teachings of subsequent events to be convinced that the Imperial government was tolerating, if not encouraging, the operations of Slidell and Bullock, and that so long as the result of the struggle beyond the Atlantic was so uncertain that the accession of one of M. Arman's rams might suffice to determine it in favor of the Confederates, little heed would be given to Mr. Dayton's remonstrances. It would never do to leave the disposition of these ships to the secret and tedious processes of diplomacy. In three months' time, if the work were permitted to go on—and under one pretext or another the government refused to stop it—they might be afloat. The government was obviously disposed to afford them every facility, which could be permitted without compromising the letter of its engagements with the United States, to embark upon their work of devastation; nor was it to be hoped for, much less expected, that respect for those relations would have any weight should a serious disaster befall the Union arms. The only way that remained to reinforce the weapons of diplomacy and to make the emperor respect his neutral engagements was for us to take an appeal, if we could, to the only power of which he stood in awe. How this appeal should be made, under a despotic government like that under which France was groaning at this time, was the problem. The press was enslaved, the government hostile, and the people quite ignorant of the schemes which seemed to be maturing at the Tuileries. After a careful survey of the whole ground, it was finally decided to procure, if possible, the best legal authority in France to denounce the contracts of Bullock and Arman as both unlawful and criminal. Fortified with such an opinion, we counted upon getting the facts before the European public through the Corps Legislatif, by forcing discussions in that body where the government would labor under the great disadvantage of having no resource but silence or retreat. The press would give to the debates in the national legislature a publicity which it would not be permitted to give to the same facts emanating from any other source.

Among the members of the French bar there was one whose position was unique, and whose alliance I determined, if possible, to secure at once. This was M. Berryer.* For more than twenty years he had been the recognized head of his profession, and at this time was a member of the Corps Legislatif— a by no means secondary qualification for usefulness to us in this crisis. He was a Legitimist in politics, which, in itself, gave him more influence with the Chamber in those days than if he had been a Republican—as were most of the opposition with whom, on all party questions, he habitually voted.

The opposition at this time was fortunate enough to embrace five or six of the best debaters not only in that but in any other legislative body in the

---

* Antoine Pierre Berryer, born, 1790; died, 1869.

world. There were besides M. Berryer, M. Thiers, M. Jules Favre, Eugene Pelletan, Emile Olivier, and M. Ferry. Either one of these was a more effective popular debater than any of the deputies of the administration. But of all the members of his parliament there was no one whose criticism the emperor would make greater sacrifices to avoid, or whose word in behalf of the American Republic would carry as much weight with the people, as that of the most eminent and most eloquent of the living representatives of the Bourbon dynasty.

I at once took measures to put myself in relation with M. Berryer. Finding he had not yet returned from his summer vacation, I made known to my friend, M. Henri Moreau, also an advocate and professionally associated with M. Berryer, my desire to pay my respects to his distinguished colleague, and in a day or two I received an invitation, of which I promptly availed myself, to visit him at Augerville, his country place. In the course of my visit, after referring to the somewhat tense relations which had been growing up between his government and mine as my excuse for mixing a little business with pleasure, I called his attention to the Imperial declaration of neutrality,* which by a sin-

---

* The imperial declaration was as follows:

"PARIS, 10th June.

"DECLARATION.

"His Majesty of the French, taking into consideration the peaceful relations existing between France and the United States of America, has resolved to maintain a strict neutrality in the

gular coincidence appeared in the *Moniteur* the very same week in which the authorization to build the Confederate ships was accorded by the Minister of

struggle between the Union government and the States which pretend to form a special confederation.

"Consequently, his majesty, in consideration of article 14 of the ordinance of the marine, of the month of August, 1861; of article 3, of the law of the 10th of April, 1825; articles 84 and 85 of the penal code; 65, and following ones, from the decree of the 24th of March, 1852; 313, and following ones, of the maritime penal code, and the article 21 of the code Napoleon,

"Declares:

"1. It will not be permitted to any ship-of-war or corsair of one or other of the belligerents to enter and sojourn with their captures in our ports or harbors for more than twenty-four hours, excepting in cases of distress.

"2. No sale of captured objects can take place in our said ports or harbors.

"3. It is forbidden to any Frenchman to take orders from either party to arm ships-of-war, or to accept letters-of-marque for privateering, or to concur in any manner in the equipment or armament of a ship-of-war or corsair, of either party.

"4. It is likewise forbidden to any Frenchman, residing either in France or foreign countries, to enroll himself, or to take service in the army, or either on land or on board vessels-of-war or corsairs, of either belligerent.

"5. Frenchmen, residing in France or in foreign countries, will likewise abstain from any act which, committed in violation of the laws of the empire or of the rights of nations, might be considered as an act hostile to either party and contrary to the neutrality which we have resolved to observe.

"All persons offending against the prohibitions and recommendations contained in this declaration will be prosecuted in conformity with the provisions of the 10th of April, 1825, and articles 84 and 85 of the penal code: subject, however, to the said offenders of the provisions of article 21 of the code Napoleon, and of articles 65, and the following, of the decree of the 24th of March, 1852, in relation to the merchant marine, number

Marine. When he had run his eye over it—he had not seen it before—I told him somewhat in detail of the Confederate operations at Bordeaux and Nantes, of the contract approved by Slidell, and the payments guaranteed by Erlanger.

He expressed considerable astonishment, and finally said emphatically that, if the emperor permitted the contract of Arman with Bullock to be executed it would be only because he had determined to abandon his attitude of neutrality, for there could be no doubt that the vessels constructing under that contract fell within the restrictions of his declaration of neutrality. But, he added, in a half-angry tone, nothing can be done in the courts that does not suit the emperor. He then launched out into a thrilling enumeration of the grievances under which his countrymen were groaning, "so humiliating to an intelligent people." They are kept in dense ignorance, he added, of what it does not suit the government to have them know; the journals are told what they may and may not say; the foreign press is sifted of everything calculated to open the nation's eyes, and even the courts of justice are servile ministers of the Imperial policy.

313, and the succeeding provisions of the penal code for the marine force.

"His majesty declares further that every Frenchman who shall not conform to the preceding directions shall have no claim to any protection from his government against any act or measure whatsoever which the belligerents may do or decree against him. "NAPOLEON.

"The Minister of Foreign Affairs,
"E. THOUVENEL."

Having satisfied myself as to the main object of my visit, that Berryer's sympathies were cordially with us, that he had neither professional nor political reasons for declining to use our ammunition against the common enemy, and that a professional appointment must be made with him for more definite and practical results, we went for our hats to take a stroll through his grounds. He paid little attention to the familiar beauties of nature which were dividing with him my interest and attention, but seemed absorbed with the questions to which the information I had communicated had given additional importance.

He deplored the Mexican expedition, which he said he could not comprehend; neither could he comprehend the emperor's passion for expeditions to the ends of the earth, which were exhausting the energies of France, without giving her wealth or glory. He seemed surprised and incredulous when I told him that I had information which led me to believe that the Archduke Maximilian would accept the crown of Mexico. He asked if the uncle, of Belgium, would approve of such an arrangement. I gave my reasons for thinking that any objections King Leopold might have entertained had been overcome. He said he had known the archduke personally; that he was *un esprit vague*, and was no doubt influenced through some of the infirmities of his character to yield to this temptation; "but," he asked, with some vehemence, "what is the good of all this to France?"

"That she may collect the seven hundred thousand

francs that are owing to her citizens in Mexico," I answered, with affected gravity.

"Yes," said he, with a grim smile, "to fill the pockets of speculators."

His expression then becoming more serious, he said that he feared that the Mexican enterprise was destined to embroil France with the United States, which he thought would be a result every way to be deplored. He then asked, with increased earnestness, what were our chances of maintaining the Union. I recapitulated the familiar reasons on which all loyal Americans nourished their faith; spoke of our marvellous artillery, of the one hundred war-vessels we were building, and the inconvenience they might prove to England's commerce if she violated her neutral obligations.

"But," said he, interrupting me, "how about *our* commerce? would we not suffer equally?"

I replied that France had comparatively little oceanic commerce. He shrugged his shoulders, and said, "How lucky we have no commerce!" and then he told the story of a steady-going shop-keeper in the time of the first revolution who comforted himself with the reflection that, while many of his friends and neighbors were in a good deal of trouble, he had a place in the National Guard; that the duty of patrolling the streets at night was not very hard, and, to crown his good luck, there was no business doing, *point du commerce.*

"So we," said Berryer, "shall be fortunate, I suppose, having no commerce, if we stumble on a war, to keep us occupied till our business revives."

He said he could no longer stand the way things were going on. Though an old man, he was determined to do what he could to make the nation comprehend its position. He went on to say that there was a very large number of *soi-disant* Imperialists who were dissatisfied with the Mexican expedition, and who thought just as he did about recognizing the Confederate organization in America, but who, nevertheless, would not vote against the government. The reason they gave to him for this refusal was, that a defeat of the government would bring on a crisis, ruin the public credit, and then would come all the evils, tried and untried, which usually follow in the train of revolutions in France.

When I said that I had lost no opportunity with my government and compatriots to cultivate the friendly dispositions which I found everywhere among the French people for our republic, he said:

"You are very right to do so; in this business the people and the government are quite distinct. The French people are indisposed to take any steps unfriendly to the United States. Unfortunately the emperor has one great advantage over us French people. He can pursue his plans steadily, and without being led aside by his *amour propre*, whereas we French people always make our interests secondary where our national pride is involved. In that way he is leading us a chase whither nobody seems to know but himself; and before we are aware of it, or can help ourselves, he may get our vanity on his side."

Of England and of her policy towards the United

States as well as towards France he spoke in a tone of extreme bitterness. He denounced the Anglo-French alliance, said it had been fatal to every sovereign in France who had embraced it, that it had brought Charles X. and Louis Philippe to grief, and that in the end he believed it would prove equally disastrous to the emperor. It certainly would if it should lead him into any combination against the United States. He then remarked that, as I might suppose from his past political associations, he favored the policy of Louis XVI. towards America, and he felt that the substantial interests of France were identified with our unity and strength.

I left him perfectly satisfied that, what with his prejudices—shall I call them—against the Imperial government, his reverence for the traditions of his party and his respect for national rights, there was no danger, to say the least, of his giving, consciously, any aid or comfort to our enemies.

Immediately upon my return to Paris I proceeded to make up a case for his opinion and sent it to him, with all the documentary evidence in my possession.

Meantime, under instructions from Washington, Mr. Dayton had formally remonstrated with the Imperial government for permitting its ports to be made the bases of warlike operations against the United States. In describing one of his interviews with the Minister of Foreign Affairs about this time Mr. Dayton wrote to Mr. Seward:

"M. Brouyn de Lhuys seems to be quite restive under this recent and constant use of the French ports by the Confederates. He says it cannot have resulted from accident, but that it is intended to compromise his government. I told him that this was doubtless so, when he added that they would not be compromised; that they meant to remain neutral. He said that if there was any person to whom he might properly address himself he would give them to understand that their action upon this subject was disagreeable."

Towards the end of November I received M. Berryer's opinion. It was all that we could have wished. It filled about thirty foolscap pages. After reciting the facts, it set forth the provisions of laws and decrees which had been violated, then the parties inculpated by the operations at Bordeaux and Nantes, and finally the courses of procedure by which they could be punished.*

---

* For the text of this opinion see Appendix A, No. 1.

Chapter III.

An Instruction from Secretary Seward.—The French Press Forbidden to Publish Berryer's Opinion.—The Emperor's Address from the Throne.—The Corps Legislatif not Permitted to Discuss the Arman Amendment.—Protest from Mr. Seward.

How to get Mr. Berryer's opinion and the facts which it recited before the public was the next question, and one not easy of answer. It was idle to ask the hospitality of any administration journals for such a document, and the penalties for publishing anything not acceptable to the government—this certainly would not be acceptable—were so very serious that I had little hope of success with the journals of the opposition. There was one print, however, upon which I was encouraged to make the experiment. The *Opinion Nationale* was an opposition paper of Republican tendencies, and commonly regarded as the organ of Prince Napoleon, who, in those days, affected popular principles, at least so far as hostility to the occupants of the Tuileries was a popular principle. The editor, M. Gueroult, was an accomplished man, and, after the *Debats*, his paper of all the opposition journals then enjoyed rather the largest share of public esteem. Its American department, too, was edited by a gentleman who was in fullest sympathy with the Union cause, and with whom I was in almost daily communication. Through him I sent to M. Gueroult a copy of M. Berryer's "consultation," and authorized him to say that I would be very much gratified to see it at length in the columns of his journal. I received a prompt assurance that it would appear immediately, and I proceeded to make arrangements for a liberal distribution of it, not only in France, but throughout Europe; but M. Gueroult as well as I had reckoned without our host. The "consultation" was all in type, and ready to go upon the press, when notice arrived from the Minister of the Interior that its publication could not be allowed. Though disappointed, I was not surprised, for I was already familiar with the difficulty of getting anything printed in Paris that was not likely to prove acceptable to the government. I took my revenge in mentioning the existence of such a document, and its suppression by the imperial censor, wherever and whenever I met any one by whom the bearing and significance of these facts would be appreciated. I knew that the suppression of an opinion by Berryer on an international question did not need the press to get it into circulation, though it might, to secure the advantages of a public discussion. About this time Mr. Dayton's remonstrances were effectually reinforced by an admirable "instruction" from Mr. Seward, bearing date December 17, and written with Paris dates before him to November 17. In this despatch he said:

> "You will persevere in these remonstrances if occasion shall warrant, and represent to M. Drouyn de Lhuys that for more

than two years this government has borne, but has never acquiesced in, a policy of France and Great Britain in which they have recognized as a naval belligerent a domestic insurrection in this country which has not held nor had a port or harbor, either in the region it claims or elsewhere; all of whose ships are built, manned, and equipped in the waters of Great Britain and France themselves, and all of whose nautical proceedings are conducted either in those waters or on the high seas, as an outlaw from their own country and from all other civilized states. These proceedings have been the subject of unremitting complaints and remonstrances.

"For all the loss and damages which the citizens of the United States have sustained by the depredations of the vessels in question, the United States, as they believe justly, hold the governments of the countries from which they have proceeded responsible, whenever they have been duly forewarned and have omitted proper measures to prevent the departure of said hostile expeditions. During all this time we have been at peace with France and Great Britain. We have practised absolute non-interference between them and their enemies in war, and have even lent them the advantages of counsel with moral influence, to enable them to attain, without dishonor, the advantages of peace. We have excused the unkindness of which we have complained, on the ground that our own disloyal citizens, whom we could not effectually control, have been active and skilful in misleading public opinion in regard to the merits and probable results of our civil war.

"The evil, nevertheless, is becoming very serious, and is rapidly alienating the national sentiments of the United States. Our commerce is forced to seek protection under the flags of the very governments which afford the shelter of which we complain to the enemies engaged in devastating it. We fully believe that in like circumstances neither France nor Great Britain would endure such injuries as we are suffering through the policy they have established, unless, indeed, like the United States, they were at the same moment engaged in a formidable war, either at home or abroad. The political drama is inconstant; the scene may soon change. We may, at no distant day be at peace; and in the chances of the hour, European maritime powers may become belligerents. Is it wise to leave open between them and the United States questions which, in such an unfortunate conjuncture, would produce confusion with regard to our own practice of neutral rights."*

Early in January an opportunity for getting our case before the public presented itself, which promised to be even more auspicious than that which had measurably failed. M. Arman offered an amendment to the address of the emperor in the Corps Legislatif, by which the Imperial government was recommended to encourage the peace-at-any-price party in the United States, and by all means in its power to discourage the further prosecution of the war. This amendment ran as follows:

"We are united in the hope of seeing realized the good results foreseen by your majesty, and we pray that a friendly mediation may finally accomplish the reconciliation of the various states of the American Union, for which the interests of the people and of European commerce more loudly call."

I immediately called upon M. Berryer and told him of Arman's amendment, which he had not noticed, and to which, singularly enough, no allusion had been made by any Paris journal, a silence which could not have been accidental. I remarked to M. Berryer that, according to the best information I had been able to obtain, M. Arman intended to call up his motion in about eight or ten days, and I suggested that while he should be on his feet, an admirable opportunity would be presented to some member to ask whether the vessels he was building at Bordeaux were calculated or designed to pro-

---

* Diplomatic Correspondence, 1864-5, part iii. p. 7.

mote the kind of peace which he was, by his resolution, commending the government to cultivate. Such an inquiry, I suggested, would put M. Arman on his purgation; would furnish the opportunity of bringing before the country his and its unlawful relations with the Confederates, in such a way as to bring on a general discussion of the subject, and, I hoped, compel the government to respond to Mr. Dayton's remonstrances a little more categorically and promptly. M. Berryer thought well of the suggestion, but he said it would not do for a deputy to proceed upon knowledge obtained from the documents I had exhibited to him until they had been published, and in some way authenticated, so as not to expose the deputy who should make the interpellation to the necessity of revealing the source of his information. I told him that many of the facts had already appeared in the papers, of which I would furnish him copies, and that I would endeavor to persuade M. Gueroult to get the rest in one way or another into the columns of the *Opinion Nationale.* I at the same time directed his attention to the joint application of the French and English government made in 1854, to the government of the United States to join in an engagement not to equip vessels to prey upon the commerce of their respective countries in time of war, an engagement which Arman had audaciously invoked in behalf of his amendment. I at the same time gave him the points made on that subject in the following extract from a letter I had received not long before from Mr. Cobden:

"In 1854, on the breaking out of the Crimean war, a communication was sent by England and France to the American government, expressing a confident hope that it would, in the spirit of just reciprocity, give orders that no privateer under Russian colors shall be equipped, or victualled, or admitted with its prizes in the ports of the United States, etc. It has occurred to me to call your attention to this, although I dare say it has not escaped Mr. Dayton's recollection. But I should be curious to know what answer the French government would now make if its own former language was quoted, against the course now being taken at Brest, in repairing, and, I suppose, victualling the *Florida*. If the answer be that this vessel is not a privateer, but a regularly commissioned ship-of-war, then I think the opportunity should not be lost to put on record a rejoinder to this argument showing the futility of the Declaration of Paris against privateering; for, if a vessel sailing under a form of authority issued by Jefferson Davis, and called a 'commission,' can do all the mischief to your merchant vessels which another would do carrying another piece of paper called a letter-of-marque, it is obvious that the renunciation of privateering by the Paris Congress is a mere empty phrase, and all the boasted gain to humanity is nothing but a delusion, if not a hollow subterfuge.

"I think it might be well if Mr. Dayton were to take this opportunity of justifying the policy of the United States, in refusing to be a party to the Declaration of Paris, unless private property at sea was exempt from capture by armed ships of all kinds. The argument would be valuable for reproduction at a future time, when the question of belligerent rights comes up again for discussion."

By the introduction of this topic into the debate, it was suggested that it would broaden the issue, increase the difficulties of evading a discussion, compel the government either to annul the contracts of Arman with the Confederates or disclose its purposes and expose the hollowness of the so-called Paris Declaration for which the Imperial government and press had taken to themselves much credit at our expense. M. Berryer seemed to fall in with these views entirely, and at his request I lost no time in furnishing him with all the materials likely to be required for the proposed interpellation.

Meantime, on the 1st of February, 1864, Mr. Dayton, in pursuance of an intimation from Washington, addressed to the Minister of Foreign Affairs a formal protest against the facilities extended to the Confederates for fitting and arming vessels in French ports to prey upon our commerce. On the same day Mr. Seward wrote Mr. Dayton as follows:

"Your proceeding in giving notice to the French government that the United States will feel themselves entitled and obliged to look to that government for indemnity for the injuries she may produce, is approved. It will be necessary that you proceed one step further, and inform M. Drouyn de Lhuys that this decision of the French government, co-operating with other causes, will be a trial of friendship of this country towards France for which, after the protests you have made, not this government, but that of the emperor, will be responsible."*

Three days after Mr. Dayton's protest was handed to M. Drouyn de Lhuys they met at the Foreign Office, when M. Drouyn de Lhuys said that Arman (the builder of those iron-clad rams at Bordeaux) had just informed him that he had sold them to the Danish government, but before he, M. Drouyn de Lhuys, acted upon that assumption, this government would have the best and most satisfactory evidence of this statement. "At present," adds

---

* Dip. Cor. 1864–5. p. 28.

Mr. Dayton, "he does not consider the statement of the fact to me as official, but says he will make it as soon as he shall receive the necessary proof. In the meantime, I shall write to Mr. Wood, our Minister at Copenhagen, to put the facts in an authentic shape."*

The doubt which M. Drouyn de Lhuys expressed to Mr. Dayton about the Arman statement had an importance which could scarcely have been suspected by Mr. Dayton. It was a falsehood; Arman knew it was a falsehood, and he was no doubt sent by some one to tell the falsehood to M. Drouyn de Lhuys with the expectation that it would be used by that minister to quiet the apprehensions of Mr. Dayton until the time—then supposed to be not far distant—when the steamers would be at sea and his remonstrances would trouble no one but M. Drouyn de Lhuys, who was to be left in as good a shape as possible for insisting that he could not help it. M. Drouyn de Lhuys knew very well that such a statement should have reached him through the Minister of Marine and not through the one party who had the largest pecuniary interest in deceiving him.

While absorbed in my preparations for the Arman amendment, a paragraph copied from the *Morning Star* of London appeared in the *Moniteur*, which stated that the government had withdrawn the authorization which had been given to Arman for the construction of the Confederate ships. As

---

* Dip. Cor. 1864–5, p. 80.

this was not an official statement of the *Moniteur*, I was uncertain whether to regard it as another blind to quiet our apprehensions or as an unofficial way of announcing an event to which the government did not care to give unnecessary *éclat*.

When the time arrived that Arman was expected to call up his motion, I watched the official reports of the legislative debates from day to day, but found no allusion to the subject. At last I instituted some inquiries through one of the deputies, and ascertained that when that amendment had been reached in the order of business, it was passed *sub silentio*, doubtless at the instance of the Duc de Morny, who was the presiding officer of the Corps Legislatif. The government had evidently become aware there was danger ahead, that it had gone far enough in that direction, and that it would not be prudent to allow a discussion of such an inflammatory nature, at least until the fortunes of the Confederates looked more encouraging than they did at that time. This was the first and a by no means insignificant indication that the government was on the retreat.

The work on the ships continued, however; the force somewhat reduced, it is true, but that might have been due to the scarcity of money with the Confederates rather than to a change of policy in the government. We could learn nothing that justified a relaxation of our exertions. It was evident that publicity was what the government dreaded, therefore publicity was our most effective weapon.

Chapter IV.

The Press and the Imperial Ministers.—The 'Opinion Nationale.' —The Mexican Loan Failure.—Imperial Sympathy with the Insurgents.—Embarrassments Resulting from the Exposure of the Conspiracy.—Delivery of the Iron-clads to the Insurgents Forbidden.—The Emperor Charged with Bad Faith by the Confederates.

M. GUEROULT, the editor of the *Opinion Nationale*, was in sympathy with the Unionists, and none the less so because of the unreasonable interference of the government with his publication of Berryer's opinion. I went to see him again myself, and satisfied him that we were fighting his battle as well as our own; that we were not appealing from France, but to France, and finally urged him to let the public into our confidences as far as he prudently could. He could not resist the temptation, and the consequence was an article in the *Opinion* entitled "*Les Corsairs du Sud*," in which both M. Arman and the government were indirectly charged with and convicted of a conspiracy against the very existence of a friendly power.

A few days before the article appeared, M. Gueroult sought an interview with both Arman and Rouher* to give them an opportunity of correcting

---

* The Minister of State; practically the Prime-Minister.

his impressions if they were erroneous. Of this interview a member of the staff of the *Opinion Nationale* furnished me with the following account written or dictated by Gueroult himself.

"On Wednesday, the 27th of April, M. Gueroult went to M. Arman in the Corps Legislatif with the proof of the article '*Les Corsairs du Sud*,' when the following conversation in substance occurred :

"M. GUEROULT. 'As you are my colleague in this body, I am unwilling to publish an article which formulates a grave accusation against you without advising you of its tenor. My object is to give you the means of defending yourself if you have a serious defence. What I wish is light, not scandal.

"M. ARMAN reads the article, appears much excited, and says : 'That is all old; the proceedings exposed occurred in 1863; all is changed since then.'

"M. GUEROULT. 'Have you, or have you not been building for the Confederates ?'

"M. ARMAN. 'Yes; but there is nothing now between the Confederates and me ; I have very large interests compromised which I am seeking to protect, and I am trying to sell to some government.'

"M. GUEROULT. 'Of two things one, either you must give me authentic, indisputable proofs that these ships are not for the Confederates, or I must publish.'

"M. ARMAN. 'I am at this moment negotiating with M. Rosales, acting as the agent for the government of Chili.'

"M. GUEROULT. 'If you do not give me the proof which I ask of you, I shall make every effort by publication or otherwise to prevent these ships from sailing. I do not wish that, to promote any private interests, our relations with the United States should be compromised. I shall publish.'"

M. Gueroult then sought the Minister of State, and laid the subject before him as he had done before M. Arman. M. Rouher pretended to be greatly astonished, said he would have an interview with M. Drouyn de Lhuys and with M. Chasseloup-Loubat on the following day, after which he would be prepared to satisfy M. Gueroult. It was then agreed to delay the publication of the article until M. Rouher should have an opportunity of communicating with these gentlemen. The details of that interview were set forth to Mr. Seward in the following letter:

BIGELOW TO SEWARD.

"(*Confidential*.)

"PARIS, *May* 3, 1864.

"*My dear Sir*,—I sent you by the last mail a copy of the *Opinion Nationale* of Saturday, 30th of April, containing the article on the Confederate steamers building in France. M. Gueroult asked M. Rouher, a few hours before the paper was to appear, for his answer proffered two days previous on behalf of the government to the implications of the article. M. Rouher replied that he had spoken to the Minister of Foreign Affairs and the Minister of Marine, whom the subject more particularly concerned, and he said they were occupied with the subject and would do whatever was proper to be done, etc. M. Gueroult replied that he must have something more definite than that, and so they parted and the article appeared.

"The next day M. Boudet, the Minister of the Interior, sent for M. Gueroult, scolded him for devoting so much space in his paper to the prejudice of the ship-building interests of France, which the government was trying in every way to encourage, and said that M. Arman threatened to proceed against the government in the courts if it interfered with his ships which were built for commercial purposes. M. Gueroult replied that M. Arman had no case at law; that he was a liar and the truth was not in him; that he pretended without a shadow of foundation to be building these ships first for one government, then for another; that it was the duty of the government at all risks to arrest the vessels, which certainly would compromise the friendly relations of France with the United States if they should escape, and that the government should have no difficulty in choosing between the hostility of M. Arman and the hostility of the United States.

"The following day M. Boudet sent again for M. Gueroult and went over the same ground, showing the greatest solicitude to prevent any further discussion of the matter. Meantime he had made use of the ample means in his hands for securing that result by notifying the official journals that it was the pleasure of the government that no allusion should be made to the subject in any way whatever, and by circulating the report among the opposition prints that M. Arman had instituted legal proceedings against M. Gueroult for what he had already printed. Hence the utter and absolute silence of the city press upon this matter, which, however, has produced a profound sensation in the Corps Legislatif and disturbed the government, as I have explained.

"In order to be ahead of the government I sent a copy of the *Opinion* the evening it appeared to Montagnie [our consul at Nantes], requesting him to have it at once in the *Phare et Loire*.* It appeared there in full the next day, so that the necessary publicity is now assured to it. What the effect will be I am unable to say, but it is the opinion of persons more competent than myself to judge that the government will be compelled to abandon the protection of Messrs. Arman and Voruz, and put themselves right, very soon, before the Corps Legislatif and the country.

"I told you that the Mexican loan had proved a failure, but the failure was more complete than I had suspected. It is the custom here, when subscribing for government loans, for the subscriber to put down his name for three or four times more than he wants, as the excess subscribed over the sum required has always rendered it necessary to cut down each individual subscription about in that proportion. So if a man wants 100,000 francs, he subscribes for 500,000, and if he wants 10,000 he subscribes for 40,000 or 50,000, and so on. The resolution of the House of Representatives about Mexico reached here in the middle of the subscriptions.† All the large subscriptions

---

* A strong anti-Imperial print and friendly to the United States, published at Nantes.

† The resolution here referred to was offered by the Hon. H.

ceased abruptly, and when the lists were examined it was found that, taking all the subscriptions at their full amount, they had received but about one third of the amount advertised for, barely enough to cover the sum allotted to the indemnification of France. The government immediately gave orders to award the full amount to each subscriber, and, what is worse, it directed that the full amount should be paid up at once. The consequence was that many subscribers of limited means, who had only expected the allotment of a fraction of their subscription, were obliged to sell out, hence a fall in the quotations of the loan yesterday of 3½ per cent., and unless the government interferes there will be another fall to-day.

"Apropos of Mexico, you will find in the Paris papers a paragraph taken from the *Moniteur*, stating that the Emperor has received from the United States government satisfactory explanations of the resolution of the House of Representatives. That paragraph appeared in the *Moniteur de Soir*, published on the 1st of May, but did not, however, appear in the *Moniteur Officiel*.

"I cannot but regret that Mr. Dayton had any authority to furnish a pretext for this article, as the subject stood very well where the House and the Senate left it. I think the resolution was having a wholesome effect here. The government is supposed to presume upon our embarrassments, and we encourage them by a tone of propitiation and courtesy which has precisely

---

Winter Davis, of Maryland, on the 4th of April, 1864, and passed the House of Representatives unanimously. It ran as follows :

"*Resolved*, That the Congress of the United States are unwilling, by silence, to leave the nations of the world under the impression that they are indifferent spectators of the deplorable events now transpiring in the Republic of Mexico; and they therefore think fit to declare that it does not accord with the policy of the United States to acknowledge a monarchical government, erected on the ruins of any republican government in America, under the auspices of any European power."

Though this resolution never passed the Senate, it had all the moral effect in Europe that could have been expected from its adoption by both houses of Congress.

the contrary effect from that designed. They are, in point of fact, in greater embarrassment than ourselves; they can bear nothing which affects their credit, and the least demonstration from the United States they feel in every fibre, as was shown by the nervousness of the official journals about that resolution, and by the fate of the loan; while the opposition would be much more courageous in reference to American affairs if they could feel sure of an ally in the American government. But when they received your charming compliments to the French government, which they know is doing all it can to cut our throats, they are indisposed to venture an attack. I think you will find before you get much farther with this government that you will have to take a more decisive tone with it, and require of it less temporizing and equivocation. At least I am convinced that that is the surest and quickest way of bringing public opinion to bear in our favor on one or two questions. Pardon me if your shoemaker has gone beyond his last. You expect me to give you frankly my impressions in regard to matters of public concern, and I am anxious you should not be misled with soft words (and nothing else), with which your representative at this Court has been entertained ever since his arrival here."

Could we have known what had already taken place in the enemy's camp, and which the government concealed from us so far as it was able to do, we should have been disturbed with fewer apprehensions. The recent publication of Captain Bullock furnishes the complement of the picture, and explains so many things that were unintelligible to us that I place his statement before the reader, reminding him, however, that at the time we had not the advantage of any such light:

"The construction of the corvettes at Bordeaux and Nantes and the two iron-clad vessels progressed rapidly, and for some months there did not arise any question which suggested a doubt in regard to the purposes of the Imperial government in respect to their departure when completed. On the 23d of November, 1863, I reported that the armored vessels were quite three fifths finished, and that the corvettes would probably be ready for sea within the contract time; but by that date things began to change in their aspect. The American papers began to discuss the probable destination of the ships, and it was stated that Mr. Dayton, the United States Minister, had addressed a protest to the French government against their completion, and it was even affirmed that he had been assured by the Minister of Marine that none of the ships would be allowed to leave France. Commenting upon these uncomfortable rumors in a subsequent despatch (November 26, 1863) to the Secretary of the Navy, I wrote as follows:

"'The extent to which the system of bribery and spying has been and continues to be practised by the agents of the United States in Europe is scarcely credible. The servants of gentlemen supposed to have Southern sympathies are tampered with; confidential clerks, and even the messengers from telegraph offices, are bribed to betray their trust, and I have lately been informed that the English and French post-offices, hitherto considered immaculate, are now scarcely safe modes of communication.

"'Mere suspicion is not, I regret to say, the basis of Mr. Dayton's protest. He has furnished the French government with copies of certain letters alleged to have passed between the builders, which go to show that the ships are for us. The confidential clerk who has had charge of the correspondence of M. Voruz, one of the parties to the contract, has disappeared, and has, unfortunately, carried off some of the letters and papers relating to the business. M. Voruz has not yet discovered the full extent to which he has been robbed, but is using every effort to trace the theft to its source, and to discover how far he can prove complicity on the part of the United States officials. We know that the stolen papers contain evidence that the ships are for us, for *the fact has been so stated by the Minister of Marine to one of the builders;* but the French government has only thus become aware of a transaction it was perfectly well informed of before. Indeed, I may say that *the attempt to build ships in France was undertaken at the instigation of the Imperial government itself.* When the construction of the corvettes was in process of negotiation *a draft of the proposed contract was shown to the highest per-*

son in the empire, and it received his sanction; at least, I was so informed at the time. At any rate, I have a copy of the letter addressed to the builders by the Minister of Marine, giving authority to arm the corvettes in France, and specifying the number of guns; and I have the original document, signed by M. Chasseloup-Loubat himself, granting like authority for the rams. It can never, therefore, be charged that the Confederate States government, through its agent, has violated the neutrality of France by attempting the construction of ships in her ports;[*] and if Mr. Dayton has received the assurances we see printed in the American papers, the time is rapidly approaching when the policy of the Imperial government in reference to American affairs must be positively and definitely expressed.

"'The builders are still sanguine that they will be allowed to send the ships to sea; but I confess I do not see any such assurance in what they say, and the manner in which the protest of the American minister has been received is well calculated to confirm my doubts. When Mr. Dayton went to the Minister of Foreign Affairs with a complaint and with copies of certain letters to substantiate it, the minister might have said, "These are all alleged copies of the private correspondence of two prominent and highly respected French citizens; they could have only come into your possession by bribery or treachery; I cannot, therefore, receive them as evidence, and must insist that you produce the originals, and explain how you came to be possessed of them."

---

[*] We shall see later that the alleged sanction of the contract between Bullock and Arman by "the highest person of the empire" was upon conditions of which he must have been kept in ignorance or had overlooked when he wrote the paragraph. He also overlooks the fact that the authorization was for building vessels to ply the China seas. That subterfuge was not resorted to by the French government to deceive itself, but for its defence when, if ever, it should be called to account for letting the vessels be built, supposing the secret of their real destination was kept until they had got beyond the jurisdiction of the French government. The disclosure of the secret at any time before the escape of the vessels, it will soon be shown, dissolved all engagements which were made upon the strength of any givings-out of the emperor.

"'It strikes me that such a course would have effectually silenced Mr. Dayton, and we could have felt some assurance of getting our ships to sea. Instead, the stolen letters have been received without hesitation, and the United States officials profess to be satisfied with the action, or promised action, of the French government. The builders are sent for, and warned by the Minister of Marine; and though those gentlemen come from their interviews still possessed by the belief that the ships will be allowed to depart, and thus, as I said before, with hopes, I cannot be blind to the significancy of the above circumstances.

"'My belief is that the construction of the ships will not be interfered with; but whether they will be allowed to leave France or not will depend upon the position of affairs in America at the time of their completion. If at that time our cause is in the ascendant the local authorities will be instructed not to be too inquisitive, and the departure of our ships will be connived at. If, on the contrary, the Federal cause prospers, the affairs of the "Confederate ships" will be turned over to the responsible ministers of the empire, who will justify their claims to American gratitude by a strict enforcement of the neutrality of France. Hoping always for the best, I shall not permit any fears to create delay in the progress of work. The ships shall be ready as soon as possible, and every effort shall be made to get them to sea in the manner least calculated to compromise the French authorities, if they choose only to be judicially blind.'

"On the 18th of February, 1864, I reported further to the Secretary of the Navy as follows:

"'I have the honor to enclose herewith my despatch of November 26, 1863, on the subject of the iron-clads and corvettes building for us in France, wherein I ventured to express some apprehension as to the policy the Imperial government would pursue when the ships approached completion. That policy has been pronounced sooner than I anticipated, and the emperor, through his Ministers of Foreign Affairs and Marine, has formally notified the builders that the iron-clads cannot be permitted to sail, and that the corvettes must not be armed in France, but must be nominally sold to some foreign merchant and despatched as ordinary trading vessels. I believe that M. Arman has acted in a perfectly loyal manner thus far in these transactions, and he sincerely regrets the present turn of events. *He* *has proposed that a nominal sale of the vessels should be made to a Danish banker, and that there should be a private agreement providing for a redelivery to us at some point beyond the jurisdiction of France.* This would simply be substituting France for England, and then Denmark for France, and the Danish banker for Messrs. Bravay; and if the two most powerful maritime nations in the world have not been able to resist the importunities of the United States, it would be simply absurd to hope for success through the medium of Denmark, a weak power at best, and just now struggling almost hopelessly for her very existence.* The proposition was therefore declined, as it only involved an increased and useless expenditure of money without a hope of profit. This case may be summed up in a very few words.

"'It is one of simple deception. I never should have entered into such large undertakings without the assurance of success. I was—not as a private individual, but as an agent of the Confederate States—invited to build ships-of-war in France, and, so far at least as the corvettes are concerned, received every possible assurance† that they might be actually armed in the ports of construction. During three or four months after the contracts were made the work advanced very rapidly, but latterly there has been a gradual falling off, which caused me to fear that the builders had received some discouraging intimations from the government. I am not fully convinced on this point, but the result would seem to indicate that my suspicions were not unfounded. By affording refuge to our ships at Calais, Brest, and Cherbourg, the Imperial government has shown us more favor than that of her Britannic majesty; and I presume that the emperor, trusting to the chances of war and diplomacy, hoped that, before the completion of the ships, affairs both in America and Europe would be in such a condition as would enable him to let them go without apprehension. He now favors us so far as

---

* Then engaged in war with Prussia and Austria in respect to the Holstein-Schleswig provinces.

† This is considerably overstated. He, or at least his principals, was very far from receiving every possible assurance, or, indeed, any assurance, from the emperor, except upon a condition that was not complied with, as will appear by and by.

to tell us frankly to sell out and save our money, but this can scarcely ameliorate the disappointment.

"'The two Bordeaux iron-clads and the four corvettes would have proved a formidable attacking squadron, and would have enabled their commander to strike severe and telling blows upon the northern seaboard. The loss of the iron-clads changes the whole character of the force, and deprives it of its real power of offence. It is difficult to predict what will be the state of Europe even a month hence, and how the progress of events may affect the chances of getting the wooden ships to sea. I shall, however, make every effort to get at least two of them out, to supply the places of our present cruisers should the casualties of the sea reduce their present number. There really seems but little for our ships to do now upon the open sea. Lieutenant Commanding Low, of the *Tuscaloosa*,* reports that, in a cruise of several months, during which he spoke over one hundred vessels, only one proved to be an American; and she, being loaded entirely on neutral account, he was forced to release her after taking a bond. The *Alabama*, also, only picks up a vessel at intervals, although she is in the East Indies, heretofore rich in American traffic. Nevertheless, if all our ships should be withdrawn, the United States flag would again make its appearance; and it is therefore essential to provide the necessary relay of vessels. There is, however, no resisting the logic of accomplished facts. I am now convinced that we cannot get iron-clads to sea, and, unless otherwise instructed, I will make no more contracts for such vessels, except with such a pecuniary guarantee for actual delivery upon the ocean as will secure us against loss.'" †

---

* Prize of the *Alabama*, commissioned by Captain Semmes.

† Bullock's "Secret Service of the Confederate States," vol. ii. pp. 38–43.

CHAPTER V.

The Plot to Secure One of the Iron-clads by a Fictitious Sale.—The Emperor Waiting for Lee to Take Washington to Recognize the Confederacy.

WHILE doing our best to compel the emperor to withdraw his support from the Confederates, our soldiers at home were using a far more effective logic. The strength of the Confederacy was rapidly wasting. The fall of Vicksburg, which gave us the control of the Mississippi from its mouth to its sources, and cut the Confederate States in two, together with the disastrous repulse of General Lee at Gettysburg, had almost as prompt and decisive an influence upon the politics of Europe as of America. "Up to the date of these events," to use the words of Captain Bullock, "the South was able in the main to beat back invasion, and sometimes, by a supreme effort, to assume the offensive. But by that time the drain of battle and disease had greatly diminished her fighting population, and the stringency of the blockade had become so great that it was impossible to supply the reduced numbers in the field with effective arms and ammunition, and all the necessary supplies could only be obtained at uncertain intervals and in insufficient quantities." The extent of its influence upon the attitude taken by the Imperial government of France towards the

Confederates was not at the time so apparent to us as, from the following statement of Captain Bullock, it appears to have been to their agents in Paris:

"M. Arman having received positive instructions not to attempt to send the iron-clad vessels to sea, but being still permitted to suppose that the corvettes would not be stopped if sent to sea without their guns, it was arranged with him to push the completion of the latter vessels to the utmost, and to go on with the armored ships more leisurely, while we were considering what might be done with them. The course of events and the *dénouement* is more clearly and fairly explained in the following despatch, written to the Secretary of the Navy at the time, than by any version I could give of the transaction now. The despatch referred to was written June 10, 1864, and was as follows :

"'It is now my painful duty to report upon the most remarkable circumstance that has yet occurred in reference to our operations in Europe. Previous despatches have informed you under what influences, impressions, and expectations I undertook the construction of ships-of-war in the building yards of France, and how smoothly and satisfactorily the work progressed for several months after it was begun. I reported to you when it became evident that the government was interfering and checking the progress of the work, and finally informed you when the authorities forbade the completion of the rams, and directed the builders of the corvettes to sell them.

"'When the consultation between Messrs. Mason, Slidell, and myself was held in Paris, the result of which has already been reported to you, it was unanimously agreed that the iron-clads must of necessity be sold, but it was thought that the corvettes should be completed, as the builders were confident that the government would not interfere with their departure, if despatched as commercial vessels, and under the assumed ownership of private individuals. Thus fortified by the opinions and advice of Messrs. Mason and Slidell, I gave M. Arman, the principal builder, written instructions to sell the ships, upon his representation that such a course was necessary in order that he might be able to show to the Minister of Marine that his business connection with me had ceased. There was at the same time an express understanding between M. Arman and me *that the sale of the corvettes should be purely fictitious,* and that the negotiations in respect to the rams should be kept in such a state that we might get possession of them again if there should be any change in the policy of the emperor's government before their completion. Scarcely a month since I had a long consultation with M. Arman regarding all of these matters, M. Eustis * being present.

"'M. Arman showed me a contract of sale of one of the iron-clads to the Danish government, and told me he was then negotiating for the sale of the other to the same government. As Denmark was then at war, it had been arranged that the nominal ownership of the rams should vest in Sweden,† and that government, I was informed, having consented to do this piece of good service for Denmark, M. Arman said that a Swedish naval officer was then at Bordeaux superintending the completion of the rams as if for his own government. In the contract of sale M. Arman had agreed to deliver the ships at Gottenberg in Sweden, and he told me that he had made this unusual stipulation in order that he might be able to send the ships to sea under the French flag and in charge of men of his own choice. "Now," said he, "if you are willing to sacrifice one of the rams, and will consent to the *bona fide* delivery of the first one, I am sure that the second one can be saved to you. When the first ram is ready to sail," continued M. Arman, "the American Minister will no doubt ask the Swedish Minister if the vessel belongs to his government. The reply will be 'Yes;' she will sail unmolested, and will arrive at her destination according to contract. This will avert all suspicion from the second ram, and when she sails under like

---

* Slidell's secretary.

† I reported this fact just as I understood M. Arman to state it, at the time of the consultation referred to ; but upon subsequent inquiry I learned that he did not mean me to infer that any public official of the Swedish government took part in the transaction, but that a Swedish banker had undertaken to carry out the arrangement. However, the whole plan fell through ; the ship was actually sold to Denmark, and was sent to Copenhagen without any disguise and under the French flag with a French commander and crew.

circumstances with the first, my people having a previous understanding with you, will take her to any rendezvous that may have been agreed upon, or will deliver her to you or your agent at sea."

" 'The above is almost a verbatim report of the proposition made by M. Arman, which after some discussion upon matters of detail was accepted, and I have since felt a reasonable assurance of seeing one of our rams at work upon the enemy. A day or two after, I called on M. Arman again, taking with me Captain Tessier, my agent in France, a man of intelligence, a capital seaman, and of course master of the French language. The object of the visit was to discuss the arrangements necessary to get the corvettes to sea, and to send to them their armament and crews. I told M. Arman that it would take a long time to set everything afloat when the proper moment arrived, but that the undertaking was one which not only involved a large expenditure of money, but which required to be managed with great caution and secrecy. When the expedition was ready, I said it would be absolutely necessary for it to sail promptly, because delay would cause exposure, and certain interruption and failure would follow, and having due regard to such a contingency, it was very important, and indeed essential, that I should, if possible, get some assurance that when we were all ready to move the government would permit the vessels to leave Bordeaux. M. Arman replied that he thought there was no doubt about the corvettes being allowed to sail unarmed, but he was to have a personal interview with the emperor in ten days or a fortnight, and would then bring the matter to a close, by direct appeal to his imperial majesty.

" 'Many details relating to the best mode of shipping the guns, the engagement of reliable captains, and the possibility of getting seamen from the ports of Brittany were discussed, all in a most satisfactory manner. Before separating, M. Arman expressed great regret at the delay and interference we had met with, and said that as he had made the contracts for building all the ships in perfect good faith, and with the assurance that his government understood the whole transaction, and would permit him to carry it out, he felt doubly bound to assist in every possible way, and to assume any responsibility that might be necessary.

"'In face of the foregoing statement you will readily imagine my astonishment when Captain Tessier arrived here (Liverpool) yesterday afternoon bringing me a letter from M. Arman, informing me that he had sold both the corvettes to governments of the north of Europe, "in obedience to the imperative orders of his government." He (M. Arman) could not write particulars. Captain Tessier was charged to deliver further verbal explanations as follows:

"'M. Arman obtained his promised interview with the emperor, who rated him severely, ordered him to sell the ships at once *bonâ fide*, and said, if this was not done, he would have them seized and taken to Rochefort.

"'Captain Tessier also brought me word that the two corvettes at Nantes were ordered to be sold, and the builders of those ships sent me by him a copy of the letter of the Minister of Marine conveying the order to them. The order is of the most peremptory kind, not only directing the sale, but requiring the builders to furnish proof to the Minister of Foreign Affairs that the sale is a real one. The Minister of Marine writes the order in a style of virtuous indignation; specifies the large artillery, the power of the engines, the space allotted to fuel, and the general arrangements of the ships as proving their warlike character, and dogmatically pronounces the one to which he especially refers *une véritable corvette de guerre*.*

"'When you call to mind the fact that this same Minister of

---

* I am indebted to the kind offices of the late United States Minister to Paris, the Hon. Levi P. Morton, with the French Ministry of Marine, for a copy of what may be presumed to be the letter to M. Arman, of which Captain Bullock professes here to give the substance. It gives some particulars which do not appear in the authorization, but as he is quoting, not from the document, which he does not profess to have seen, but from an oral report of M. Tessier of an oral statement by M. Arman, both made many years before, it is easier to suppose that he ascribed to the document some statements which may have been only uttered in the discussion, than that a second remonstrance of a similar purport to this should have emanated from the Department of Marine at or about the same date:

Marine, on the 6th day of June, 1863, wrote over his own official signature a formal authorization to arm those very ships with fourteen heavy guns (*canons rayé de trente*), the affectation of having just discovered them to be suitable for purposes of war is really astonishing.

"'When Captain Tessier brought me the unwelcome and discouraging report of the forced sale of our French ships, I was so fully occupied with pressing affairs in England that it was im-

"Paris, *le* 1*er Mai*, 1864.

"*M. Arman, Député, à Paris,*—Par une lettre, en date du 22 Avril, le Ministre des États-Unis a fait connaitre à S. E. le Ministre des Affaires Étrangères qu'il resultait des informations, prises a Stockholm que les deux batiments de guerre construits par vous, à Bordeaux, et dont vous aviez annoncé que la vente avait été faite au gouvernement Suedois, n'avaient réellement pas été vendus à ce gouvernement.

"M. Drouyn de Lhuys, qui m' a donné communication de la lettre de M. Dayton ainsi que des documents qui l'accompagnaient, a en conséquence, appelé de nouveau mon attention sur ces constructions et la destination de ces batiments.

"Vous vous rappelez, Monsieur, que sur les renseignements fournis par une correspondance dont M. le Ministre des États-Unis avait eu connaissance, j'ai eu, pour la première fois, à la date du 21 8bre dernière, à vous faire remarquer que vous assumiez sur vous une grave responsabilité par des actes qui se commettraient en contravention à la declaration du 10 Juin, 1861. Enfin, je vous prévenais que je ne saurais autoriser l'armement des navires qui vous etaient signalés comme construits pour les Confédérés.

"Aujourd'hui je viens vous faire connaitre que sous aucun pretexte, je ne laisserai armer les batiments que vous avez annoncé avoir vendus, avant que vous n'ayez justifié au Département des Affaires Étrangères de la vente qui en aurait été faite, par vous, à un gouvernement étranger.

"Les ordres les plus formels seront donnés aux autorités maritimes pour s'opposer à l'armement des navires dont il s'agit jusqu'a ce que S. E. M. Drouyn de Lhuys m'ait fait connaitre qu'il en peut être autrement. Recevez, etc."

possible for me to go to France at once, but I sent him immediately back with a letter to Mr. Slidell, and with instructions to arrange with M. Arman to meet me in Paris, and followed in a few days. A consultation with Mr. Slidell resulted in nothing but the conviction that the Imperial government had changed the views which had been previously expressed, and that it would be impossible to retain possession of the ships, or to prevent their delivery to the purchasers by any process of law. It was manifest that the builders of the ships were as much surprised and disappointed by the action of the government as we were. They would not have undertaken the transaction unless they had been impressed with the belief that the supreme government fully understood and approved what they were doing, and they were ready and willing to comply with their engagements and to assume any reasonable responsibility in the effort to fulfil them.'"

In giving this statement of Captain Bullock I have enabled my readers to considerably anticipate my knowledge of what was going on in the camp of the enemy. I have borrowed this light as it were from the future, that my readers may more readily understand, as my narrative proceeds, the shameless duplicity with which we had to contend during this protracted and anxious struggle with the Confederate and Imperial governments combined.* Of course I knew nothing of the new attitude taken by the emperor towards the Confederacy, nor

---

* I will here cite a letter which I had occasion to address to Mr. Seward on the 6th of August, 1864, to show that the emperor had required Arman to get rid of his ships from no feeling of respect for his neutral engagements, nor with any thought of befriending our government:

"(*Confidential.*)

"PARIS, *August* 6, 1864.

"*My dear Sir,*—M. Ancel, the deputy to the Corps Legislatif from Havre, finding himself at Vichy the other day, sought

of the order to sell the ships and rid France of any political responsibility for their construction.

---

and obtained an interview with the emperor. After discussing the local matters of his district which prompted his request for an interview, he remarked a map spread out upon the table, which proved to be a map of the United States. M. Ancel expressed his regret that the emperor's benevolent design to stop the terrible slaughter in the United States had thus far proved ineffective. 'Yes,' the emperor replied, 'it would have all been stopped three years ago if England had been willing to act with me' (or follow my advice, or example, or something of that kind).

"'However,' he added, 'Lee will take Washington, and then I shall recognize the Confederates. I have just received the news that Lee is certain to take Washington, and he is probably in possession of the capital now. As soon as the fact transpires, I shall be justified in recognizing the Confederate government, and then England will regret her course. England always likes to be on the side of the strongest.'

"This is almost textually the language of the emperor, as reported to me by a personal friend of M. Ancel, who places implicit faith in the report; nor do I entertain any doubt of its substantial accuracy. It furnishes a new motive and explanation of Lee's recent expedition north, which, without some such explanation, wore an aspect of rashness and recklessness not characteristic of his movements.

"If any new motive were needed for making the defences impregnable, here you have it.

"Yours very faithfully,
"JOHN BIGELOW."

Chapter VI.

A Confederate Iron-clad Escapes.—Its Arrival on the French Coast.—Takes Refuge in Spain.—Watched by the United States Frigate "Niagara."—Double Dealing of the Imperial Government.

On the first of December, 1864, the mission at Paris became vacant by the sudden decease of Mr. Dayton. On the 12th of January I was charged with its duties.

As soon as my letters of credence had been presented I proceeded to verify a report which had reached me, that two of Arman's vessels had been sold to the Peruvian government. I was assured by M. Barreda, then the Peruvian Minister in Paris, that he had bought the corvettes *Shanghai* and *San Francisco* for the Peruvian navy, and that both had sailed fully armed, under orders of the Peruvian government.

In a few days more it transpired that the remaining corvettes and one of the rams had been sold to Prussia, and the second to Denmark. I was beginning to feel that at last the dangers which threatened us from that quarter of the horizon were conjured; that we need no longer apprehend the destruction of our commerce and the devastation of our seaports by the rams, nor any serious disturbance of our relations with France, which must have followed the appearance of either of them in American waters at any time before the termination of the war. But my respite from anxiety was destined to be of short duration. It was true that the *Shanghai* and *San Francisco* had been bought in good faith by Peru and had been delivered. It was also true that negotiations were pending, which were ultimately consummated, for the sale of one of the rams and some of the corvettes to the Prussian government, but it was not true that the sale to Sweden had been consummated. Late in the afternoon of Saturday, the 28th of January, our consul at Nantes notified me that the ram which Arman pretended to have sold to the Danish government, and which had left Bordeaux for Copenhagen under the name of the *Stoerkodder*, had sailed from that port again under the name of *Olinde*, and was now lying in the bay of Quiberon, on the French coast, where she had discharged her Danish crew of forty-two men on board a vessel sent from the yard of Messrs. Dubigeon fils of St. Nazaire, which vessel had brought to the ship a load of coal; also that a British steamer had been alongside of the *Olinde* with a supply of guns, ammunition, and a crew, which were also put on board.

I immediately communicated these facts to the Minister of Foreign Affairs, and on the following day, although it was the Sabbath, I betook myself at an early hour to the Ministry of Marine. M. Chasseloup-Loubat professed ignorance, but said that he would telegraph at once for information, adding that Arman had deceived him twice and might try to do it again; if so, they could not help it, as the point where these vessels lay was not under any guns of the government. I replied that the transfer had occurred in French waters, that the vessel had been coaled clandestinely from a French steamer, and that intelligence of these facts had reached me indirectly through a French government officer. He repeated that the waters in which this vessel was lying were not under government surveillance; then, as if beginning to realize the weakness of that position, he took the ground that the vessel had been sold to the Danish government, which had thereby become responsible for the use that should be made of it. I asked if he had any evidence that the Danish government had accepted the vessel before she left France. He replied that, as it was a vessel-of-war, it could not have received his authorization to leave without first exhibiting a contract for its purchase by some neutral government; that it did produce one from the Danish government, and if that government did not intend to keep the ship, it should, by a proper notification, have placed it once more under French jurisdiction; till then, Denmark and not France was responsible for the vessel.

This brief but animated discussion had greatly simplified the issue between us. The question left to be settled was whether the Danish government had or had not made itself responsible for the future career of the steamer. I betook myself immediately to the Danish Legation, but as Count Moltke, the Danish Minister in Paris, chanced to be absent, I called the following day, January 31, 1865, when I learned from him that there had been negotiations pending between his government and Arman; but the Danish inspector had informed Arman before the vessel left Bordeaux that she would not be accepted, as she had not been delivered according to the conditions of the contract. Count Moltke said, further, that Arman sent her to Copenhagen in spite of this notice, with a French crew in charge of a M. Arnous de la Rivière; that on her arrival the crew was sent home, and after laying there some three months, the Danish government persisting in its refusal to accept her, Arnous hired a Danish captain and crew to bring the ship to Bordeaux. Count Moltke also informed me that Arnous had been to see him the day before in company with the Danish pilot and captain, and he gave as his reason for stopping in the bay of Quiberon that his engineers were unskilful, his sailors mutinous, and his oil had given out. This last embarrassment struck the count as quite a novelty in the category of maritime disasters, and helped to confirm his suspicions in regard to the whole transaction. The count said there could be no mistake about the main fact so important in determining where the responsibility must rest for the escape of the *Stoerkodder*—the name under which the *Olinde* had sailed from Bordeaux—that she never for one moment passed out of the control of Arman and his agents, and therefore was never for one moment under the control of the Danish government. In speaking of the alleged defective construction of the *Stoerkodder*, Arnous admitted to Count Moltke her predatory destination in the remark "that she was a terrible vessel, and was going to make terrible havoc among the blockading squadrons of the Federals."

Whether in her make-up and speed the *Stoerkodder* did or did not conform to the terms of the contract of Arman with the Danish government, there was one reason more decisive than all others for its availing itself of any pretext for not accepting the steamer. His contract with Denmark bound Arman to deliver the vessel, at that time known as the *Sphinx*, by the 14th of June, 1864, under a penalty of 1000 francs for every day's delay. The time of her delivery was of vital importance to Denmark, then engaged in a supreme but very unequal struggle with the combined forces of Prussia and Austria for the retention of the duchies of Schleswig and of Holstein. Having but a small land force, she relied mainly upon her fleet, which was not to be despised. The acquisition of a ram like the *Stonewall** at that moment would have proved to her of incalculable importance. Arman, however, could not, or at least did not, tender the vessel until October, and after the Schleswig-Holstein question was settled and Denmark had submitted to the terms which her enemies dictated.

Of course the *Stonewall* had by this time become an article of luxury which Denmark had neither

---

* This was the significant name for which that of *Stoerkodder* had been exchanged after she left Copenhagen.

disposition nor means to indulge herself with, and she did not hesitate to take advantage of Arman's neglect to comply with the terms of his contract.

In order to put upon the files of the French Foreign Office an official record of what I regarded as established facts in regard to the escape of the *Stoerkodder,* alias the *Olinde,* alias the *Stonewall,* from the waters of France and her return to it, I addressed a communication to the Minister of Foreign Affairs on the 2d of February, reciting the false pretences under which she obtained leave to sail for Copenhagen, and a history of her subsequent career until she received a Confederate crew, armament, and coals in the bay of Quiberon; I concluded my statement with the following assignment of reasons for sending it:

"I take leave to bring these statements, which all come from authentic sources, thus promptly to the notice of your Excellency in the hope that you will be pleased to inform me if they differ in any important particulars, and if so in what, from the reports which have reached the Imperial government, that my own government may be assisted by an undisputed record of facts, in determining precisely where the responsibility should rest for the depredations which are to be apprehended from the irregular and presumptively piratical manner in which the *Olinde* quitted the waters of France.

"While I sincerely hope these apprehensions may prove to have been groundless, I do not feel sufficient doubt of the final destination of the *Olinde* to justify me in neglecting any precaution which it would be proper for me to take if my apprehensions were convictions."*

My remonstrances seemed to have been not with-

---

* Dip. Cor. 1864-5.

out effect upon the Imperial government, for only two days after this letter was received at the Foreign Office, I received a telegram from Mr. Perry, our *Chargé* at Madrid, informing me that the *Olinde*, which had practically avowed her piratical genealogy and destination by taking the name of *Stonewall*, had arrived at Ferrol in Spain, and had gone into the dock for repairs. I immediately waited upon M. Drouyn de Lhuys, and suggested to him the propriety of instructing his ambassador at Madrid to detain the *Stonewall*, at least until the inquest which the Minister of Marine was making was completed. M. Drouyn de Lhuys replied that he had written twice to the Minister of Marine for his report, upon which he could order an inquest by the Minister of Justice—another device for evasion and delay—but had received as yet no answer. He hesitated to give any order upon the subject until he had the official report of the minister before him. His greater trouble obviously was, lest, in giving such an order, he might be assuming for his government a greater degree of responsibility for what had occurred in Quiberon Bay than was consistent with his theory that the *Stonewall* was a Danish and not a French vessel. I insisted that a crime against the laws of France had been committed, and hence the inquest upon which the Minister of Marine was engaged; that until the author and the extent of that crime were ascertained and punished, France was interested in detaining the vessel and all on board as contingently liable in damages; that this right was quite independent of the nationality of the vessel; and, finally, that the *Stonewall* was the *Corps de delit*, and France had the right to insist on her remaining at Ferrol to await the impending investigation.

From the Minister of Foreign Affairs, partly at the suggestion of M. Drouyn de Lhuys, I went to the Minister of Marine. He informed me that the report was ready and that he was just then about sending it to M. Drouyn de Lhuys. When I had seen it placed in the hands of a messenger—for I let him see that I was waiting till it should go—I returned to the Ministry of Foreign Affairs, with the intention of reinforcing my suggestion made at the previous interview. I was told the minister had gone out to drive, which was highly probable, for I am sure he did not wish to see me again, while he must have been morally certain that I would soon be back. Returned to my Legation, I addressed him a note urging the expediency and importance of instructing his ambassador at Madrid at once to request the Spanish government to detain the *Stonewall* until the inquiry which the Minister of Justice had been or was to be instructed to institute into the circumstances attending the *Stonewall's* equipment and departure from France had been completed. I also suggested to him as a precedent by which to prove to the Spanish government that the Imperial government would be asking no more than it was willing to concede the case of the *Rappahannock*, a Confederate vessel then lying at Calais, by virtue of a procedure precisely similar in all important particulars to that which I proposed to have instituted against the *Stonewall*. "If your Excellency," I concluded, "should estimate the importance of preventing this steamer from leaving the west coast of Europe under the flag of the so-called Confederate government as highly as I do, you will pardon the earnestness with which I press a course of proceeding which promises a speedy, natural, and satisfactory solution of what threatens to become a very troublesome case." Three days after this communication was sent to M. Drouyn de Lhuys, I received from him the following reply:

M. DROUYN DE LHUYS TO MR. BIGELOW.

(Translation.)

"PARIS, *Feb.* 7, 1865.

"*Sir*,—Upon the receipt of the letters which you did me the honor to write me the 28th of January last and the 2d of this month, I hastened to call the attention of his Excellency M. the Minister of Marine to the facts which you mention, begging him to be pleased to communicate to me all the information which he could possibly collect concerning the appearance and sojourn upon the coast of France of a vessel-of-war sailing under the Danish flag, and which your information indicates as destined to cruise on behalf of the Confederate States. I have just received from the Count de Chasseloup-Loubat the information which permits me to answer the questions which you have addressed to me. The *Olinde* (this is the name which the vessel bore which appeared upon our coast) being in your opinion—as, indeed, certain indications also authorize us in supposing—the same vessel which under the name of *Sphinx* last year went out from the ship-yard of M. Arman, a French ship-builder, I think it my duty here first to recall the circumstances under which the *Sphinx* was authorized to leave the port of Bordeaux. When it was a question of her delivery to her purchaser, the government of the emperor took care to assure itself that the sale of this vessel was not a cloak to any operation contrary to the neutrality which it observed, and which it has constantly watched pursuant to the provisions of law, in order that no violation should occur from its own subjects. It proceeded, therefore, to the strictest investigation, and it was only when M. Arman had established, by the most unexceptionable proof—that is to say, by the production of his bill of sale—that the *Sphinx* was really sold to a European non-belligerent power, that its exit from the port of Bordeaux was authorized.

"The 1st of October, the testimony of M. the Minister of Denmark at Paris, supported by that of his minister at Copenhagen, fully confirmed the declaration of M. Arman, and the authenticity of the title which he had produced. There could then be no doubt as to the real destination of the vessel, which in effect, on quitting France, was sent to Denmark.

"Here, according to what you write me, sir, arose a new order of facts, a consequence of which was the transfer into other hands of the ownership of the vessel in question. Upon this point the government of the emperor does not possess any other information than that which you have been pleased to transmit to me, and the absence of M. Arman at Berlin at this moment has not permitted us to ask any from him. One cannot be astonished, however, at the ignorance in which the French administration finds itself concerning what passed during the stay of the *Sphinx* in Denmark, since this vessel had then ceased to be a French vessel. We have neither any reason nor any right to make an inquiry into the matter. It would, indeed, have been, on the part of the government of the emperor, passing the limits of what comports with the most scrupulous neutrality to pretend to exercise a control over the ulterior destination of a vessel having become the property of a neutral power and definitively escaped from its jurisdiction.

"As to the arrival of the *Olinde* in French waters, the report which M. the Minister of Marine has addressed to me, and of which I have the honor to send you herewith a copy, establishes, as you will see, sir, that she presented herself there under the Danish flag, manned by a Danish crew—that is to say, with every quality which constituted for her a Danish nationality.

"Her arrival upon our coast had nothing unusual in it nor anything which would call particular attention to her if she was joined there by an English vessel; that was but a very ordinary fact, not being, either, of a nature to arouse any special attention.

"There is, therefore, no occasion for being surprised that the stay of this vessel should have passed unnoticed, particularly if one considers the insufficiency of the means of surveillance in open roadsteads, such as those where she anchored. Upon all these points the accompanying letter of M. le Comte de Chasseloup-Loubat will furnish you the most conclusive information.

"In announcing to me, sir, by your letter of the 5th of this month, that the vessel which you consider as at present belonging to the Confederates had, under the name of *Stonewall*, entered the port of Ferrol, you expressed the wish that the government of the emperor would intercede with that of her Catholic majesty, with the view of procuring her detention. I would be happy to be able to respond to the desire which you have done me the honor to express to me, but it is not possible for me to understand by what right I would be permitted to do so. I need not say that the police of her ports appertains to the Spanish government alone; and in this case no particular circumstance would authorize the intervention of the government of his majesty. As results from the facts which I have just recalled, the regular sale which has been made of the vessel in question, to a neutral power, took from her her character as a French vessel, and we had no longer any right to ask then that under this title in a port of Spain she be subjected to special measures of surveillance or of coercion. You will understand, sir, that to act thus without any right of our own, and in an interest that is foreign to us, would be to depart by an unjustifiable step from the attitude of strict abstention which we ought to preserve in the war, and to infringe, to the detriment of one of the parties and to the profit of the other, the neutrality which we desire to observe towards both. The Danish government might, perhaps, if it judged proper, take the initiative in this matter, which to us is in any case interdicted. The government of the emperor would certainly regret, sir, as deeply as any one, that the *Stonewall* should ultimately receive the destination of which you were apprehensive, and the injury which might result thereby to the commerce of the United States. But, unfortunately, it does not depend upon it to place an obstacle to this. It is only conscious of having taken the greatest possible care not to depart from the rules which it has laid down for itself, and which evinces, at the same time, its kindly feelings towards the United States, and its wish to relieve itself from all responsibility. In this case, as in all circumstances, it has strictly conformed to the principles of neutrality which have not ceased to govern and to inspire all its actions.

"I will finish, sir, by a last observation upon the subject of the analogy which the situation of the *Stonewall* in the port of Ferrol seems to you to offer to that of the *Rappahannock* in the port of Calais. Even were the situations of these two ships the same, the government of the emperor would not be held to account for it, as far as it is concerned, since the *Stonewall* is in a Spanish port, where we have no jurisdiction.

"But, in my opinion, the circumstances under which the two vessels presented themselves—the one at Calais, the other at Ferrol, are entirely different. You will in effect remember, sir, that the *Rappahannock* was, as supposed, a vessel of commerce having left a port of England, and which, having taken refuge in a French port, attempted to transform herself there into a vessel-of-war. Faithful to its principles, the government of the emperor did not permit this transformation to take place in its waters, and opposed the going out of the ship. The vessel whose presence at Ferrol you mention seems to have presented herself there under circumstances entirely different, which it seems to me do not allow of any assimilation to the precedent which you recall.

"Receive, sir, the assurance of the very distinguished consideration with which I have the honor to be,

"Your very humble and very obedient servant,

"DROUYN DE LHUYS."

THE MINISTER OF MARINE TO THE MINISTER OF FOREIGN AFFAIRS.

(Translation.)

"PARIS, *Feb.* 5, 1865.

"*Dear Mr. Minister and Colleague*,—You did me the honor to transmit to me the copy of a letter which M. the *Chargé d'Affaires* of the United States had written to you, and in which he mentioned the arrival at Belleisle and off the island of Houat of two vessels recently constructed in France, sailing at present under the Danish flag, but which, according to him, are destined to cruise on behalf of the Confederate States.

"Mr. Bigelow thinks that the ram vessel is the *Sphinx*, constructed by M. Arman of Bordeaux. Your Excellency remembers that this vessel, as also the other ships-of-war which left the yards of this ship-builder, were stopped by my orders until M. Arman should have proved to the Department of Foreign Affairs their regular sale to a neutral power.

"The 3d of October last, your Excellency having made known to me that the proof had been produced by M. Arman, and that the *Sphinx* had been really sold to the Danish government, which had just concluded the preliminaries of peace, there was no longer any motive for detaining the vessel. She left then for Helsingport, and she does not appear to have carried any other but the Danish flag.

"According to what Mr. Bigelow tells me (but what no official document has made known to me), it would appear, in consequence of difficulties raised between the Danish government and M. Arman, this vessel was refused, and the latter, remaining the owner, had arranged with the agents of the Confederate States to deliver her to them.

"However this may be, it is certain that the vessel which appeared in the waters of Belleisle was of a construction similar to that of the *Sphinx;* she carried the Danish flag and had a Danish crew when she anchored in the roadstead of Calais. She afterwards went to the island of Houat. A side-wheel steamer under the English flag joined her there, it appeared, and the bad weather might naturally cause the belief that this vessel had also put into port. At length the French steamer, the *Expeditif*, brought coal to these vessels. These incidents could not but appear very natural; similar cases constantly occur, and it is not customary to make inquiries into what a foreign vessel-of-war comes into port to do, particularly in bad weather, upon a friendly coast.

"I think it my duty to direct your Excellency's attention to the fact, also, that we have not the means of exercising an effective surveillance over vessels which anchor in our open roadsteads. Upon the other hand, I would add that, on account of prevailing bad weather, communications have been infrequent with the island of Houat, situated opposite the bay of Quiberon, near which the vessels were anchored; and finally, that there exists upon this little island neither telegraphic bureau nor semaphore.

"However, I have asked the maritime authorities of Belle-isle, and at the different points of the coast which are contiguous to the waters of Houat Island, for information upon the movements of the vessels mentioned by M. the *Chargé d'Affaires* of the United States.

"As far as the supposition of Mr. Bigelow is concerned, that the ram vessel was destined to cruise under the flag of the Confederate States, it would be for Denmark to respond to him, since her crew was Danish, she carried the Danish flag, and, as you have remarked, she had been regularly sold to the Danish government.

"The facts in question could not then, in any case, concern us, and I believe it unnecessary to recall the fact that, under all circumstances, the government of the emperor has always made it a duty to observe and to cause to be observed the most strict and loyal neutrality between the two parties who at present divide the United States of America."

Chapter VII.

The Spanish Government Asked to Detain the Stonewall.—Commodore Craven's Embarrassment.—Report of the United States Chargé d'Affaires at Madrid.—The Career of the Stonewall Described by her Captain until her Final Surrender to the United States Authorities at Havana.—Vindication of Commodore Craven.

It required all my self-control not to betray the disgust with which the obvious bad faith of these letters inspired me, but it was not until many years after the events I am describing that I realized the extent of it. The subject upon which this correspondence threw most light was the hopeless extent to which the Imperial government had compromised itself with the Confederates and with Arman. No resource was left it but silence or evasion. I immediately wrote to Mr. Perry, then in charge of our Legation at Madrid (who meantime had informed me that the *Stonewall* could be detained for a few days), the following despatch:

MR. BIGELOW TO MR. PERRY.

"*February* 8, 1865.

"*Dear Sir*,—I was gratified to learn by your telegrams of Monday and to-day that the *Stonewall* can be detained a few days; that will suffice for the frigate *Niagara*, Commodore Craven, which I presume left Dover on Monday, to reach Ferrol.

"The French government decline to meddle with the *Stonewall* in Spain. Their theory, to which they will naturally adhere as long as possible, is that she was a Danish vessel until she went into Confederate hands, and that it is for Denmark, and not for France, to intercede with Spain for her detention.

"As no assistance is to be expected from this quarter, you will need no suggestion from any one to use every proper influence with the Spanish government to detain the *Stonewall*, at least until you hear from our government.

"I do not know the relative strength of the two vessels, but the result of a conflict between the *Stonewall* and the *Niagara* might be sufficiently uncertain to make it bad policy to risk one unnecessarily. Upon that point, however, Commodore Craven is authority.

"The *Stonewall* carries one 300-pounder and two 120-pounders I am told, in addition to any guns she may have received the other day from the *Duke of Richmond*.

"I remain, dear sir," etc.

On the 25th of February I received the following note by a private messenger from Commodore Craven:

COMMODORE CRAVEN TO MR. BIGELOW.

"U. S. SHIP 'NIAGARA,'
FERROL, *February* 20, 1865.

"*Dear Sir*,—Your letter of the 13th instant I have just received. As I have already informed you by telegrams, I arrived at Corunna on the morning of the 11th instant, and there learned that the rebel ram *Stonewall*, Captain Thomas J. Page, had put into that port on or about the 2d instant in a leaky condition; and after remaining there three days went to Ferrol for repairs, and that she would be ready for sea on or about the 14th instant. On the evening of the 15th I came here and was informed on the following morning, by the military and civil governors of the place, that the *Stonewall* had been reported as being ready for sea, but her commander had not appointed a day for sailing. On the morning of the 17th our consular agent came on board and in great glee informed me that the governor had called upon him, and said that Captain Page had asked if there would be any objection on the part of the Spanish government to his absenting himself for a few days for the purpose of visiting Paris; that his vessel still leaked badly, and he wished to confer with the Confederate Commissioners in relation to selling the *Stonewall*, or compelling the contractors to take her back, as she did not come up to the contract and was not seaworthy. On the evening of the 17th, Page took passage in a Spanish war steamer for Corunna, *en route* for Madrid and Paris. On the evening of the 18th our consular agent came on board and informed me that Page had given out to the people at Corunna that his repairs were all completed, and that he was going to Paris for the purpose of purchasing another vessel.

"When I arrived at this port, there was lying lashed to the port side of the ram a Spanish government hulk, in which were deposited her stores, ammunition, etc., and for the first two or three days these symptoms of leakage have disappeared. The Spanish corvette (hulk) was hauled off from her side yesterday morning, and to-day she is taking in coal and appears otherwise ready to sail at any moment. I am inclined to suspect all reports relative to the continuance of her leak as being a humbug, or, in other words, she is playing 'possum.'

"She is a very formidable vessel, being completely cased with 5-inch plates of iron. Under her topgallant forecastle is her casemated 300-pounder Armstrong gun. On her quarter-deck in a turret are two other rifled guns, 100 or 120 pounders; besides these she has two smaller guns in broadside.

"If she is as fast as reputed to be in smooth water, she would be more than a match for three such ships as the *Niagara*. So, sir, you will readily perceive I am placed in a most unenviable predicament, and that our only chance for cutting short her career rests upon the possibility of detaining her here until such time as our government sees fit to send out the necessary reinforcements."

I immediately addressed the commodore the following letter:

Mr. Bigelow to Commodore Craven.

"United States Legation,
Paris, *February* 27, 1865.

"*Dear Commodore*,—I received your despatch by private messenger yesterday morning. I hope, and incline to believe, that your apprehensions in regard to the *Stonewall* are unfounded, though the risks are sufficient to justify every precaution. I think the French government has signified to the Spanish government as decided a wish for the detention of the *Stonewall* as could be reconcilable with its theory of irresponsibility for its movements. It insists, moreover, that the *Stonewall* was a Danish vessel, which, it is true, abused the hospitality of French waters, but escaped before her presence there was recognized by the official authority. I have as yet no official evidence which authorizes me to dispute the allegation that the *Stonewall* was actually a Danish vessel when she entered Quiberon Bay, though I am daily expecting the Danish view of the case from our Minister at Copenhagen. I have not neglected to present to this government every view of the case which seemed likely to dispose it to assist in detaining the *Stonewall*, and have insisted, with as much pertinacity as I thought became my position, upon their concurrence with the Spanish government and our own to this end. That steps have been taken to punish some of the parties engaged in equipping the *Stonewall* and conniving at her escape there can be no doubt. To what stage these efforts will be carried time will determine.

"In regard to your own position I hardly feel competent to advise you. If you have reason to apprehend any danger to your vessel from the *Stonewall* in the harbor, you have but one of two courses to pursue—either you must go out into the open sea where you may encounter your enemy on fair terms, or you may take steps to deprive her of the means of injuring you. What these means should be you alone are competent to judge. Captain Page has certainly made very public the statement that his ship was in a very distressed condition when it entered Ferrol, and unable to cross the ocean. A letter from one of the officers has reached Paris of the same tenor. Whether these statements are made to mislead or are genuine, you can best judge. I would counsel extreme prudence in all your relations with the Spanish authorities. The United States cannot afford to establish a precedent which it would not be willing to accept as a rule. The position of our affairs at home is not so desperate as to afford us any justification for irregular or lawless warfare, even if justifiable under different circumstances. An act of lawless violence perpetrated upon your vessel by the *Stonewall* in a port of Spain would probably do your country and its cause more good and the Confederates more damage than the *Niagara* ever has accomplished, or can hope to accomplish in any other way.

"But it does not become me to repeat such commonplaces to an officer of your experience and reputation. I hope most sincerely that you may pass through your difficulties with success, as I am sure you will pass through them with honor. I shall wait most anxiously for news from you and from your gallant companions. I only regret that I have nothing more definite and satisfactory to offer you in the way of counsel.

"I am," etc.

On the day succeeding that on which the foregoing note was written, Commodore Craven addressed the following to our *Chargé* at Madrid:

COMMODORE CRAVEN TO HORATIO J. PERRY.

"U. S. SHIP 'NIAGARA,'
CORUNNA, *February* 28, 1865.

"*Dear Sir*,—I had the honor yesterday of receiving your despatch of the 23d instant, with its accompanying copies of your several despatches to our Secretary of State at Washington and to our *Chargé d'Affaires* at Paris, giving full and very interesting information of what has been done in the matter of the pirate ram *Stonewall*.

"You ask my opinion as to the capability of her going to sea in her present condition. I can only answer this by stating that, from the information I received on my arrival here, and from what I have been able to see of that vessel and learn from our agent and the authorities at Ferrol, providing the information received can be relied on, she is not at this time in a seaworthy condition. The leak has been but imperfectly stopped and might at any time break out and become as inconvenient as ever.

"Notwithstanding the pledges given you by the Spanish ministers that strict orders had been issued to the commandant at Ferrol not to allow any repairs except such as were indispensable for the safety of the crew of the *Stonewall* at sea to be put upon her, notwithstanding the assurances of the naval commandant at Ferrol that those orders had been strictly obeyed, and notwithstanding I place implicit confidence in the honesty of those assurances, I cannot help feeling that in spite of their care and watchfulness to prevent it, the pirates have had the opportunity and have clandestinely improved their time, and have done much more than they had proposed to do towards, not only the repairs, but to the fitting out of their vessel in the bay of Ferrol.

"Besides other occupations, they were busily engaged for one or two days after my arrival at that port in filling up their shells and otherwise preparing their battery for work.

"The *Stonewall* is a very formidable vessel, about one hundred and seventy-five feet long, brig-rigged, and completely clothed in iron plates of five inches in thickness; under her topgallant forecastle is her casemated Armstrong 300-pounder rifled gun, in a turret abaft her mainmast are two 120-pounder rifled guns, and she has two smaller guns mounted in broadside. If as fast as reported to be in smooth water, she ought to be more than a match for three such ships as the *Niagara*. Should we be so fortunate, however, as to catch her out in rough weather we might possibly be able to put an end to her career. Our main chance now depends upon the possibility of detaining her where she is, until the government sees fit to send out the proper reinforcements. In the meantime, and in any event, I shall strive to do my duty.

"As the Spanish authorities have acknowledged their inability to prevent the egress of the *Stonewall* from Ferrol, why *have I not the right 'in self-defence' to seize upon the opportunity to run her down in that harbor? I feel sorely tempted to try it, and were she in a French port, with the same good reasons holding, I should not long hesitate hazarding the die.*

"In order that you may understand fully the part that I have taken in this matter, I enclose, herewith, a copy of a part of a letter which I addressed to Mr. Bigelow on the 20th, and which he has just acknowledged the receipt of by telegram on the 20th. I wished to send you an entire copy of that despatch, but it has not been copied in my letter-book, and I cannot lay my hand on the finishing clause, which, however, was merely introductory of a gentleman who kindly volunteered to bear my despatch to Paris, and is of no importance.

"Thanking you, sir, for your kind consideration in loaning me those press copies of your correspondence, which are herewith returned,

"I am, with great respect, etc., Js. CRAVEN."

On the 6th of March I notified the Minister of Foreign Affairs, upon the authority of our consul, Mr. Dudley, at Liverpool, that the crew of the Confederate steamer *Florida* had been shipped on board the *Stonewall* while lying at Ferrol. "I hasten to bring this information to your Excellency's knowledge," I said, "that the parties who may be concerned in the perpetration of this crime may, by the laws of France, receive speedy and condign punishment."

The Imperial government assumed to have a sufficient pretext for taking no further responsibilities upon itself for the career of the *Stonewall*. Of that pretext it seemed determined to make the most. In a few days we learned that the *Stonewall* had sailed to parts then unknown, and that Commodore Craven did not consider his force sufficient to justify him in pursuing her. Her career, from the time she left Quiberon Bay until she finally passed into the hands of a foreign power is recited by Captain Bullock in his recent work, with some details which had not before transpired and with an authenticity which entitles them to a place in this record:

"Captain Page wrote from Isle d'Houat, near Quiberon, giving a full account of his tedious delays, and the disappointment he felt at not getting a full supply of coal, but he did not like to wait for the return of the coal-tender from St. Nazaire. He advised me that he had taken charge of the ram on behalf of the Confederate government, and that M. Arman's agent, who was with him, had complied with all engagements satisfactorily, and was, therefore, entitled to receive the stipulated commission for his services. The Danish crew was discharged and sent to St. Nazaire, and the ram was chartered and commissioned in due form as the Confederate ship *Stonewall*. In the heavy weather, after leaving Quiberon Bay, the *Stonewall* made a good deal of water, and it was thought that she had sprung a leak somewhere, but owing to the crowded state of the ship a satisfactory examination could not be made. This apparent defect was an additional reason for making a harbor, and, when the gale had moderated, Page bore up and ran into Corunna, and the day after arrival there he took the *Stonewall* across the bay to Ferrol, where all facilities were politely tendered by the officers of the naval arsenal.

"The first advice of the *Stonewall* from Ferrol was without date, but she arrived there about February 2, and Page soon began to lighten the ship by discharging some of the heavy weights into a good dry hulk which the naval authorities had kindly put at his disposal, with the purpose of finding the leak.

"It appears, however, from his correspondence, that the facilities granted him upon his first application were quickly withdrawn. Writing to me, under date of February 7, he says: 'To-day there came an officer to inform me that in consequence of the protest of the American minister the permission to repair damages had been suspended,* and I must restore the things in the hulk of the ship.' Page added, however, that the commanding officer told him that his case was under consideration at Madrid, and that he thought all would be right in a few days. In the end, permission was given to make all necessary repairs, but many difficulties were met with, the authorities appearing to be very desirous to hurry the ship off, yet not willing to turn her out of port in an incomplete state.

"On the 10th of February, Page wrote that the United States frigate *Niagara*, Captain Craven, had arrived; and a few days after the United States ship *Sacramento* joined the *Niagara*, and both vessels anchored at Corunna, about nine miles distant, from whence they could watch the *Stonewall*. Their presence, Page said, gave the Spanish authorities much uneasiness. It was now manifest that the *Stonewall's* movements were known. The two United States ships at Corunna would either attack her when she attempted to leave Ferrol, or they would follow her across

---

* This was four days after my despatch to M. Drouyn de Lhuys, cited above, p. 61.

the Atlantic. Besides, this advice of her being at sea would be sent to New York, and preparations would be made by the United States naval authorities to give her a warm reception. The leak was discovered to be in consequence of defective construction in the rudder-casing, and this, together with other injuries caused by the rough handling the ship had encountered during the tempestuous voyage from Copenhagen, satisfied Page that the repairs would detain her several weeks at Ferrol. He took also into consideration the latest news from America, which appeared to indicate that the South could not resist much longer. Finally, he determined to go to Paris for consultation, and he directed Carter meanwhile to push on with the repairs. While Page was absent, the *Niagara* and *Sacramento* ran across the bay from Corunna and anchored at Ferrol. In a letter, reporting the incident, Carter said:

"'We of course got ready for accidents, and in lighting fires sparks flew from the funnel. In a few minutes a barge from the navy-yard, with an officer of rank, came alongside, asking if we meant to attack the *Niagara*. I replied that we had no such intention, but proposed to defend ourselves from an attempt to repeat the affair at Bahia.* He said, "This is not Brazil. The admiral requests that you will let your fires go out, and warns you against any attempt to break the peace." Two guard-boats were also stationed near us, and remained there every night while the *Niagara* was in port. However, we kept steam all night and the chain unshackled, so as to get the ram pointed in case the *Niagara* moved our way.'

"It was decided, after consultation with the Confederate commissioners, that in spite of the gloomy prospects across the Atlantic, no possible effort that could be made from Europe should be abandoned. Page, therefore, returned to Ferrol with the purpose to pursue his enterprise, which, I may just say in brief phrase, was to go to Bermuda, get some additional ordnance stores and a few picked men from the *Florida* waiting there for him, and then attempt to strike a blow at Port Royal, which was then supposed to be the base of General Sherman's advance through South Carolina.

---

* This was in allusion to the capture of the *Florida*, at Bahia, by the United States ship *Wachusett*.

"Vexatious delays detained the *Stonewall* at Ferrol until March 24, when Page got to sea. The United States ships *Niagara* and *Sacramento* had manifested every purpose to follow and attack the *Stonewall* when she left Ferrol. The *Niagara* was a large, powerful frigate, mounting ten 150-pounder Parrot rifled-guns; and the *Sacramento* was a corvette, very heavily armed for her class, the principal pieces being two 11-inch and two 9-inch guns. The *Stonewall* was protected by four-and-three-quarter-inch armor, and mounted one one quarter 300 pounder and two 70-pounder Armstrong guns; but she was a small ship and low in the water, and the *Niagara* battery could have commanded her decks. Page, being quite sure that he would be followed out and attacked as soon as he had passed the line of Spanish jurisdiction, cleared for action before getting under way, in full sight of the two United States ships. The upper spars to the lower masts were struck and stowed on deck and the boats were detached from the davits.

"In this trim the *Stonewall* steamed out of Ferrol on the morning of March 24, 1865, accompanied by a large Spanish steam-frigate. At about three miles from the shore the frigate fired a gun, and returned to Ferrol. The *Stonewall* then stood off and on all the remainder of the day, with her colors flying in full plain view of the two United States vessels, which remained at anchor. Carter, in a letter, says, 'We could see the officers standing in the *Niagara's* tops using spyglasses.'

"At dark the *Stonewall* stood close in to the entrance of the harbor, and then, being satisfied that the enemy did not intend to come out and fight, Page bore away and steamed down the coast to Lisbon, where he arrived in due course, the *Niagara* arriving about thirty-six hours after him.

"Commenting upon the failure of the *Niagara* and *Sacramento* to follow the *Stonewall* and attack her, Page wrote me from Lisbon as follows: 'This will doubtless seem as inexplicable to you as it is to me and to all of us. To suppose that those two heavily-armed men-of-war were afraid of the *Stonewall* is to me incredible, yet the fact of their conduct was such as I have stated to you. Finding that they declined coming out, there was no course for me but to pursue my voyage.'

"Captain Thomas T. Craven, who commanded the *Niagara*, was not the officer who was mentioned in another chapter as the commander of the United States ship *Tuscarora*, and who had a correspondence with the governor of Gibraltar in respect to the Confederate ship *Sumter*. Captain Thomas T. Craven was an elder brother of the latter-named officer. His conduct in making so much parade of a purpose to stop the *Stonewall* and the subsequent failure to accept her invitation to come out and engage her was a good deal criticised at the time. I have no means of knowing what explanation of his conduct he made to his own government, and I should be sorry to repeat any of the gossip of the period which might suggest a slur upon his courage. His reputation in the United States navy, while I held a commission in that service, was such as to place him above any suspicion. He was certainly an able and efficient officer, and I mention the incident with the *Stonewall* as an historical fact and without the slightest purpose to cast an imputation upon his memory.

"At Lisbon, Page was made to feel that he was the representative of a losing cause. He was permitted to get a supply of coal, but it was manifest that the authorities wished him clear of the port. He got away as soon as possible, proceeded to Santa Cruz, in the island of Teneriffe, replenished his fuel there, and thence stood down into the northeast Trades. On April 25 he hauled up for Bermuda, but encountered northwest winds and heavy head swell immediately after leaving the Trade winds, and being in rather short supply of coals he shaped his course for Nassau, arriving there May 6. From Nassau he proceeded to Havana.

"At the time of Page's arrival at Havana the war was practically at an end. In a few days he learned of General Lee's surrender, and, soon after, of the capture of Mr. Davis. Manifestly he could now venture upon no offensive operation. The small amount of funds he took from Ferrol was exhausted. Major Helm, the Confederate agent, could do nothing for him in that way. The position was perplexing and quite exceptional. As a last resource negotiations were opened with the Cuban authorities for the surrender of the ship to them, if they would advance the money necessary to pay off the crew. When it was known, through a resident merchant, that the captain-general was willing to make the necessary advance and take the ship, Carter was sent to state the requirements and get the money, and his brief report of the interview was as follows:

" 'After five minutes' conversation, the captain-general asked what sum we required. I said, "$16,000." He said, "Say $100,000." I replied that my orders were to ask for $16,000. He then turned to an official at a desk and bid (*sic*) him write, continued asking questions, and when the document was handed to him for perusal he looked at me again and said, "Shall we make it $50,000?" But I obeyed orders, and $16,000 was ordered to be paid.'

"Upon the receipt of the money Page paid off the crew to May 19, 1865, and delivered the *Stonewall* into the hands of the Captain-General of Cuba. In July, 1865, she was delivered to the government of the United States, and the conditions of the surrender are set out in the annexed correspondence between the Spanish minister at Washington and Mr. Seward, the United States Secretary of State. She was subsequently sold by the United States to the government of Japan."*

Commodore Craven's version of the story was set forth in a letter written from Lisbon on the 4th of March, 1865, to the Navy Department.†

COMMODORE CRAVEN TO THE SECRETARY OF THE NAVY.

U. S. SHIP "NIAGARA," LISBON, *March* 29, 1865.

"*Sir,*—I have the honor to inform you of the arrival of the *Niagara* and *Sacramento* at the port of Lisbon, on the evening of the 27th instant, two days from Corunna.

"Since the date of my despatch to you of February 28, No. 4, and up to the 24th instant, the pirate *Stonewall* has been still lying in the harbor of Ferrol, where, as I anticipated, she succeeded in adding to the number of her crew, in finishing her equipments, and fitting out for sea in the most thorough manner.

"On Tuesday the 21st, and on Thursday the 23d instant, having stripped ship to her lower masts, she left her anchorage and stood out some two miles from the entrance of the harbor; but the state of the sea was not favorable for her purposes, and as

---

* Bullock's "Secret Service of the Confederate States," vol. ii. p. 96.

† I am indebted to the courtesy of Mr. Secretary Whitney for a copy of this letter.

the *Niagara* and *Sacramento* were steaming out of the Bay of Corunna to meet her she turned and ran back to her old berth. After showing ourselves off the mouth of Ferrol, we returned to our former positions in the Bay of Corunna.

"On the morning of the 24th, a dead calm prevailing, with a smooth, glassy sea, she again made her appearance outside, and to the northward of Corunna, accompanied, as on the two former occasions, by the Spanish steam-frigate *Conception*. At this time the odds in her favor were too great and too certain, in my humble judgment, to admit of the slightest hope of being able to inflict upon her even the most trifling injury; whereas, if we had gone out, the *Niagara* would, most undoubtedly, have been easily and promptly destroyed. So thoroughly a one-sided combat I did not consider myself called upon to engage in. As she had left her boats behind her, my impression was that she would return again to Ferrol; but on Saturday morning she was reported as being still outside and lying under a point of land to the northward of Ferrol. In the afternoon, however, I learned that she was last seen early in the morning steaming rapidly to the westward, when, immediately after paying our bills on shore, for coals, etc., we got under way and made the best of our way to this port, our progress being considerably retarded by the inability of the *Sacramento* to keep up with us.

"On our arrival in the Tagus, an officer from the Portuguese guard-ship came on board, and informed me that the *Stonewall* had arrived here on Sunday, the 26th instant, thirty hours from Ferrol; that she had just finished coaling, and in conformity with a positive order given by his government to leave the port, she was at that moment in the act of getting under way; at the same time this officer stated that it was the urgent desire of his king that I should anchor where I then was, about half a mile to the eastward of the tower of Belam, and not attempt to go out of the harbor until twenty-four hours had elapsed after the departure of the *Stonewall*. Contrary to his promises, he, Captain Page, did not sail until about 11 o'clock yesterday morning, at which time I was at the residence of our minister, Mr. Harvey.

"By telegrams from the several signal stations upon the coast, the pirate was reported to be (when last seen) steering north; but had gradually drawn off from the land.

"From the foregoing you will learn, sir, that after forty-five days of constant watchfulness, at times buoyed up with the hope that she might be detained definitely at Ferrol, or until reinforcements should reach us from home, I have been compelled to lose sight of one of the most formidable iron-clad vessels now afloat.

"It may appear to some that I ought to have run the hazard of a battle, but, according to my judgment, I shall ever feel that I have done all that could properly be attempted towards retarding the operations and progress of that vessel.

"All of my suspicions (which I have freely expressed to our Ministers at Paris and Madrid) as to the truth of her reported leaks and unseaworthiness, and my convictions that she would make a convenience of the harbor of Ferrol to finish her equipments, etc., have been most fully verified.

"I am now awaiting the arrival of two blockade-runners, reported to be on their way here from Liverpool, and, after remaining here a reasonable time, shall run down as far as Madeira and thence back to the English Channel *via* the Western Islands.

"While at Ferrol, and during their brief stay here, Captain Page and his officers had talked freely of their intention to visit some of our Northern cities, and particularly New York, where they contemplated levying heavy contributions, or destroying the towns. Very respectfully,

"Your obedient servant,

"THOS. T. CRAVEN, *Commodore U. S. Navy.*

"The Honorable GIDEON WELLES."

The surprise expressed by Captains Page and Bullock that the *Stonewall* was permitted to leave the ports of Ferrol and Lisbon unmolested was not creditable to their magnanimity, and the hesitated slur upon the courage of the Union commander cannot be allowed to pass unchallenged. I will judge their criticisms by their own standards.

Captain Bullock previously had built, at the Laird's ship-yard in England, for the Confederate navy, two armored rams, which were then indisputably the most formidable vessels that had to that time ever been floated. "I designed these ships," he said, "for something more than for coast defence, and I confidently believe, if ready for sea now, they would sweep away the entire blockading fleet of the enemy." In his letter to the Secretary of the Confederate Navy, dated July 9, 1863, he says: "They would thus be able to overcome any wooden ships or a fleet of them. I respectfully propose, then, that the ships, when ready for sea, should be ordered to proceed as quickly as possible to Wilmington, North Carolina. One could fall in with the land at New Inlet and the other at the main 'ship-bar' at the mouth of Cape Fear River; by steaming quietly in at early daylight they might entirely destroy the blockading vessels. Not one should be left to steal away and make known the fact that the iron-clads were on the coast; crews might be ready at Smithville or Fort Caswell, to be put on board the ships as soon as they had destroyed or dispersed the blockaders, and in a very few hours afterwards the two vessels would be ready to strike a decisive blow in any direction. When the departure of the iron-clads from Europe can be definitely determined, say within two weeks, a special messenger is to be sent to report specifically to you, so that all necessary steps can be taken and arrangements made to carry out the further views of the department.

* * * * * * * *

"The Atlantic coast offers enticing and decisive

work in more than one direction. Without a moment's delay, after getting their crews on board at Wilmington, our vessels might sail southward, sweep the blockading fleet from the sea-front of every harbor from the capes of Virginia to Sabine Pass, and, cruising up and down the coast, could prevent anything like a permanent systematic interruption of our foreign trade for the future. Again, should Wilmington still be held by the enemy, our ironclads could ascend the Potomac, and, after destroying all transports and gunboats falling within their reach, could render Washington itself untenable."

The English government seized this ram, and immediately placed at the disposal of Captain Inglefield, in order to prevent its escape, her majesty's ship *Majestic*, sixty guns, her majesty's ship *Liverpool*, sixty guns, three gunboats with one pivot gun each. It also proffered to reinforce them with her majesty's ship *Prince Consort*. Such was the view which the English government entertained of the effective powers of this vessel.

We have already seen that Captain Bullock himself estimated this ram to be more than a match for all our Monitors, and they had already proven themselves capable of destroying any number of wooden vessels that could be brought against them.

Now the *Stonewall*, as will be apparent to experts from her description, was a far more formidable instrument of destruction than the English ram; she was superior in armament, more easily handled than any vessel then afloat, and she had been planned and constructed for the specific purpose of destroying, first our great Atlantic blockading fleets, and then the Mississippi squadron. Her cruise from Bordeaux to Copenhagen established her speed against a head wind and sea of from ten to ten and a half knots an hour. And, finally, she was equipped with twin-screws, working separately, so as to be capable of a simultaneous counter-motion.

On the other hand, the *Niagara* was a wooden vessel. She had been one of the most powerful vessels in our navy, and a fast sailer—perhaps the fastest ship afloat. She was, also, when her engines and boilers were in good condition, fast under steam (for those times), as she could steam between ten and eleven knots. She had, however, been more than two years in commission, and had never been without fires under her boilers for a moment during all this time. She had, while on the European coast, been compelled to use soft English coal, while her boilers were intended for anthracite. She could not at that time steam more than eight to eight and a half knots under the most favorable circumstances. Her battery had been condemned by a board of survey as unserviceable. The "Reports of Target Practice" show that shot fired from her guns would "tumble" and be deflected from the object to which they were pointed, "wabbling about" to the right and to the left and from left to right. Under steam it required fifteen minutes for the *Niagara* to turn around. Running at a speed of eight knots an hour, she would have to travel two miles and more to get about, and she required a space of at least three quarters of a mile in performing this evolution, whereas the *Stonewall* could turn on her centre while going either forward or backward, in something *less than one and a half minutes.* The *Sacramento*, the crippled consort of the *Niagara*, could at her best scarcely make six knots an hour, and her boilers were burned out and in such a condition that she would have been of no practical assistance in a fight with a ten-knot ship, even had they been anywhere nearly equal in other respects.

Fully a month before the *Stonewall* escaped from Ferrol, Commodore Craven wrote to our *chargé* at Madrid that "if she" (the *Stonewall*) "is as fast as reported, in a smooth sea she would be more than a match for three such ships as the *Niagara*. In a rough sea we might worry her considerably. Our only chance for cutting short her career rests upon the possibility of detaining her here until such time as our government sees fit to send out reinforcements."

The reinforcements, however, never came.

It does not appear in Captain Bullock's report, though I think, in fairness, it should have appeared there, that the *Niagara* did go out twice with intent to give the *Stonewall* battle, in spite of all the disadvantages with which she had to contend; the first time on the 21st of March and the second time on the 23d. On these two occasions a breeze was blowing and the sea was a little rough, which somewhat neutralized the disparity of force of the antagonists. On both these occasions the *Stonewall* ran back to her anchorage, Captain Page declining the risk of a battle in which all the advantages were not on his side. On the 24th the sea was as smooth as a mirror, and Captain Page was as brave as a lion, for he had no doubt of his ability, under such conditions, to destroy the *Niagara* before she could be turned around. Neither had Captain Craven, and therefore he had the courage to save his ships, and deprive the Confederates of the prestige of such an inexpensive victory as the more popular course of action on his part would have given them. His view was, practically, sustained by his government. A court-martial was ordered, as a matter of course, at the commodore's request, on his return. The results of this trial* established the facts that neither the court, embracing several of the most experienced officers of our navy, nor the Secretary of the Navy himself, believed that Craven had failed in his duty in not attacking the *Stonewall*, though some of them no doubt thought, as the country generally was disposed to think, that it was an opportunity for a commander to take the risk of losing his ship, of which a man willing to subordinate the interests of his country to his personal ambition would have made a mistake in not availing himself.

That the government at Washington had lost none of its confidence in the commodore was evidenced by his reappointment to an important command and his remaining in active service until retired by age.†

---

* The details of this trial will be found in Appendix B.

† In July, 1866, Commodore Craven was placed in command of the navy yard at Mare Island, California. On the 10th October, 1866, he was commissioned Rear Admiral. In August, 1868,

With the cruise of which we have given the somewhat inglorious termination the career of the *Niagara* as a vessel-of-war may be said to have ended. She lay at anchor in the Boston Navy Yard after the war until the 6th of May, 1885, when she was sold at auction, in the twenty-first year of her age, for $12,350. She had cost originally $754,000. The purchaser was Peter Butler, a junk-dealer, who, in June following, had her towed down to Apple Island and burned for the metal in her structure.

---

he was placed in command of the North Pacific Squadron. In March, 1869, he was ordered to resume the command of the navy yard at Mare Island, where he continued until, on attaining sixty-two years of age, he was retired. He was immediately appointed Port Admiral at San Francisco, where he continued on active duty until the office of Port Admiral was abolished, in October, 1870. The commodore died at the Charlestown navy yard, on the 23d of August, 1887.

Chapter VIII.

Prosecution of Arman to Recover the Price of the Confederate Steamers Sold to Foreign Powers.—Berryer's Argument.—Strange Rules of Evidence in French Courts.—Arman's Balance Sheet.

As the Confederate navy had now done us all the mischief it could, I determined to see if it could not be turned to some use in the settlement of impending difficulties with the Imperial government. Though the termination of the war and the surrender of the *Stonewall* extinguished one source of profound anxiety, our relations with the emperor were anything but serene. His attempt to take advantage of our domestic troubles to destroy the autonomy of a sister republic and to impose a dynastic government on the people of Mexico had produced in the United States a feeling of profound discontent. But wisely concluding that one war at a time was enough, Mr. Seward contented himself till the close of the war with quietly declining to recognize the military organization in Mexico, of which the Prince Maximilian of Austria was the ostensible head. This attitude was fatal to the consolidation of the new empire.

No sooner had peace been established within our borders than I received instructions to give more formal expression to the discontent of our government with the Franco-Austrian intervention in Mexican affairs. Determined as we were that the French army should leave Mexico to decide for herself whether Maximilian's government or that of Juarez suited her best, but anxious to avoid any proceeding that would have a tendency to wound the pride of the French people and rally their patriotism to the support of the emperor, we limited our resistance to measures tending to render the emperor's occupation of Mexico as expensive to, and as unpopular with, his subjects as possible. Looked at from that point of view, I did not feel that we could afford to allow the emperor's treacherous connivance with the Confederate agents to sleep. I thought that so long as he annoyed us with his army in Mexico we should neglect no opportunity of annoying him at home, and for that reason more than any other, I asked and obtained from Mr. Seward permission to institute proceedings in the French courts for the recovery of the money which Arman and his associates received for the ships built by him and his associates for account of the Confederates, and also for damages sustained by the United States in consequence of their construction.

Arman had been twice paid for his ships, first by the Confederates as they progressed, and a second time, for all but the *Stonewall*, by their respective purchasers. We claimed that the second price belonged to us.

The publicity which would necessarily be given to the duplicity of the Imperial government by a judicial investigation could hardly fail to strengthen the hands of our friends in the Legislative Assembly and among the people.

A suit was accordingly instituted in the upper chamber of the civil tribunal of the Seine, on the 6th of July, 1866. The United States were plaintiffs of record, and Messrs. Arman, Erlanger, Voruz, Dubigeon, Jollet & Babin, Mazeline, and the *Société des Chantiers et Ateliers de l'Océan* were defendants.

After several hearings during the months of June and July, 1868, Henry Moreau and M. Berryer appearing for the United States, and MM. Lacan and Andrel for Arman and associates, the case was finally submitted.* Neither the eloquence of our coun-

---

* It is worthy of record here that this was the last occasion in which the voice of the great Berryer was ever heard at the bar. For this reason, if for no other, it may be pleasing to those who shared the hopes and fears of the Unionists in the war of 1861–5 to read an extract from the introductory portion of M. Berryer's last professional address, which exhibits the sentiments towards the United States which animated him in the closing years of his life:

"The Confederate States have been warmly commended for their enterprise, and for the manner in which they have sustained this long and bloody war. Of this as a matter of opinion I have nothing to say. When a foreign nation finds itself in face of a people rent by intestine dissensions and civil war it may think what it pleases of the causes, motives, and reasons which have animated the insurgent party. The freedom of opinion is entire; that I perfectly comprehend.

"But if opinions are free in such a situation, permit me to say that actions are not. Duties are imposed on individuals, not only by the law of nations which prevails among all the civilized nations of the earth, but also by the law of the country to which the individuals belong, and the question to be settled by these

sel nor the strength of our case were sufficient to cope with the adverse influences operating upon the court, and our claim was rejected, on the grounds

---

proceedings is, what were the duties and obligations which the French government imposed on French citizens in relation to the conflict which disturbed the United States? Let it be said, if you please, that the Southern States had a noble cause, that they even maintained it in the name of liberty; that they were justified in breaking the federal bond and separating themselves from the nation of which they formed a part; that they have wished to reconquer their independence, one of the rights of liberty. Gentlemen, I have a great respect for the rights of liberty and its principles. I cherish and will always defend them when they represent the moral force of a people, uniting all its members by the respect which each has for the rights which belong to all.

"The liberty which unites, which makes nations strong, that is the liberty which I wish; but I repel all theories which tend to disorder in society or in families. The war of the Confederates has been compared to the American war of Independence.

"What! will you compare people who break their political bonds, their social bonds, their federal bonds, with those colonies which endured all the vexations of foreign domination, which were subjected to the fiscal laws of England without any part in her government, and who, seconded by us, bravely conquered their enfranchisement.

"Ah, gentlemen, in this contest between the United States and the Confederate States I leave to others the eulogy of an insurrection which had no other purpose but one which no one here would dare to sustain or avow, the perpetuation of slavery. This was the sole object of the rash leaders who put themselves at the head of the insurrection, of which they left no doubt by proclaiming in the first article of their constitution that slavery should forever be maintained in the Confederate States.

"Such was the end which they proposed to themselves and which they are come here to defend in the name of freedom, in the name of liberal principles, against what? Against the effort

that the declaration of neutrality of 10th of June, 1851, was an act of sovereignty which imposed duties upon French subjects, but created no rights by which the belligerents could profit; that the price of those ships was not proven to have been paid out of American funds, and, finally, that the correspondence upon which the plaintiffs relied to prove their cause must necessarily have been originally procured by improper means from their legitimate owner, and therefore could not serve as the basis of any judicial conclusions.

I forbear to discuss the judicial merits of this decision, for the reason that before it was deliv-

---

made, nobly made, against this great and beautiful federation, this federation which in France we ought to respect and for which we ought to pray that it may be protected against insurrection tending to dissolve it; this federation, our work, to the birth of which France contributed so gloriously in the last years of her ancient monarchy; this federation which has constituted a great people, magnificent by the liberal tone of its institutions, by the principles of justice which rule so austerely its society, and by everything else which make of it an immense nation—this nation grows every day, gathering into its embrace all who suffer in other parts of the world, and who, desiring to be prosperous, respectable, and happy, come to be made citizens of the United States.

"It is this work of the federation that they wish to shake, and against which they are trying to arouse the prejudices of France at the very time that we are bound by so many liens—by the memories of its origin, by all the relations of social and industrial interests—to this nation which has become such a power in the world and which, perhaps, will some day be the necessary and most available ally of France. Behold the sentiments, if this is a question of sentiments, which ought to be uppermost in our hearts when we contemplate the struggle in which the states of the American Union engaged in 1861."

ered the result of the litigation had lost its original and chief importance. The emperor had been compelled, under peculiarly humiliating circumstances, to withdraw his troops from Mexico; Maximilian had been shot, and the French people had amply expiated the criminal folly of their sovereign in conspiring to cripple the United States with the view of maintaining a Franco-Austrian dynasty upon the ruins of a sister republic.

There was one feature of the decision, however, upon which self-respect constrains me to submit a few observations. I refer to the exclusion of a portion of the plaintiff's testimony on the ground that it was procured by unjustifiable means. This was a wanton perversion of justice. The plaintiff's agents in Paris were never asked how they became possessed of the documents; none of the parties to the Confederate's contracts, if put upon the stand —neither Bullock, nor Arman, nor Erlanger, nor Voruz, nor Mazeline, nor Dubigeon fils—could have denied any of the plaintiff's allegations, but must have admitted all; the ministry were cognizant of the whole transaction, both from the lips of Arman and the emperor. The correspondence which I furnished Mr. Dayton was of no more importance, when this trial took place, to prove the character and purpose of those ships, than the identical apples which Newton saw fall are necessary to prove the law of gravitation. In fact there were no witnesses to be found who could throw a doubt upon the plaintiff's view of them.

Captain Bullock and Mr. Slidell professed to be

very much shocked that Mr. Dayton presented these documents. "The agents and emissaries of the Washington government," wrote Mr. Slidell, "not satisfied with the establishment of a vast organized system of espionage and the subornation of perjured informers, now unblushingly have recourse to theft and forgery to attain their ends."

The defeat of a scheme from which such important results were fairly to be expected, by its exposure, was enough to try the patience and temper of more disciplined natures than either Slidell's or Bullock's. "Lambs could not forgive, nor worms forget it." But how absurd in an official communication to characterize a transaction of which, so far as the agents of the Washington government were concerned, they knew absolutely nothing wrong, as "theft and forgery." Bullock and Slidell would have been ashamed to admit to each other, or to anybody else, that they would have hesitated a moment to secure, upon any condition, the means of doing one half the mischief to the Federals which the exposure of their plot deprived them of the means of inflicting. What did the agents do? A man comes to my office, tells me the Confederates are building several vessels-of-war—some of them more formidable than any in the English or American navy—in the ports of Bordeaux and Nantes, in violation not only of the neutral obligations of the Imperial government, but in violation of the laws and police regulations of the empire, to prey upon the commerce and ravage the seaports of a friendly nation of which I was an officer. He exhibits unmistakable evidence of the truth of his story. He then adds, if you will pay me a certain sum of money, you can communicate this information to whom it may concern. Having that information without money and without price, I pay for the privilege of communicating it to the prime-minister of France, whom it most concerns. I bought this privilege for a price, and then freely, and without charge, gave the information, that the laws of France were being violated and its relations with a friendly power compromised, to the French government. That was all there was of it. How Mr. X became possessed of the documents I did not know, nor do I know now, except what is alleged in Slidell's correspondence.* Nor would

---

* As the French judges, in their opinions, treated as proven the fact that the documents put in evidence by the United States had been procured by some illicit means, I applied through our obliging minister in Paris, in June last, and since the preceding pages were written, for a copy of the record, taking it for granted that there must have been some testimony before the court to justify, judicially at least, the language with which they had allowed themselves to characterize the testimony submitted by the plaintiffs. To my infinite surprise, I learned from the reply of the French Minister of Justice that no testimony had ever been taken at all in the case; that the court had accepted the statements of Arman's counsel as testimony, and upon them, in part at least, rested their decision.

Another extraordinary fact is disclosed by this correspondence, a copy of which follows· and that is that Petermann, the alleged unfaithful clerk of M. Voruz, was never held for trial, nor did M. Voruz ever enter any complaint against him. Why this forbearance was extended to Petermann by his employer is a question to which a correct reply could hardly fail to be edifying. Lacking such a reply, it may be profitable to meditate

5

it have made any difference if I had known. Slidell & Co. were engaged in a criminal act. If they were betrayed by their confederates, that was their

on the suggestion thrown out by Mr. X when asked how those documents came into his possession, that everybody was not as anxious as Mr. Bullock was that those vessels should be finished and equipped to be used against the United States.

THE FRENCH MINISTER OF JUSTICE TO THE AMERICAN MINISTER.

(Translation.)

"PARIS, *June* 27, 1887.

"*Sir*,—By your favor of the 23d May last, you have been pleased to advise me that Mr. John Bigelow, former Minister of the United States, desired, for purposes purely historical, to have a copy of the record of proceedings which had been instituted before the Tribunal of Nantes against a Mr. Petermann, for subtracting from M. Voruz, a builder, various papers relating to an order for ships-of-war for the account of the Confederate States of America.

"In reply to this communication, I have the honor to send you, under this cover, a note emanating from the Minister of Justice, from which it appears, as you will see, that no proceedings have been instituted at Nantes, nor any inquest opened by the *parquet* of this city against the said Petermann.

"Accept assurances of the high consideration with which I have the honor to be, sir,

"Your very humble and very obedient servant,

"FLOURENS.

"MR. MACLANE, United States Minister at Paris."

"NOTE.

"From researches made by M. the *Procureur-General* of Rennes, it appears that no proceedings have been instituted, and that no inquest has been opened at Nantes against M. Petermann on the occasion of his subtraction from M. Voruz, builder, of various papers relating to an order of ships of-war for account of the Confederate States of America.

"During the War of Secession M. Voruz had received from

affair, not mine. Had I failed to secure these letters because I found upon inquiry that Mr. X had not been to the confessional since they came into his possession, I should never have dared to return to the United States. There may possibly be a higher plane of duty than that which we occupied, but no one who proposes to occupy that plane has any right to accept office under any civil government. Dr. Franklin was called a thief, by the King's Solicitor-General in the House of Lords, for receiving and sending home the Hutchinson and Oliver letters, but no one questioned the propriety of his conduct save those whose treacherous schemes he

---

the States of the South an order for two ships-of-war. Petermann, who was employed by this constructor, allowed himself to be corrupted, and sold the papers which passed between the States of the South and Mr. Voruz, for money.

"The *Phare et Loire* published these contracts. M. de Chasseloup-Loubat, at that time Minister of Marine, notified M. Voruz that the delivery of the ships might lead to trouble, as a cruiser was then guarding the entrance of the port of St. Nazaire.

"The Confederate States of the South then urged M. Voruz to sell the ships, even at a loss, to recover a portion of their advances.

"M. Voruz was so fortunate as to dispose of them to Peru, and they were delivered without difficulty to the government of Peru.

"*Petermann was not prosecuted. M. Voruz, in fact, has never made any complaint against him.*"

The originals of these documents will be found in Appendix C.

Curiously enough, according to our American notions of judicial as well as of official responsibility, the Minister of Justice of the French republic assumes as proven, and states as officially established facts, what in the same document he shows was never proven at all.

thwarted. Defeated lawyers have a prescriptive right to swear at the court, but men whose judgments are not warped by disappointment reason in those cases like Edgar, in "King Lear," over the papers he found in the pockets of Oswald:

> "Let's see his pockets; these letters, that he speaks of
> May be my friends.—He's dead; I am only sorry
> He had no other deathsman.—Let us see:
> Leave, gentle wax; and, manners, blame us not:
> To know our enemies' minds, we'd rip their hearts;
> Their papers, is more lawful."

Captain Bullock reproaches the French Minister of Foreign Affairs for paying any attention to the documents submitted to him by Mr. Dayton, and says he should have said to him, "They could only have come into your possession by bribery or treachery. I cannot, therefore, receive them in evidence, and must insist that you produce the originals and explain how you became possessed of them."

It never seems to have occurred to Captain Bullock that if M. Drouyn de Lhuys had thus challenged Mr. Dayton to produce the originals, the originals, which were in my possession, would have been produced; that M. Drouyn de Lhuys may have refrained for that very reason from offering such a challenge to Mr. Dayton, not wishing to increase the difficulty of adhering to the indecisive policy which was traced out for him by his master.

Besides, M. Drouyn de Lhuys knew that the documents were genuine. What was it to him how they were obtained. The question between his government and ours was simply this, had the neutrality laws and engagements of France been violated, as charged by Mr. Dayton? Knowing they had been, how absurd for him to ask for additional proof, or to pretend to Mr. Dayton that he could not proceed against the accused parties because he did not believe they were guilty. Besides, the idea of the ministers of the third empire having any scruple about using a document or anything else till they knew where and how it was obtained is inexpressibly ludicrous. That the same objections to these documents as evidence was subsequently made with success in the French courts would not make it sound any the less preposterous in the mouth of M. Drouyn de Lhuys.

We took an appeal from the decision of the Tribunal of the Seine, more as a protest against its absurdity than from any interest in the final result. This appeal was set down for hearing on the 11th of July, 1870. M. Berryer had died on the 29th of November, 1868, and M. Jules Favre was retained in his place. Before the second hearing the emperor was a prisoner at Coburg, Jules Favre was called to the Ministry of Foreign Affairs, and our case was argued by M. Moreau, M. Lacan again appearing for Arman and his associates. The decision of the Court below was sustained.

Arman died shortly after these events, bankrupt and broken-hearted. "It is due to his memory," says Mr. Bullock, "that I should say that he offered to settle his accounts with me after the close of the war; but, when he did so, we did not agree as to the balance due, and I was not willing to assume any further responsibility with reference to Confederate affairs. Subsequently, he proposed to pay over to the United States, by way of compromise, a considerable amount, if I would certify the statement of accounts and the United States would accept a compromise and refrain from taking legal proceedings against him. I declined to give the certificate because the statement did not exhibit the balance which I should have claimed on behalf of my principals, and I had no authority to make an arrangement or compromise for their successors."

Mr. Bullock adds, in a note, that the disagreement between M. Arman and himself was not in respect to the amounts received and disbursed by him, but in respect to the large commissions charged by Arman for effecting the forced sale of the ships by order of the government.

Mr. Bullock does not give the account submitted to him and which he refused to certify. This omission I think I am in a condition to supply. At all events, the following balance-sheet from Arman's office and bearing date the 1st of July, 1866, can hardly be any other than the one referred to by Mr. Bullock. It presents a curiously interesting and entirely authentic summary of the fiscal transactions of the Confederate agents with M. Arman.

Doivent les Navires "Yeddo," "Osacca," "Sphinx," et "Cheops," leur Compte Spécial de Vente.			A voir.		
1864, Juin 22.	Solde dû par J. Bullock sur le prix de construction de 4 navires	2,320,000	1864, Juillet 3.	Reçu de la Prusse ⅓ du prix du *Yeddo*	1,000,000
" Juillet 19.	Débit du compte de vente du clipper *Yeddo*	257,152.91	" " 4.	Reçu de la Prusse ⅓ du prix du *Osacca*	1,000,000
" "	Débit du compte de vente du clipper *Osacca*	253,752.07	" " 12.	Reçu de la Prusse 2de mortié du prix du *Yeddo*	1,000,000
" "	Compte sur remises sur Londres	1,000,000	" " "	Reçu de la Prusse 2de mortié du prix du *Osacca*	1,000,000
" Août 26.	Compte sur remises sur Londres	250,000	" Déc. 29.	Reçu de la Prusse 1re au compte du prix du *Cheops*.	725,000
" " 30.	Compte sur remises sur Paris	250,000	1865, Sept. 23.	Reçu de la Prusse 2de à compte du prix du *Cheops*	1,350,000
1865, Avril 4.	Artillerie achetée pour compte J. D. Bullock, frets, assurance, consignations avances et commissions	425,000			
" Mai 6.	Débit du compte du bélier *Sphinx* au moment de son désarmement à Copenhague	729,131.02			
" "	Débit du compte du bélier le *Cheops*	462,440.25			
		5,947,476.25			
	Solde créditeur	127,523.75			
	Francs	6,075,000.00		Solde créditeur.... Francs	127,523.75
					6,075,000.00

Paris, le 1er Juillet, 1866.   Sauf erreurs ou omissions

(Signé) L. ARMAN.

PART II.

PART SECOND.

CHAPTER IX.

Slidell's First Interview with the Emperor.—Thouvenel Talks "Banalties."—Slidell Submits Benjamin's Proposal to Hire the Emperor's Fleet to Break the Blockade.—Proposes to Make Common Cause with the French in Mexico.

FROM a reluctance to interrupt the preceding narrative, I have passed without remark several statements and allegations in the correspondence of the Confederate agents which invited remark, and which I cannot be expected to dismiss without some further notice.

In the first place, I am unwilling to take final leave of Captain Bullock without correcting a very serious error into which he was betrayed, partly, no doubt, by his hopes, but chiefly by the highly colored bulletins of Slidell and Benjamin. He assumed in all his operations in France, and has assumed in his commentaries, that the emperor was pledged to allow Arman's ships to be built for and delivered to the Confederates, and was guilty of a breach of faith in refusing them exit under the Confederate flag. That this was Captain Bullock's firm conviction, I have no doubt; and that this conviction was authorized by Slidell's reports, I have no doubt. I have as little doubt that in this conviction, so far as the emperor was concerned, he was entirely mistaken. The emperor dealt falsely with the United States from the outset, but there is no evidence that he did not faithfully keep all his engagements with the Confederates. He promised that the ships might be built and allowed to sail *if their real destination was concealed;* if they could be got out of French waters without compromising his neutrality. This was all he ever promised Slidell or any one else. That the ships should be built; that the secret should be kept; and that the vessels should get out and decide the transatlantic struggle in favor of the Confederates, he, no doubt, ardently desired. If he was guilty of treachery and duplicity, it was towards the United States, not towards the Confederates. But the secret of the destination of the ships was not kept. When the documentary evidence that they were destined for the Confederate States was placed in the hands of his Minister of Foreign Affairs he was no longer bound to let them go. It was through no fault of his that the secret got out, but being out, to let the vessels sail would have been not only a violation of his neutral obligations, but, practically, a declaration of war upon the United States, as much as if he had sent one of his own frigates to prey upon our commerce, to break our blockade, and to ravage our coast, the very exigency which he meant to guard against by stipulating that the destination of the Arman ships should not transpire until they were beyond the jurisdiction of France and ready to become her efficient allies in the war that must have inevitably ensued between her and the United States. As the error of Captain Bullock has more or less infected popular opinion on both sides of the Atlantic, I will present what Captain Bullock will himself accept as incontestable evidence that the emperor never gave any such unconditional promise as that upon which these charges of duplicity and treachery are founded. That many people about the emperor, the De Mornys and the Fleurys and other parasites of less degree, gave both Slidell and Mason such unconditional assurances is very likely, but it was their own fault if the diplomatists allowed themselves to be deceived by a class of men who were notorious speculators upon the credulity and ignorance of the public, and whom Slidell, at least, was not the man to engage with, unless he was reasonably sure that he had more and better cards in his sleeve than they had.

There were but two sources from which Slidell could have received the assurances upon which Captain Bullock's charges of duplicity and treachery on the part of the Imperial government could be sustained. One was the emperor and the other was Drouyn de Lhuys, his Minister of Foreign Affairs. These were the only two men in the empire competent to bind the Imperial government to any engagement with a foreign power. I will now show from Mr. Slidell's own testimony that he never received any assurances from either. Beginning with the emperor, Mr. Slidell never met the emperor on official business but three times. He gave full reports of these interviews to Mr. Benjamin. Of these reports I am so fortunate as to have copies, and, as they have never been in print, I cannot perform a more acceptable service to the reader than to give them entire, not only to show how entirely contingent upon the fortunes of the war was the emperor's promise, but to what an extent Mr. Slidell allowed his judgments and undertakings to be affected by his hopes and dreams. His first interview with the emperor was procured through the intervention of the Count de Persigny, and a few days after the receipt in France of the first intelligence of the battles of the 26th and 27th of June and the strategical movements of McClellan across the Chickahominy and towards James River. The interview occurred while the emperor was at Vichy in the summer of 1862, and was thus reported by Slidell. The italics are mine.

I shall preface their interview with the letter from Slidell to Benjamin, in which he states the circumstances under which the interview was accorded, as well as of a very unsatisfactory interview he had held with M. Thouvenel, the Minister of Foreign Affairs, on the subject of recognition. It will be seen in this and in Slidell's subsequent letters to Benjamin that he really at no time had any substantial footing in the French Foreign Office.

SLIDELL TO BENJAMIN.

"PARIS, *October* 20, 1862.
"Hon. J. P. BENJAMIN, Secretary of State, Richmond:—
"*Sir*,—My last was of October 9. I had hoped before this to have had it in my power to communicate something definite as

to the emperor's intentions respecting our affairs, but new complications in the Italian question have entirely absorbed the attention of the government. Mr. Thouvenel has resigned and has been succeeded by Mr. Drouyn de Lhuys. For two or three days a general disruption of the cabinet was imminent. Messrs. de Persigny and Fould tendered their resignation, which, if accepted, would have been followed by two or three others. They were, however, induced to withdraw them by the earnest appeal of the emperor, and at present it seems probable that no further change will take place in the ministry.

"Since my last, I have had reason to be less hopeful of early joint recognition by France and England. Some days past I learned from an English friend that Lord Cowley (the British Ambassador) declared most emphatically that his government had no official knowledge of the emperor's views on the subject of recognition—that he had spoken, it was true, very freely to various persons of his warm sympathies for the South, but that such conversations had no public significance, and until he gave them an official form her majesty's ministers would be presumed to be ignorant of them. I have entire reliance on the truthfulness of the gentleman who gave me this information, coming directly to him from Lord Cowley. On inquiring at the *Affaires Étrangères*, I was informed by the friend to whom I have alluded in previous despatches that Mr. Thouvenel expressed great surprise at Lord Cowley's assertion, saying that it had to him the appearance of a *mauvaise plaisanterie tres réel;* that there had been between the two governments *pour parlers* on the subject of American affairs; that England was not as well disposed to act as the government of the emperor; that it was from London that a communication was expected, and that the object of France was to bring about an armistice as a necessary preliminary to peace; that Lord Lyons was decidedly opposed to any action until the result of the Northern elections should have been ascertained, and that his views would probably prevail in the cabinet council, shortly to be held, when the tenor of the instructions to be given him would be decided. The discrepancy between the statements of Lord Cowley and Mr. Thouvenel is such that, giving, as I do, full credence to the latter, I can only suppose that Lord Cowley is not kept informed of his government, or *that he deliberately misrepresents the position of* *affairs.* On this alternative I do not venture to express an opinion.*

"Count Persigny had promised to ask for me an interview with the emperor on his return from Biarritz. He tells me that he has done so; that the emperor says he will give me an audience as soon as the excitement of the Italian imbroglio, which now throws all other questions into the shade and which engrosses his attention, shall have subsided. I hope in my next despatch to put you in possession of the emperor's purpose. From present appearances it seems probable that he will not be as much disposed as he has hitherto been to defer to the suggestions of his friends on the other side of the channel. The *entente cordiale* no longer exists, or at least is very seriously impaired.

"Mr. Drouyn de Lhuys has always been understood to be very favorably disposed towards our cause.

"I have the honor to be, with great respect,

"Your most obedient servant, JOHN SLIDELL."

SLIDELL TO BENJAMIN.

"Hon. J. P. BENJAMIN, Secretary of State,' Richmond:—

'*Sir*,—My last was of 1st June, No. 9. I have allowed so

---

* Slidell had but an indifferent opinion of English statesmen during this part of his public life, especially of the upright and exemplary class to which Lord Cowley belonged, and for the same reason, I presume, that rogues have but a poor opinion of the law. In another letter written about this time to "My dear Benjamin" he says: "You will find by my official correspondence that we are still hard and fast aground here, and nothing will float us off but a strong and continued current of important successes in the field. I have no hopes from England, because I am satisfied that she desires an indefinite prolongation of the war until the North shall be entirely exhausted and broken down. Nothing can exceed the selfishness of English statesmen except their wretched hypocrisy; they are continually canting about their disinterestedness, magnanimity, and abnegation of all other considerations than those dictated by a high-toned morality, while their active policy is marked by egotism and duplicity.

long an interval since to elapse, because Mr. Billault's declaration that France would not act in our matters without the co-operation of England was so unqualified and peremptory that I considered it quite idle, for the time at least, to importune those who were friendly to our cause, and therefore had nothing new to communicate.

"In the meanwhile, however, I had corresponded with Mr. Mason, expressing the opinion that the time had arrived when we should make simultaneously a formal demand for recognition, and, if it were refused, should say that it would not be renewed until we should receive from the respective governments to which we are accredited an intimation that they are prepared to entertain it favorably. Mr. Mason agreed with me in this opinion, and I accordingly prepared a letter to Mr. Thouvenel which I expected to present about the 20th ultimo; but Mr. Mason having consulted several members of Parliament friendly to our cause, was advised to defer making his demand; he accordingly decided so to do, and I consequently determined to withhold mine.

"Subsequent events have shown that nothing has been lost by the delay.

"On Thursday, the 10th instant, we received the first intelligence of the battles of the 26th and 27th of June, and the 'strategical movements' of McClellan across the Chickahominy and towards James River. On the strength of this news and of your despatch No. 3 (which with numbers 1, 2, and 4 had been delivered by Mr. De Leon) I was about to call on Count de Persigny, when I received a message from that gentleman, who had recently returned after an absence of some weeks in England, saying that he desired to see me. I, of course, lost no time in complying with his request. I communicated to him confidentially the substance of my new instructions, and he advised me to proceed to Vichy, where the emperor would be on Saturday, but he thought would be much occupied for a day or two in receiving the authorities, etc. The count gave me a very warm letter to General Fleury, who is a great favorite of the emperor and constantly accompanies him, urging him to procure an audience for me. I went accordingly to Vichy on Tuesday, arriving there in the evening. The next morning I sent a note to General Fleury, enclosing that of Mr. de Persigny soliciting his good offices to procure me *une audience officieuse* with the emperor. I very soon received a reply saying that the emperor would receive me at two o'clock.

"You will find herewith full details of my interview marked No. 1.

"Mr. Thouvenel having returned from London, whither he had gone to attend the Exhibition, I addressed him on Sunday evening a note asking for an interview. The next morning I received an answer, saying that he would with pleasure see me on Wednesday, 23d July, at 1 o'clock.

"He received me very cordially, and after some preliminary conversation about his visit to London and the state of affairs in America, I said that I had asked to see him for the purpose of presenting a formal demand of recognition, which I wished to accompany with some oral explanations. He said, 'Had you not better withhold it for the present? In a few weeks, when we shall have further news from the seat of war, we can better judge of the expediency of so grave a step, and the English government may perhaps then be prepared to co-operate with us, which they certainly are not now; that the refusal to acknowledge us, however worded, could not fail to be prejudicial to our cause; that the answer could only be couched *en banalites* (commonplace phrases) and unmeaning generalities.' I replied that my own decided opinion had been in favor of presenting the demand several weeks since; that I had yielded to the better judgment of my colleague at London, who had consulted several of our leading friends in Parliament as to the expediency of such a step, but that I could no longer consent to defer it with any regard to the interests of the government or to self-respect; that if it were not to be recognized now after such signal demonstration of our will and ability to maintain our independence, I could see no reason to hope for recognition excepting at some distant future, when it would be of no value to us, and when we should not want it; that with all due deference to his friendly suggestions I must persist in my purpose. I then asked him if he had seen or heard from the emperor since his return from England? He said that he had not seen him, but that he had received from him a short note saying that he would very soon write to him about American affairs. I said, 'Your Excellency does not probably know that I have had the honor of an audience with the emperor.'

He replied that he did not, and asked whether I had seen the emperor at Vichy. He then entered into a long conversation, which, as it referred principally to what had passed in my interview with the emperor, and was a paraphrase of the arguments I then used, it is not necessary to repeat. It appeared to produce a very decided impression on Mr. Thouvenel, and he made no further attempt to dissuade me from presenting my demand. He asked me whether Mr. Mason would send a similar letter to Earl Russell? I said that he had either done so to-day or would do so to-morrow. He said that he was glad to know it, as it was all important that the same application should be made simultaneously to both governments. He said that Lord Lyons and Mr. Mercier were both decidedly of opinion that an offer of mediation now would only create additional exasperation at the North, and could only be attended with mischievous results. I said that while it was not desired by us, it would not be refused; all we asked for was recognition, which we thought could no longer be deferred without violating the principles which the emperor cherished and England professed, and without ignoring all the precedents of the last thirty or forty years. I asked him if Mr. Mercier did not consider the re-establishment of the Union impossible? He said, 'Yes;' that it was not only his very decided opinion but of every one in France. In reply to my suggestion that we should be allowed to correspond with our government by French ships-of-war, he said that the privilege was not even allowed to their own subjects writing of their own private affairs; that it would be a breach of neutrality. I referred him to Hauteville, the most eminent modern French publicist, as negativing this opinion. He said if we were recognized, the privilege might be granted; to do so before would not be loyal. Although I could not see the force of the distinction, I, of course, could not say so, as I hope that I shall have an opportunity of availing myself of it. I then handed my letter to Mr. Thouvenel, of which I send copy marked No. 2, with a memorandum on the subject of the blockade, substantially your No. 2. Mr. Thouvenel promised me that he would have them translated without delay, and copies sent to the emperor. He said that he was going to Germany on Saturday to accompany his wife, who was unwell; would be absent about ten days; that in the meanwhile he would fully examine the whole matter and especially the question of boundaries, of which he had spoken at large. I consequently cannot expect an answer before the 12th or 15th of August, and its character then will of course very much depend upon the more or less favorable accounts we may receive of the progress of the war.

"As I was taking leave, Mr. Thouvenel asked me to give him a brief written memorandum of the propositions in confidence, for his own use and that of the emperor.* I sent him one, unsigned, copy of which you will find herewith, marked No. 3. He asked me if any similar propositions had been or would be made to England? I replied, certainly not, that our commissioner there was ignorant of them, although I intended to give him the information so soon as I found a safe opportunity.

"With this full narrative of what has passed here, you will be enabled to form as safe an opinion as I can of the prospect of recognition. While I do not wish to create or indulge false expectations, I will venture to say that I am more hopeful than I have been at any moment since my arrival in Europe.

"With great respect,
"Your most obedient servant,
"JOHN SLIDELL.

"P.S.—I have also received since my last, despatches numbered respectively Nos. 3 and 5, the latter in the form of a copy forwarded from London by Mr. Mason."

SLIDELL'S ACCOUNT OF HIS FIRST INTERVIEW WITH THE EMPEROR.

"On Wednesday evening, July 16, at nine o'clock, I enclosed to General Fleury, *aide-de-camp* and *premier écuyer* of the emperor, a letter from Count de Persigny, and asked him to procure me the honor of an unofficial audience with the emperor. Before twelve o'clock I received from Mr. Fleury a note stating that the emperor would receive me at two o'clock. The emperor received me with great kindness, and, after saying that he was very happy to see me and regretted that circumstances had prevented his

---

* These were proposals from Benjamin to the emperor to hire his fleet to break the blockade by a present among other things of one thousand bales of cotton, the emperor to send his ships for them. See these proposals *infra*.

sooner doing so, invited me to be seated. He commenced the conversation by referring to the news contained in the evening papers of the previous day of the defeat of the Federal armies before Richmond, which appeared to give him much satisfaction. He spoke of Lincoln's call for three hundred thousand additional troops as evidence of his conviction of the desperate character of the struggle in which he had been engaged and of the great losses which the Federal forces had sustained. That although it was unquestionably for the interest of France that the United States should be a powerful and united people, to act as a *contrepoids* to the maritime power of England, yet his sympathies had always been with the South, whose people are struggling for the principle of self-government, of which he was a firm and consistent advocate; that he had, from the first, seen the true character of the contest, and considered the re-establishment of the union impossible and final separation a mere question of time. That the difficulty was to find the way to give effect to his sympathies; that he had always desired to preserve the most friendly relations with England, and that, in so grave a matter, he had not been willing to act without her co-operation; that he had several times intimated his wish for action in our behalf, but had met with no favorable response, and that, besides, England had a deeper interest in the question than France, that she wished him to 'draw the chestnuts from the fire for her benefit.' He asked me to give my views of the state of affairs and of what could be done to bring the war to a close. The conversation had thus far been in French, with occasional remarks from me; but as I knew that the emperor spoke English well and fluently, and was said not to dislike having an opportunity to converse in our language, I said that, if it would not be disagreeable to him, I would prefer speaking English—I could better express myself in my own tongue. He assented, and during the remainder of the interview the conversation was in English. He inquired the amount of our army. I estimated the number of men now under arms at about two hundred and fifty thousand, although at certain previous periods, before we had abandoned the impossible idea of defending all the points of our immense coast and frontier, the number had probably been nearer five hundred thousand, but since we had adopted the policy of concentrating our forces, three hundred and fifty thousand men were, I thought, as many as we could advantageously employ. That our difficulty was not to find men; of them we had and always would have more than enough, but that what we wanted were arms, powder, and clothing. I explained the composition and character of our army; that with us every man was a soldier, that very many of the *élite* of our country were serving in the ranks; spoke of the devotion and enthusiasm of our women; that our men were badly clothed and fed, most of them with inferior arms, and all insufficiently and irregularly paid, but submitting patiently to all the privations. That, on the contrary, our enemies were admirably equipped and armed, as a general rule profusely fed, having many luxuries in abundance, such as tea and coffee, of which our troops were entirely deprived; but that the very large majority were mercenaries, who served for pay and food, not being able to find employment and wages [the emperor expressed his great surprise at our troops not having coffee, which, he said, was considered essential to the health of the soldiers]; that probably one half of the privates were foreigners, principally Germans and Irish, while our troops were almost exclusively born on our soil; that this difference made them much more than a match for their enemies when they met with equal numbers, but that this advantage was more than compensated by the greater moral value of those whom we lost—carrying mourning into every Southern family, while no interest was felt at the North for the mercenaries who were fighting their battles, so long as they could supply their places by new levies.

"I spoke of the submission of the neutral powers to a blockade, which for more than six months had existed only on paper, as having inflicted on us incalculable injury; that the submission to a blockade, not enforced in accordance with the principles of international law and the 4th article of the Treaty of Paris, the voluntary renunciation of the right to trade with ports not really blockaded, were, in fact, a violation of the neutrality which the European powers professed to observe, and that we were especially disappointed that France, who had always championed neutral rights, should for the first time have failed to assert them. The emperor said that he had committed a great error, which he now deeply regretted. France should never have respected the blockade; that the European powers should have recognized us last summer, when our ports were in our possession and when we were menacing Washington. But what, he asked, can now be done? To open the ports forcibly would be an act of war; mediation, if offered, would be refused, and probably in insulting terms, by the North; and mere recognition, while of little advantage to us, would probably involve him in a war. To this I replied that a large portion of our coast was not even now effectually blockaded; vessels were constantly arriving at and departing from Charleston, Wilmington, and numerous other small ports; they might be declared open, and the declaration, if necessary, enforced by arms; that the Northern press and government would bully and menace, but that experience had fully shown what value should be placed on their threats. They had first instructed their ministers to say that our simple recognition as belligerents would be considered as an act of hostility; that we had been so recognized; then that any communication with our agents, even unofficial, would be so considered and followed by the like consequences; that our privateersmen would be hanged as pirates; they had threatened Holland with war because she had permitted the *Sumpter* to take supplies of provisions and coal in her ports; yet in all these instances, and many others that could be cited, finding that their menaces had been disregarded, or, as in the case of the privateers, retaliatory measures would be adopted by the Confederate States, they had, with bad grace it is true, but very quietly, abandoned their absurd and insolent pretensions. The crowning instance of loud boasting and ignominious backing-out was the affair of the *Trent*. The commander of the *San Jacinto* had been fêted wherever he went as a conqueror; that his journey from his landing at Boston to his arrival at Washington was one continuous ovation; the Secretary of the Navy officially endorsed his action; the House of Representatives voted him a sword by acclamation; the President and his Cabinet openly declared that the prisoners should never be surrendered; and the entire press, without exception, denounced as cowards and traitors all who ventured even to hint that the seizure was illegal. Yet they had succumbed so soon as the peremptory demand to give up the prisoners was made by England, backed by the significant letter of Mr. Thouvenel. The emperor asked me how I had been treated while prisoner. I answered, not discourteously; but that we had been very indifferently lodged at Fort Warren. His majesty occupies, by the way, a small house at Vichy, and received me in his only *salon* there, and one of very modest proportions. I told him that we were four prisoners in a room, of about one fourth the dimensions of the one in which we were sitting, which served us for bedroom, *salon*, and dining-room, at Fort Warren, but that fortunately we had found there a very agreeable mess, established in a kitchen. I took this occasion to say that I regretted not to have had an earlier opportunity of presenting, on behalf of my wife and children, my thanks for his friendly interposition, to which I mainly attributed my release; but that I had always regretted it, because if we had not been given up it would have caused a war with England, which would have been of short duration, and whatever might have happened to myself, the result must have been advantageous to our cause. The emperor said that he thought I was right; that he regretted to say that England had not properly appreciated his friendly action in the affair of the *Trent;* that there were many reasons why he desired to be on the best terms with her; but that the policy of nations necessarily changed with circumstances, and that he was constantly obliged to look forward to the possible contingency of not always having the same friendly relations as now existed.

"This gave me an opportunity of saying about Mexican affairs substantially what will be found in my letter to Mr. Thouvenel of 21st instant. I went still further, and said that as the Lincoln government was the ally and protector of his enemy Juarez, we could have no objection to make common cause with him against the common enemy.

"I asked him if he had seen Count de Persigny since his return from England, or if the count (to whom I had confidentially communicated the substance of your despatch, No. 3) had written him about our affairs. He said that he had neither seen nor heard from the count. I then stated to the emperor what I had been instructed to propose.* It did not seem disagreeable. He said, "How am I to get the cotton?" I replied, "*That*, of course, depends upon your majesty." He will soon have a fleet

---

* This refers to Benjamin's effort, already noted, to tempt the emperor, by an offer of cotton, to send a fleet to invade our coast and break the blockade.

in the neighborhood of our coast strong enough to keep it clear of every Federal cruiser.

"I gave him in a few words a description of the American marine—some second-class steamers constructed for war purposes, and a large number of merchant vessels hastily purchased and fitted up for the blockade and transport service. I said that the *Gloire*, the *Garonne*, or the *Normandy*, could pass the fortifications of New York and Boston, and hold those towns at their mercy; or could enter the Chesapeake, destroy all the vessels there, and Fortress Monroe, by bombardment.

"He agreed with me in this. I expressed my regret at having heard that some of his first-class steamers were armed *en flute*, and asked if his armament could not be completed at Martinique and Guadeloupe, and suggested that, if not, guns could be sent there for the purpose. He appeared to be pleased with the suggestion.

"He then spoke of recognition, saying that simple recognition would be of no value, and as to mediation, that would be refused by the North. I replied that, as to mediation, I agreed with him that, if offered, it would be refused by the North, but would be accepted by us, but that such refusal and acceptance would be of vast advantage to our cause, and enlist the sympathies of the civilized world in our favor, and afford sufficient reason for more potent intervention. But we did not ask for mediation; all we asked for was recognition; that there was a large majority in the Northern States in favor of peace and separation, but that a reign of terror existed which, for the present, stifled all expression of such opinions; that the Congressional elections were approaching, and that recognition would give the peace party courage to organize, and perhaps place them in the majority. He said that he was pleased to see that there had been a great peace meeting in New York. I said that recognition would at once bring out many similar demonstrations. I then said that, although we did not place ourselves on that ground, the interests of humanity might be urged as calling on Europe, and especially on him who exercised so potent an influence over the destinies of the world, to put an end to the strife, which was not only devastating the South and exhausting the North, but paralyzed the commerce and industry of Europe. He replied, 'What you say is true, but the policy of nations is controlled by their interests, and not by their sentiments, and ought to be so.' I replied that I fully admitted his proposition, but that the interests to be consulted should not be those of the hour; that England seemed to have abdicated the great part which she had been accustomed to play in the affairs of the world, and adopted a tortuous, selfish, and time-serving policy, which had only served to make all nations either her bitter enemies, or, at least, fair-weather friends. That we at first had been well-disposed towards England, but that having, for selfish, ulterior purposes, to revive for her advantage the old, exploded principles of blockade, and to secure the monopoly of cotton for her Indian colonies, given a false interpretation to the Treaty of Paris, we should never hereafter consider her our friend. The emperor remarked, 'I have already told you what I thought of the blockade, and as to the culture of cotton in India supplanting yours, I consider the idea entirely chimerical. If you do not give it to us we cannot find it elsewhere.' I then said, 'Your majesty has now an opportunity of securing a faithful ally, bound to you not only by the ties of gratitude, but by those, more reliable, of a common interest and congenial habits.' He said, 'Yes, you have many families of French descent in Louisiana who yet preserve their habits and language.' I replied that he was right, and that I could give him an instance in my own family where French was habitually spoken.* He asked me whether we anticipated no difficulty from our slaves. I replied that they had never been more quiet and more respectful, and that no better evidence could be given of their being contented and happy. This was the only allusion made to slavery during the interview.

"The emperor asked me if I expected that England would agree to co-operate with him in our recognition. I replied that he, of course, must have much better information than I, but that our friends in England were more hopeful than they ever had been before, and that our commissioner at London, for the first time since his arrival, wrote encouragingly. That the motion of Mr. Lindsay recommending recognition would be brought

---

* Mr. Slidell was born in New York City, where he was an unsuccessful tradesman before he went to New Orleans to mend his fortune.

up on Friday, and that probably the debate would bring out Lord Palmerston with a declaration of his purposes. He asked how Cobden was disposed. I said that he was unfriendly to us, but not so much so as Bright. That it was conceded on all hands that an immense majority of the House of Commons was in our favor, but that Lord Derby was not prepared to take office, and nothing would be done that would cause Lord Palmerston to resign.

"While I was advocating recognition the emperor, with a very significant smile, said, 'It is very singular that, while you ask absolute recognition, Mr. Dayton is calling upon me to retract my qualified recognition of you as belligerents.' I replied that such a demand was but another evidence of the insolence of the Washington government.

"The emperor asked me, if France and England intervene, on what terms can a peace be made? The question of boundaries is a most difficult one; what will you do with the border states? You will not be willing to accept what the North, even if she submits to separation, will accord. I replied that the question appeared, indeed, to be difficult, but it seemed to be susceptible of an easy solution, and one which he would willingly receive. In all the states where the people had, in full conventions, voted for separations, there could be no difficulty; that in Kentucky, Missouri, and Maryland the question whether they would join our confederacy, form a separate one for themselves, or remain with the United States, should be submitted to the popular vote, and that I had no fear of the result; that such had been the emperor's policy in Italy, and the whole world approved it. That the Chesapeake, Potomac, and Ohio were natural and indispensable boundaries, which could not be relinquished. He regretted that he had no map at Vichy, that we might trace the line.

"I should have mentioned that, when speaking of the cotton subsidy, I told the emperor that the proposition was made exclusively to France,* my colleague at London not being aware of my authority to make it.

"I said to the emperor that, in deciding upon the course he was to pursue, he might assume two fixed points of departure: First, that reconstruction on any terms was impossible. Sec-

---

* See p. 120.

ond, that without European intervention in some form or other peace was impossible within any reasonable period; that a peace must be preceded by an armistice, with our ports open to the commerce of the world.

"I omitted to mention that, in speaking of Mexican affairs, I said that Mr. Lincoln had sent to the Senate the treaty negotiated by Mr. Corwin—that it was, in fact, a subsidy of $11,000,000—to enable Juarez to carry on the war against France. He replied, 'But the Senate will not ratify it.' 'Of this,' I said, 'I had no means to form an opinion; but, at any rate, it was clear that the President approved of its principle, and the executive virtually controlled the foreign relations.' I said that I had heard, from what seemed to be good authority, although I did not pretend to vouch for the truth of the report, that Schufledt, United States Consul-General at Havana, had gone to Mexico, and placed at the disposition of Juarez $2,000,000, being the cash instalment stipulated by the treaty; and if this were so, the Mexican army was now waging war against France with means furnished by the Federal treasury. I also alluded to the presence of the Orleans princes in the Federal armies as evidence at least that Lincoln was not particularly desirous to avoid giving just cause of offence to France, and mentioned that the son of the Prince de Joinville was now serving as a midshipman on board of a Federal man-of-war, a fact of which he had been previously ignorant.

"I suggested that, without violating neutrality, we might be allowed to communicate with our government by French ships-of-war visiting our ports; that such communication was called for even by French interests; that it was important that Southern newspapers should be freely received to neutralize the false statements of the Northern press. The emperor replied that such a request seemed reasonable, and that he would consider it.

"Finding that the interview had been sufficiently prolonged, I rose to take leave, saying that I had already too much abused his indulgence; that I had, perhaps, omitted to present some arguments which, if not new to him, were from a different point of view, but that I had prepared a formal demand of recognition, in which they were embodied, and that I intended to present them to Mr. Thouvenel as soon as he should return from England, where he then was, and I would feel much obliged, if he

THE EMPEROR NON-COMMITTAL.

saw any reason to object to the course I proposed, that he would intimate his wish. He said that he saw no objection to my presenting my demand; *he, of course, said nothing to commit himself as to the answer that would be given.* At parting he said that he hoped in future there would be less difficulty in my seeing him than had heretofore existed.

"On the whole, my interview was most satisfactory. I had been led to expect, from what I had heard of his habitual manner, that he would be extremely reserved, confining himself to asking questions or intimating on what points he wished me to speak, with occasional brief observations on his part. On the contrary, he was frank, unreserved, I might perhaps say cordial, placing me entirely at my ease by the freedom with which he spoke himself. *Although he said nothing to commit himself as to his future course, I left him with the decided impression that if England long persevered in obstinate inaction he would take the responsibility of moving by himself.*

"The interview lasted seventy minutes; and as the conversation was free and animated, I cannot rely sufficiently on my memory to repeat everything that was said by the emperor, but I am sure that I have not omitted anything important, and that I have given substantially what he said."

It will be observed that in this interview, on Mr. Slidell's own admission, the emperor committed himself to nothing. Instead of the commissioner interviewing the emperor, the emperor interviewed the commissioner; and though his majesty "was frank and unreserved, I might say cordial," he courteously permitted the commissioner to do all the talking.

The commissioner's next interview with the emperor was at St. Cloud, three months later.

Chapter X.

Slidell's Second Interview with the Emperor.—Invites him again to Break the Blockade.—Proposes to Submit the Issue between the United States and the Confederate States to the Emperor, Knowing his Views.—Asks the Emperor not to Watch too Closely what was Going on in his Ship-yards.—The Confederate Government had no Objection to his Seizing St. Domingo.

Slidell's Account of his Second Interview with the Emperor.

"Memorandum of an interview with the emperor at St. Cloud, on Tuesday, October 22, 1862:

"The emperor received me in a most friendly manner. Taking me by the hand, he inquired how I had been, and invited me to be seated. He then asked me what news I had from America, and how our affairs were going on. I replied that we were entirely cut off from the reception of any news, that we were obliged to take our intelligence from the Northern press, and that he well knew how little reliable it was, being subject to the most arbitrary surveillance over everything connected with the war. But that in spite of that surveillance the truth could, after a certain lapse of time, be gleaned even from Northern journals, and especially from the private correspondence of persons at New York and elsewhere. That since I had the honor of seeing him at Vichy our position had most materially improved, and was now better than at any previous period. That our troops were as numerous and better disciplined than they had ever been; that time and opportunity had developed high military talent in many of our officers, while there was a singular absence of that quality among Northern generals; that while we anxiously desired to see the war brought to a close, we had no apprehensions whatever of the final result of the contest; that we had the immense advantage over our enemies of harmonious counsels and a thoroughly united people ready and willing to make every sacrifice, and submit to any privation for the establishment of their independence.

"The emperor replied that he was entirely satisfied of the correctness of all that I said; that he had no scruple in declaring that his sympathies were entirely with the South; that his only desire was to know how to give them effect; that the condition of affairs in Europe was very unsatisfactory, especially in Italy and Greece; that he was obliged to act with great caution, and intimated that if he acted alone, England, instead of following his example, would endeavor to embroil him with the United States, and that French commerce would be destroyed. He asked what were my views. I said that I had no hope of any friendly action from England, until the time should arrive when it would become a matter of indifference to us; that all we asked for was recognition, satisfied that the moral effect of such a step, by giving confidence to the peace party at the North, would exercise influence; that if it had been taken a few months since, it would have secured the election of a majority of the House of Representatives opposed to the war. That recognition would not afford, in the eyes of the world, the slightest pretext for hostilities on the part of the North; that there were, however, stronger reasons that would bind them to keep the peace—their mercantile tonnage was infinitely larger than that of France, and that in the same proportion would be their losses at sea; that their navy, of which they boasted so loudly, would be swept from the ocean, and all their principal ports efficiently blockaded by a moiety of his powerful marine, and that the *Gloire* or the *Normandie* could enter without risk the harbors of New York and Boston, and lay those cities under contribution. I told him the condition of Fort Warren, manned by raw militia; that the ports of New York would not be better defended, as they were only garrisoned by new levies, who so soon as they had been drilled for a few weeks were sent to the armies in the field and replaced by fresh recruits; and that, above all, the energies and resources of the North were already tasked to their utmost by the war in which they were engaged, and that mad and stupid as the Washington government had shown itself to be, it still had sense enough not to seek a quarrel with the first power of the world.

"The emperor asked, 'What do you think of the joint mediation of France, England, and Russia? Would it, if proposed, be accepted by the two parties?' I replied, that some months since I would have said that the North would unhesitatingly reject it, but that now it would probably accept it; that I could not venture to say how it would be received at Richmond. I could only give him my individual opinion. I had no faith in England, and believed that Russia would lean strongly to the Northern side; that the mediation of the three Powers, where France could be outvoted, would not be acceptable; that we might, perhaps, with certain assurances, consent to the joint mediation of France and England, but *knowing, as I did, the emperor's sentiments, I would gladly submit to his umpirage.*

"The emperor said, 'My own preference is for a proposition of an armistice of six months, with the Southern ports open to the commerce of the world; this would put a stop to the effusion of blood, and hostilities would, probably, never be resumed. We can urge it on the high grounds of humanity and the interest of the whole civilized world; if it be refused by the North, it will afford good reason for recognition, and, perhaps, for more active intervention.' I said that such a course would be judicious and acceptable; indeed, it was one that I had suggested to Mr. Thouvenel, when I first saw him in February last. That I feared, however, he would find it as difficult to obtain the co-operation of England for it as for recognition. He said that he had reason to suppose the contrary; that he had a letter from the King of the Belgians which he would show me. He did so; it was an autograph letter from King Leopold to the emperor, dated Brussels, 15th October; the date is important, as Queen Victoria was then at Brussels. The king urges, in the warmest manner, for the cause of humanity and in the interests of the suffering populations of Europe, that prompt and strenuous efforts should be made by France, England, and Russia to put an end to the bloody war that now desolates America. He expresses his perfect conviction that all attempts to reconstruct the union of the United States are hopeless, that final separation is an accomplished fact, and that it is the duty of the great powers so to treat it; that recognition, or any other course that might be thought best calculated to bring about a peace, should be at once adopted. The appeal is made with great earnestness to the emperor to bring the whole weight of his great name and authority to bear on the most important question of his day. It is universally believed that King Leopold's counsels have more influence with Queen Victoria than those of any living man; that in this respect he has inherited the succession of the late Prince Consort.

"I repeated to the emperor what I had said to Mr. Drouyn de Lhuys, of the assertions of Lord Cowley and others, that no intimation of his wishes and views on the question had been made to the British government. He smiled and said that he supposed that it was in accordance with diplomatic usages to consider nothing to exist that had not been formally written; that Mr. Thouvenel must have spoken to Lord Cowley, and intimated that *perhaps Mr. T. might not have endeavored to impress Lord Cowley with the idea that he was much in earnest.* I have had strong suspicion on this score for some time past, and am inclined to think that the feeling that Mr. Thouvenel did not fairly represent his views on this, as well as on the Italian question, may have had some influence on the decision of the emperor to dispense with the services of Mr. Thouvenel as Minister of Foreign Affairs; it is very certain that his resignation was invited by the emperor.

"The emperor asked why we had not created a navy; he said that we ought to have one; that a few ships would have inflicted fatal injury on the Federal commerce, and that with three or four powerful steamers we could have opened some of our ports. I replied that, at first many of our leading men thought it would be bad policy to attempt to become a naval power, as we had no good ports for large vessels but Norfolk and Pensacola, few seamen, and an inconsiderable mercantile marine; that we would always be essentially an agricultural people, selling freely to all the world and buying in the cheapest markets; we could rely on our peaceful disposition to preserve us from collisions with European powers, while at the same time it would be the interest of those powers to prevent our only probable enemies from abusing their superiority over us at sea; that we all now saw our error and were endeavoring to correct it, that we had built two vessels in England, and were now building others—two of which would be powerful iron clad steamers; that the great difficulty was not to build, but to man and arm them, under the existing regulations for the preservation of neutrality; *that if* the emperor would give only some kind of verbal assurance that his police would not observe too closely when we wished to put on board guns and men, we would gladly avail ourselves of it.

"He said, 'Why could you not have them built as for the Italian government? I do not think it would be difficult, but I will consult the Minister of Marine about it.'

"I forgot to mention that King Leopold, in his letter, spoke of his wishes for the success of the French arms in Mexico, and the establishment under their protection of a stable and regular government. This gave me an opportunity of alluding to the propositions I had made at Vichy, and to hold out the advantages which would result to France from a cordial and close alliance between the two countries, not so much depending on treaties and mere paper bonds as resulting from mutual interests and common sympathies. An idea prevails among some of the officers who have gone to Mexico, that as troops and ships have been sent there on a scale vastly greater than the apparent objects of the expedition require, that the emperor has some ulterior views, perhaps to occupy the old French colony of St. Domingo, as Spain has done for the eastern portion of the island. *I took occasion to say to the emperor that, however distasteful such a measure might be to the Washington government, ours could have no objection to it.*

"While the question of recognition was the topic of conversation, the emperor said that he had seen a letter from a New-Yorker which he wished me to read, to have my opinion of the correctness of the views it expressed. It was a letter that I had previously seen—it being addressed to Mr. Lindsay, M.P., who consulted me about the propriety of placing it before the emperor, as he had already done with Earl Russell. At my instance Mr. Lindsay handed it to Mr. Michel Chevalier, a senator standing high in the emperor's confidence. The letter purported to be the expression of the opinion of many leading Democrats, that recognition of the South would soon bring the war to a close. As the writer was well known to me as a man of high character and intelligence, I assured the emperor that he might confidently rely on the fairness and accuracy of his statements. In the same connection the emperor spoke of an article in a Richmond paper which had attracted his attention, and which he said had produced some impression on his mind. It was an article from the

Dispatch, I think, and which has gone the rounds of most of the European papers, especially those friendly to the North. It deprecates recognition as tending only to irritate the people of the North, and to stimulate to increased exertion, while it would be of no service to the South. I have been more than once surprised to hear this article referred to in conversation by intelligent persons well disposed towards our cause on whom it seemed also to have had some effect. I told the emperor that there were at least five, perhaps more, daily papers published in Richmond, and that, if my recollections were correct, it was the one that had the least influence; that the article was but the expression of the individual opinion of an anonymous writer who, in all probability, if he were known, would prove to be a man without the slightest position, social or political.

"The emperor inquired particularly about the character of Generals Lee, Johnston, and 'Stonewall' Jackson, and expressed his admiration of the recent march of Stuart's cavalry into Pennsylvania, crossing the Potomac at Hancock and recrossing below Harper's Ferry. He asked me to trace the route on the map, and was astonished at the boldness and success of the enterprise. He expressed his surprise at the large number of killed and wounded in various battles, and asked if the accounts were not exaggerated. I said that, so far as the enemy were concerned, they were, on the contrary, systematically very much understated; that as they had acknowledged a loss of more than fourteen thousand in the Maryland battles, there was every ground for believing that it was nearer twenty-five thousand. He remarked, 'Why, this is a frightful carnage; we had but twelve thousand *hors de combat* at Magenta.' 'But,' I replied, 'Solferino and Magenta produced decisive results, while with us successive victories do not appear to bring us any nearer to the termination of the war.'

"He asked how the Northern Congressional elections would probably turn out, and what would be the effect of the success of the Democratic party. I said that appearances indicated that the Democrats would probably have a majority in two or three states, but that, in my opinion, such partial success would exercise little if any influence on the course of the Lincoln government.

"I omitted to mention in the proper connection that the emperor said that he had very recently seen Lord Cowley, in a manner to have me to infer that he had then communicated his views respecting American affairs.

"The emperor recalling, I presume, what I had said in the memorandum submitted to him through M. de Persigny, of which I sent a copy in my No. 13, asked if we should not be probably exposed to serious losses, when the Western rivers should be again navigable. I said that we undoubtedly would, that action by France now would save innumerable lives and entitle him to the gratitude of the world; that such an opportunity to serve the cause of humanity and civilization would never again present itself.

"I have thus endeavored to give the outlines of an interview which lasted one hour. Something has, perhaps, escaped my recollection, and the order of the conversation has not been strictly followed, but you may rely on the substantial correctness of my summary.

"The whole interview was, as well in manner as in substance, highly gratifying. On taking leave the emperor again shook hands. I mention this fact, which would appear trivial to persons not familiar with European usages and manners, because it afforded additional evidence of the kindly feeling manifested in his conversation, which, by the way, was conducted entirely in English. J. S."

This interview was much like the last, except that, on separating, the emperor shook the commissioner's hand, a circumstance likely—he informs Secretary Benjamin—to be undervalued by persons not familiar with European usages and manners. The subject of building steamers for the Confederates in France was introduced, and with that perfect freedom from all popular prejudice, and any inconvenient respect for the law or plighted faith, which might be expected in two cracksmen plotting a burglary, the commissioner invited the emperor not to watch the Confederates too closely, and the emperor suggested that, if they would pretend the ships were building for the Italian government, he would not. It deserves to be remarked, however, that in this, his first allusion to the ship-building scheme, he assumes that it is to be executed in a way not to compromise his government. "Why could you not have them built as for the Italian government," was his only suggestion.

This was as distinct a caution as any cool-headed man would have required, but it seems to have made no impression upon Slidell, for, in January following, he writes as follows to Benjamin:

SLIDELL TO BENJAMIN.

"PARIS, *January* 11, 1863.

"HON. J. P. BENJAMIN, Secretary of State, Richmond:—
"*Sir,*—

* * * * * * * *

"At an interview which I had with Mr. Mocquard, the emperor's private secretary and confidential friend, on the 31st ultimo, I mentioned that I had received a despatch explanatory of the action of my government in *these cases,* and, at his request, I sent him extracts of your No. 7 and copies of the documents accompanying them to be presented by him to the emperor. I also referred to the conversation I had had with the emperor at St. Cloud in relation to the building of ships-of-war in French ports, to the emperor's promise to consult the Minister of Marine on the subject, and asked him to remind the emperor of his promise and to ascertain the result. I again saw Mr. Mocquard at his own request on the 4th instant, when he informed me that the emperor, after having consulted one of his ministers, *found greater difficulties in the matter than he had anticipated, and that for the present, at least, he could not give any encouragement.**

"But, on the 7th instant, I had a visit from Mr. Arman, a mem-

---

* The dismissal of the French consular agents at Richmond and Galveston.

ber of the Corps Legislatif, and the largest ship-builder in France. He came to offer to build iron-clad steamers. He said there would be no difficulty in arming and equipping them; that he spoke from authority; that if anything were done it should be known only to himself and me. I had heard him spoken of as a man whom the emperor consulted about all naval matters, and who enjoyed his confidence. I feel sure he came to me at the emperor's instance. I said to him that at the moment I could give him no definite answer, the financial question was first to be considered; that I was expecting daily to hear the result of certain propositions made by European bankers to our government for a loan, and suggested that some arrangement might perhaps be made for payments in cotton. He thought that mode of payment might be acceptable if the emperor would let it be understood that he favored the negotiation of cotton bonds.

* * * * * * * *

"I am, with great respect,
"Your obedient servant, JOHN SLIDELL."

Though again indirectly, but authoritatively, assured that the emperor found greater difficulties in the matter than he had anticipated, and that for the present, at least, he could not give any encouragement, Slidell was willing to accept more encouraging assurances from the man of all others in France having the greatest pecuniary interest to deceive him. The next interview between the high concocting parties took place at the Tuileries in June, 1863, and after the contracts for the ships had been signed.

CHAPTER XI.

The Emperor's Reasons for Refusing to Recognize the Confederate States.—Slidell Offers to Pledge the Confederate States to Guarantee Cuba to Spain.—The Emperor Preferred having the Whigs in Power in England to the Tories.—Refuses to Guarantee the Exit of the Confederate Steamers unless their Destination was Concealed.—Roebuck's Proposal to Interview the Emperor.—The Emperor Orders Slidell's Son to be Received as a Pupil at St. Cyr.

SLIDELL'S ACCOUNT OF HIS THIRD INTERVIEW WITH THE EMPEROR.

"Memorandum of an interview with the emperor at the Tuileries, Thursday, June 18, 1863:

"On Wednesday I received from the Duke de Bassano, First Chamberlain, a note informing me that the emperor would receive me at the Tuileries on the following day at ten o'clock. The emperor received me with great cordiality. He said that he had read the memorandum presented to him by the Count de Persigny (copy of which accompanied my despatch No. 37); that he was more fully convinced than ever of the propriety of the general recognition by the European powers of the Confederate States, but that the commerce of France and the success of the Mexican expedition would be jeopardized by a rupture with the United States; that no other power than England possessed a sufficient navy to give him efficient aid in war on the ocean, an event which, indeed, could not be anticipated, if England would co-operate with him in recognition.

"I replied that I was well satisfied that recognition by France and other Continental powers, or even by France alone, would not lead to a war with the United States, as they already found ample occupation for all their energies at home; that he could count on the co-operation of Spain, Austria, Prussia, Belgium, Holland, Sweden, and Denmark. He remarked that none of those powers possessed a navy of any consequence. I suggested that Spain had a very respectable navy and was daily increasing it. I adverted to the instructions in your despatch No. 16, of the 9th of May, and that I was authorized to give the adhesion of my government to the tripartite treaty for the guarantee of Cuba to Spain; and I thought it was probable that such an adhesion might induce Spain, if assured in advance of the concurrence of France, to take the initiative of our recognition. Would the emperor be willing to give such an assurance? He said he would. I asked, will the emperor authorize me to say so to the Spanish Ambassador, Mr. Isturitz, to whom I had already communicated the substance of my instructions. He replied that he was willing that I should do so. I then spoke to the emperor of a letter from Mr. Roebuck, of which I asked his permission to read some extracts. He assented. I asked him if I might be permitted to deny on his authority the correctness of the rumor of which Mr. Seymour Fitzgerald had spoken to Mr. Roebuck. He said that I might give it an unqualified denial.

"I then inquired if it would be agreeable to him to see Messrs. Roebuck and Lindsay, and if I might so inform them. He said that he would be pleased to converse with them on the subject of Mr. Roebuck's motion, and that I might write to that effect. He, however, after a little reflection, added, 'I think that I can do something better; make a direct proposition to England for joint recognition. This will effectually prevent Lord Palmerston from misrepresenting my position and wishes on the American question.' He said, 'I shall bring the question before the cabinet meeting to-day, and if it should be decided not to make the proposition now, I will let you know in a day or two through Mr. Mocquard, and what to say to Mr. Roebuck.'

"I then said it may, perhaps, be an indiscretion to ask whether your majesty prefers to see the Whigs or Tories in power in England, and he said, 'I rather prefer the Whigs.' I remarked that Lord Malmesbury would under a conservative administration probably be the Secretary for Foreign Affairs, and that I had always understood that intimate relations existed between the emperor and him. He said, 'That is true; personally we are excellent friends, but personal relations have very little influence in great affairs where party interests are involved.' He playfully remarked, 'The Tories are very good friends of mine when in a minority, but their tone changes very much when they get into power.'

"He then spoke of the different spirit in which the news of the fall of Puebla had been received North and South; that the Northern papers showed their disappointment and hostility, while Richmond had been illuminated on the occasion. This is reported by the newspapers. I, of course, did not express any doubt of the fact, although I considered it somewhat apocryphal. I said that there could be no doubt of the bitterness of the Northern people at the success of his arms in Mexico, while all our sympathies were with France, and urged the importance of securing the lasting gratitude and attachment of a people already so well disposed; that there could be no doubt that our Confederacy was to be the strongest power of the American continent, and that our alliance was worth cultivating. He said that he was quite convinced of the fact, and spoke with great admiration of the bravery of our troops, the skill of our generals, and the devotion of our people. He expressed his regret at the death of Stonewall Jackson, whom he considered as one of the most remarkable men of the age.

"I expressed my thanks to him for his sanction of the contracts made for the building of four ships-of-war at Bordeaux and Nantes. I then informed him that we were prepared to build several iron-clad ships-of-war, and that it only required his verbal assurance that they would be allowed to proceed to sea under the Confederate flag to enter into contracts for that purpose. He said that we might build the ships, *but it would be necessary that their destination should be concealed.* I replied that the permission to build, equip, and proceed to sea would be no violation of neutrality, and invoked the precedent of a ship built for the Chilian government under the circumstances mentioned in my despatch No. 32, of April 20. *The emperor remarked that there was a distinction to be drawn between that case and what I desired to do. Chili was a government recognized by France.*

"The conversation then closed. The audience was shorter than the two previous occasions of my seeing the emperor. It lasted half an hour, but I did not think it discreet again to go over the ground covered by my note, and the points discussed in the former interviews, although they were occasionally brought into the conversation. I give below a copy of the letter of Mr. Roebuck. In reading it to the emperor, I omitted the portion underscored." *

There was certainly no ambiguity about the emperor's language at this interview. He was willing

---

* Copy of a letter from I. A. Roebuck, M.P., to W. S. Lindsay, M.P.:

"*June* 13, 1863.

"*My dear Lindsay*,—Seymour Fitzgerald said to me last night that it was rumored that the French emperor at the present time thought it would be unwise to recognize the South, and that Lord Palmerston on the 30th would say that England thought the time for recognition had not arrived, that France he could state authoritatively, thought so too, and that therefore it was quite clear that any negotiation about the matter at the present time was utterly out of place and impossible. Now upon this an idea has come into my head, and I will explain it by a question. Could we, *i. e.*, you and I, do any good by going to Paris and seeing the emperor? *You know that I am no great admirer of that great personage, but still I am a politician, so is he, and politicians have no personal likes or dislikes that stand in the way of their political ends. I therefore would act as if I had feelings neither friendly nor hostile to him, he would do the same as regards myself, and therefore I have no fear but that he would listen to all I have to offer by way of suggestion and advice.* Whether he would take that advice is another thing. Still he would listen, and good might come of our interview. Think over this proposition and give me your opinion. If we go, we ought to go at once. The 30th is not very far off, and we must soon decide whether the motion that stands in my name shall, or shall not, be brought on. The determination of the French emperor will have an important bearing upon that question. I send this letter to Shepperton, because I believe that on Sunday you will be there. If we determine to go to Paris, we ought to start on Monday morning. Yours very truly,

"I. A. R.

"W. S. L., Esq., M.P."

enough to deceive the Federals, but was careful to define the limits of his engagement to the Confederates, and if they failed to get their ships out, it was certainly through no violation of any engagement he had made to them. "You may build the ships," he said, "but their destination must be concealed." Twelve days before this conversation was held, Slidell had clothed Bullock and Arman's contract for the ships with his official sanction, and upon the strength of such sanction Erlanger, nine days before, had formally guaranteed the price to be paid for them.

This was the last, and these three were the only official interviews Slidell ever had with the emperor. In 1864 they met casually at the races, and the emperor spoke to him, but no allusion was made to steamers. I will give the account of it which Slidell sent to Benjamin in a private note, that the reader may know absolutely everything that ever passed between him and the emperor that he thought worth reporting:

SLIDELL'S ACCOUNT OF THE EMPEROR'S SPEAKING TO HIM AT THE RACES.

"PARIS, *Sept.* 1864.

"Hon. J. P. BENJAMIN, Secretary of State:—

"*Sir*,—I was yesterday at the races of the Bois de Boulogne, where I met the emperor; he recognized me at some distance, and came towards me, greeting me very cordially with a shake of the hand. He inquired if I had been well, and asked if I had received from the Minister of War notice of an order for the admission of my son at St. Cyr. I said that I had to thank him very sincerely for his kindness in affording my son an opportunity of acquiring a good military education. He replied that it was quite unnecessary, as he was pleased to have an opportunity of showing his good-will. I have not before alluded to this circumstance because an order had not been actually given, although the emperor had very promptly promised Mr. de Persigny to grant the permission on his application made about the 10th instant, and indeed I should not probably have mentioned the matter officially had I not had occasion to report my conversation with the emperor.

"The emperor, after making inquiries about my family, asked me what I thought of our military position, especially in Georgia, and of the effect of the fall of Atlanta. I said I was happy to assure him that the abandonment of Atlanta was a much less serious matter than was generally supposed in Europe, as we had removed all the valuable machinery and material weeks before Sherman took possession; that the only effect of Sherman's advance was to increase the distance from his base of supplies and make his communications more liable to interruption; that I did not think it at all improbable that we should soon hear of his falling back upon Chattanooga. He asked if the report of the surrender of Mobile was true. I said that I was confident not only that the report was premature, but that we should be able to hold Mobile as we had Charleston. I went on to say that we might soon expect stirring news from the armies near Petersburg, and I doubted not that Lee would give a good account of Grant. He expressed his admiration and astonishment at what he had achieved against such enormous odds, and his confidence in our ability to maintain ourselves; he spoke of the impossibility of occupying a territory like ours, and his regret that our many victories had not been followed by more decisive results. I answered that this was susceptible of easy explanation; that we were always fighting against superior numbers and had no strong reserves to follow up our successes; that the troops that had been engaged were generally exhausted by fatigue; that our great battles had usually been a series of desperate fighting for several days, and while we had inflicted much heavier losses on the enemy, we had necessarily been much crippled ourselves. Besides, our cavalry, from the difficulty of renewing our stock of horses, was much less numerous and efficient than it had been, and we were unable to pursue and harass a beaten and retreating enemy with such effect as would be expected in Europe under similar circumstances.

"The emperor asked me what were the prospects of peace. I replied that had the question been put to me ten days before I should have replied that they were good; but that the letter of McClellan accepting the Democratic nomination for the presidency had completely dissipated them; that Lincoln would probably be re-elected, and that the war would be continued until a revolution should break out in the free states. I asked him if he had read McClellan's letter; he said that he had, that it had greatly disappointed him, for he had entertained strong hope that the terrible conflict would soon be ended. He then left me with another cordial shake of the hand.

"A year ago I should have attached some important political signification to this incident; as it is I merely consider it as indicating personal kind feeling towards the representatives of a cause that commands his respect and good wishes.

"I have the honor to be with great respect,

"Your most obedient servant,

"JOHN SLIDELL."

Chapter XII.

Slidell's First Interview with Drouyn de Lhuys.—The Minister Declines to Express any Opinion about Recognizing the Confederate States.

Now let us see what encouragement Mr. Slidell received from the emperor's Minister of Foreign Affairs. On the 28th of October, he sent to Mr. Benjamin an account of his first audience with M. Drouyn de Lhuys, in which the reader will see just about how far that functionary was favorably disposed to make the French dock-yards a base of military operations against the United States.

Slidell to Benjamin.

"Paris, *October* 28, 1862.

"Hon. J. P. Benjamin, Secretary of State, Richmond:—

"*Sir*,—I had the honor to address you on the 20th instant. I send under this cover despatch of the same date on a special subject.

"On the 24th instant I sent to Mr. Drouyn de Lhuys, successor of Mr. Thouvenel, a note of which you will find a copy herewith, marked A, asking an interview. I received the same day, through his secretary, a verbal answer saying that he would see me on Sunday, 26th instant. I accordingly waited on Mr. Drouyn de Lhuys, who received me very kindly. After the customary interchange of courtesies, I said that I had been pleased to hear from various quarters that I should not have to combat with him the adverse sentiments that had been attributed to his predecessors in the Department of Foreign Affairs, with what degree of truth I did not permit myself to appreciate, and that if public rumor might be credited, he had expressed his sympathy with the cause of the Confederate States.

"He replied that *he was not aware of having expressed any opinion on the subject;* that not having anticipated being called to the post he now occupied, he had not given to the American question the attention which it deserved; but he could assure me that he would examine it carefully, and with the most perfect impartiality. He invited me to give my views. I said that I had addressed to his predecessor, the 21st of July, a letter in which I had set forth at some length the reasons on which I then relied for expecting the formal recognition of my government, and that as he had informed me that he had not yet found time to look into the question, I would briefly recapitulate them. I did, stating how much our position had improved in the meanwhile. I then adverted to the audience with which the emperor had honored me at Vichy, the assurances I then had that the emperor's views and wishes were well known to the English government. I spoke of the public declarations of Lord Palmerston and Earl Russell, that the policy and purpose of France and England were identical on American affairs. That this game of misrepresentation was still kept up, although Mr. Thouvenel had authorized a gentleman high in his confidence to say to me that he had had serious conversations, '*des pour parlers tres réels,*' with the British ambassador on the subject. In confirmation of my assertion, I stated the following facts:

"1st. An English friend, who had very recently passed the day with Lord Cowley at Chantilly, told me that Lord Cowley had said without reserve or qualification that no intimation, written or verbal, had been made to the British government of the views or wishes of the emperor on the American question; that he believed it was quite true the emperor had, to various private persons, expressed very freely his sympathies for the South, but that no notice could be taken of such expressions, of which the British government was supposed to be ignorant.

"2d. That I had seen, but a few days before, a letter from a leading member of the British cabinet, whose name I mentioned confidentially to the minister, in which he very plainly insinuated that France was playing an unfair game; that she was not better disposed towards the South than England was, and only affected to be so to create unkindly feeling towards England. That nothing had been said to induce England to recognize the South or to take any other step in relation to American affairs.

"3d. I had just received a letter from a gentleman in every way reliable, that he had seen Mr. Gladstone and several other members of the cabinet, who all said 'that it was quite certain that Mr. Thouvenel had not attempted at any time to induce their government to move.'

"Mr. Drouyn de Lhuys said that he had too recently come into office, and his time had been too much occupied by the Italian question, to know precisely what had been said or done by Mr. Thouvenel, but that he was quite sure that in some form or other the British government had been invited to act with France on the American question. I then attempted to show how entirely divergent were the interests of France and England on the subject—I do not repeat these reasons, as I have already stated them in previous despatches—and asked if, in spite of this divergence, the action of France would always be contingent on that of England. He replied, *that there were very grave objections to acting without England, and that he did not see how they could well be gotten over; that he could not venture to express any distinct opinion for the reason already stated, and because he was not fully in possession of the emperor's views on the subject.* I also showed him a letter from a friend in London, the same who informed me of Lord Cowley's declarations, dated 24th October; and as he is very intimate with Lord Palmerston, I give you an extract from it: 'I have just returned from Broadlands (this is Lord P.'s country-seat), and have also seen several leading political men in town. My impression is that little or no progress has been made as regards your question. The great majority of the government are clearly adverse to recognition at present, on selfish and narrow grounds, perhaps, but on grounds they think good. Gladstone's individual expression of opinion goes for very little. The cabinet meeting has been indefinitely postponed, because there is no question demanding immediate discussion, especially in the absence of the queen. I do not think that there will be a cabinet for ten days or a fortnight, unless something extraordinary should occur.' I said to Mr. Drouyn de Lhuys, considering the source from which it came, the letter offered to my mind conclusive evidence that we had nothing to expect from England. I also read it to the emperor to-day. I then referred to the propositions I had submitted to the emperor at Vichy, and repeated confidentially in writing to Mr. Thouvenel on the 23d July last. He was evidently ignorant of their purport, but they seemed to impress him strongly. I also informed him of the reasons which had induced me not to press his predecessor for an answer to my letter of 21st of July, reasons which I have communicated in a despatch preceding.

"I said that the emperor had accorded me the honor of an audience on the following Tuesday, and that I might, perhaps, have in consequence to solicit another interview.

"M. Drouyn de Lhuys, *although extremely courteous, scrupulously avoided saying anything that would indicate his personal views and feelings*, and wound up by saying that he would carefully examine the subject and consult the emperor, when he would again see me.

"On Saturday M. de Persigny informed me that the emperor would receive me on the following Tuesday. I have just returned from that interview, and have prepared a note of the conversation, which I annex, marked B.*

"I am, with great respect, your most obedient servant,

"JOHN SLIDELL."

---

* See *supra*, report of the first interview with the emperor.

Chapter XIII.

Slidell's Second Interview with Drouyn de Lhuys.—The Emperor's Silence about American Affairs in his Address to the Chambers Excused.—Slidell's Note to the Emperor Requesting him to Order the Minister of Marine not to Interfere with the Sailing of the Rams Building for the Confederates.

In Slidell's account of his second interview with Drouyn de Lhuys, which I now submit, he quotes a letter which he had the assurance to address to the emperor, asking him, in observance of engagements and understandings between him and the writer, to give orders that the Minister of Marine should not interfere in any way to oppose the departure of the rams. This letter was written only five months after Slidell's last official interview with the emperor at the Tuileries, when he was given distinctly to understand that if any vessels were built for the Confederates *their destination must be concealed.*

Slidell to Benjamin.

"Paris, November 15, 1863.

"Hon. J. P. Benjamin, Secretary of State:—

"The speech of the emperor addressed to the Chambers of the 5th instant has excited an immense sensation throughout Europe; it is very differently interpreted by different persons and in different quarters; by the majority it is considered pacific in its tone and tendencies—the opinion of others, and as I think the better opinion, is that it foreshadows a European war at no very distant day.

"You will have observed, perhaps with some surprise and disappointment, its silence on the subject of American affairs. This was my first feeling on perusing it, but after a more careful examination and further reflection I did not construe it so unfavorably. Not choosing, however, to rely on my own impression, I at once made inquiries of my friend at the *Affaires Étrangères* and of M. Mocquard, and received the same explanation from both. The former, at my request, had a conversation with his chief on the subject. There were two reasons for the emperor's reticence:

"1st. He could not say what he had been, and was still willing to do with the co-operation of England without, by implication, contrasting his policy and feelings with hers, and throwing upon her the responsibility of the present condition of American affairs; this he was not willing to do, as he desires scrupulously to avoid everything that would be likely to produce at this critical moment any coolness or alienation.

"2d. As he could not say all that he would desire to say on the subject, he preferred to say nothing rather than confine himself to *banalités*, commonplace expressions of regret at the continuance of the war and fruitless effusions of blood, etc. As to this latter point I am very decidedly of opinion that absolute silence is more satisfactory than vague, unmeaning generalities would have been. It may not be uninteresting to know—as well as showing the habits and mode of action of so remarkable a personage as illustrating the thorough aristocracy of his government, that that address—so remarkable and important in every way, was prepared without consultation with his ministers. On the third instant I called on the Duc de Morny, who had recently returned to Paris after a considerable absence. He said that he knew nothing of what the emperor would say in his address, excepting that it would be pacific in its tone, that a cabinet meeting would be held the next day, when the emperor would read it to his ministers. The duke, although not a minister, as president of the Corps Legislatif, attends cabinet meetings, especially during the session of the Chambers. M. Mocquard, the emperor's private secretary, told me a day or two previous that it had not yet been put on paper.

"I give you, in cipher, copy of a note which I addressed on the 6th instant to a high personage:

"'The confident assertions of agents of the Washington government, and certain remarks made at the Ministry of Foreign Affairs and Marine, lead undersigned to apprehend that without consulting your majesty orders may be given that will interfere with the completion and armament of ships-of-war now being constructed at Bordeaux and Nantes for the government of the Confederate States. The undersigned has the most entire confidence that your majesty, being made aware of the possibility of such an interference, will take the necessary step to prevent it. The undersigned has no access to the Minister of Marine, and does not feel authorized to state to the Minister of Foreign Affairs the circumstances under which the construction of these ships was commenced.

"'He relies upon this reason to excuse the liberty which he has ventured to take in addressing himself directly to your majesty on a subject in which are involved not only vital interests of the government which he represents, but very grave and delicate personal responsibilities for himself.

"'The undersigned tenders, etc.   JOHN SLIDELL.

"'PARIS, *November* 7, 1863.'

"On the following day I received a note from M. Drouyn de Lhuys requesting me to call on him on the 9th instant. As I anticipated, he wished to see me on the subject of my note of the 6th instant, which had been handed to him. He at once entered upon it, and seemed at first disposed to take rather a high tone, saying that what had passed with the emperor was confidential; that France could not be forced into a war by indirection; that when prepared to act it would be openly; and that peace with the North would be jeopardized on an accessory and unimportant point, such as the building of one or two vessels; that France was bound by the declaration of neutrality.

"I then gave him a detailed history of the affair, showing him that the idea originated with the emperor, and was carried out not only with his knowledge and approbation, but at his invitation; that it was so far confidential that it was not to be communicated but to a few necessary persons, but could not deprive me of the right of invoking, as I did, an adherence to promises which had been given long after the declaration of neutrality. I spoke very calmly, but very decidedly. *The minister's tone changed completely, and I took leave of him satisfied that the builders would not be interfered with.*

* * * * * * * *

"I have the honor to be, with the greatest respect,
 "Your Excellency's most obedient servant,
  "JOHN SLIDELL."

It is difficult to say whether the burden of the letter here quoted as sent to the emperor, or the reason assigned for sending it, is the most extraordinary. The effort to hold the emperor to an engagement which he knew the emperor had never made was one of those bold procedures which even desperation would hardly advise. On the 7th of November Slidell assigns as a justification for the liberty he was taking, that he did not feel authorized to state to the Minister of Foreign Affairs the circumstances under which the construction of these ships was commenced. Three days later he tells Benjamin that he gave the Minister of Foreign Affairs "a detailed history of the affair, showing him that the idea originated with the emperor and was carried out, not only with his knowledge and approbation, but at his invitation." It is not surprising that Slidell never had another official interview with the emperor.

Now let us see how much better off the commissioner was for the change which he supposed he had wrought in the minister's tones.

CHAPTER XIV.

Slidell's Third Interview with Drouyn de Lhuys.—Referred by him to the Minister of Marine for Information about the Rams.—Rouher Gives Assurance that the Rams may Leave when Finished.—Drouyn de Lhuys Refuses Permission to Advertise the Confederate Cotton Loan in France.—His Refusal Withdrawn by Order of the Emperor.

SLIDELL TO BENJAMIN.

"PARIS, *March* 4, 1863.

"Hon. J. P. BENJAMIN, Secretary of State:—

"*Sir*,—I spoke to M. Drouyn de Lhuys of the matter mentioned in cipher in my No. 23. He said that it belonged rather to the Minister of Commerce and Marine; that it was better that he should know nothing of it; that he was quite willing to close his eyes until some direct appeal was made to him.

"The minister was extremely cordial, said that he would always be happy to see me whenever I desired it, but that unless something especial occurred it would be better that I should communicate through the friend of whom I had spoken in previous despatches.

"He asked me to send him through that channel any information or suggestion that I might desire to make. This is a very convenient and agreeable arrangement, dispensing with the delays and formalities attending personal interviews with the minister.

"On the following day I called by appointment on M. Rouher[*] with M. Voruz, deputy from Nantes, of whom I spoke in my No. 25. The express object of the appointment was to re-

---

[*] Minister of State and leader of the Administration in the Legislative Chamber.

ceive from him a distinct assurance that if we were to build ships-of-war in French ports we should be permitted to arm and equip them and proceed to sea. This assurance was given by him, and so soon as the success of Erlanger's loan is established I shall write to Messrs. Maury and Bullock, recommending them to come here for the purpose of ascertaining whether they can make satisfactory contracts.

"The partner of a large banking-house at Vienna recently called to see me. He says that the Austrian government has some very superior war steamers which can be bought thoroughly armed and ready for sea, with the exception of the crews. I shall advise Mr. Maury to look at them.

"Seward's letter to Dayton, rejecting the proposition for a conference, was published two or three days since. Its tone is considered very exceptionable, and his boasting assertions are universally received with ridicule and contempt. I have not been able to learn what impression it had produced on the emperor, but I remain unchanged in my opinion that he will not long allow our question to rest where it is.

"I send you a copy of a letter addressed by me to the Minister of Foreign Affairs with a copy of your No. 10. I am obliged to you for files of Richmond papers. Until the arrival of M. de Leon I sent you regularly the Paris papers, journals, but have not since done so, presuming that he will have kept you supplied.

"I am still without your No. 1 of new series and all except 1, 2, 3, 5 of old series. I hope that you will send copies to complete the files of the commission.

"In my conversation with M. Drouyn de Lhuys I mentioned the loan of Erlanger & Co., and invoked his good offices in carrying it out, saying that these gentlemen considered it important that it should be advertised in the Paris papers, but that the advertisement could not be made without the assent of the government. He expressed his wishes for the success of the loan, but thought that he could not consent to the advertisement, that the object could be equally well attained by circulars, etc., while advertisements would excite unfriendly comment and probably be made the subject of a protest from the Federal Minister.

"The consent of the Minister of Finance, M. Fould, had been

obtained, subject, however, to the approbation of the Minister of Foreign Affairs. Erlanger then brought the subject before the emperor, who very promptly directed his secretary to write a note to the minister requesting him to grant an audience to Mr. Erlanger on an urgent matter in which he felt great interest.

"The result of the audience was the withdrawal by M. Drouyn de Lhuys of his objections, and the loan will now be simultaneously advertised here and in London. I mention this fact as offering renewed evidence of the friendly feeling of the emperor.

"I have the honor to be, with great respect,
"Your most obedient servant,
"JOHN SLIDELL."

It is sufficiently apparent from the tenor of his conversations with M. Drouyn de Lhuys that Slidell received from that minister far less encouragement than from the emperor to embark in the shipbuilding business. The exposure of their conspiracy had made it impossible for the government to countenance the scheme, and neither the minister nor the sovereign gave him any reason to anticipate a different result. Slidell, at length, began to realize the *impasse* into which he had landed his government, and seemed not unwilling to divide with Captain Bullock the responsibility for it, as will appear in the following despatch from Slidell, in which he admits that the emperor never committed himself to the sailing of the iron-clads, "unless their destination could be concealed."

SLIDELL TO BENJAMIN.

"PARIS, *February* 16, 1864.

"Hon. J. P. BENJAMIN, Secretary of State:—

"*Sir*,—Commander Maury, C. S. N., being despatched by Commodore Barron to Richmond, I avail myself of so favorable an occasion to speak more fully of matters to which I had in previous despatches but briefly and cautiously alluded.

"Lieutenant Whittle, who was sent to the Confederacy by Captain Bullock last summer, communicated to the president and Secretary of the Navy detailed information respecting the arrangements made for the building of ships in France, and the extrication of two of those then in course of construction in England from anticipated difficulties.

"These arrangements have been seriously interfered with by the felonious abstraction of certain papers, as stated in my No. 49, and it is now asserted that by similar means papers relating to the ships in England have come into the possession of the emissaries of the Washington government. On this latter point I am inclined to think that the assertion is unfounded, as Captain Bullock is very confident that no access could have been had to his papers, and I have every reason to believe that in other quarters equal vigilance has been observed. So far as regards the corvettes that are being built at Bordeaux and Nantes, there is, unfortunately, no doubt of the fact that complete evidence of their ownership is in the hand of Mr. Dayton, and has been by him communicated to this government.

"By referring to the report of my conversation with the emperor contained in my No. 38, you will find that while fully assenting to the arming and departure of the corvettes, he consented only to the building of iron-clads for our account, and *did not commit himself to permit their sailing unless their destination could be concealed. This in the case of iron-clads could only be done by setting up an apparent ownership by some foreign government.* As to the corvettes, they were to be represented as intended for commercial purposes in the Indian Ocean, China, etc. The contract for the corvettes was concluded only after the official consent to their armament and sailing was given by the Minister of Marine, and this was given on the representation that they were intended for commercial purposes, although their real character and destination were fully known to him; he, however, reluctantly signed the order in obedience to superior authority. No such authority was given in case of the iron-clads, *and I was ignorant that any contract was in contemplation for their construction until after it had been made.* I mention these facts not with the most remote idea of implying any censure upon Captain Bullock, but to establish the distinction to be drawn between the two classes of vessels, which is necessary to bear in mind in order to come to a proper decision as to the course to be pursued in relation to them. In the first interview I had with the Minister of Marine, on the 19th of November, consequent on my note to the emperor of the 9th of November, contained in my No. 48, he drew a very broad line of distinction between the corvettes and the iron-clads, saying that with proper precautions the former might be permitted to go to sea, but that the iron-clads, being from their very build fitted for warlike purposes, their being permitted to sail in spite of the remonstrances of the Washington government and in violation of the emperor's declaration of neutrality would be an overt act of hostility.

"The question now presents itself, what is to be done with these vessels? M. Arman, the builder of these iron-clads, was informed that they will not be permitted to go to sea, except as the property of some non-belligerent government. This was before the breaking-out of hostilities between Denmark, Austria, and Prussia. Captain Bullock, after consulting Mr. Mason, Commodore Barron, and me, determined to sell the iron-clads. They could have been disposed of at a considerable advance on their cost, to Denmark or to Prussia, but the pending war may put these purchasers, as belligerents, out of the market. Commodore Barron and Captain Bullock say that the corvettes were intended to act in conjunction with the iron-clads in raising the blockade of our coasts, and this object being no longer attainable, and there being few Federal merchant vessels afloat, they are disposed to sell the corvettes, also, or at least two of them. I do not agree with them in this view of the case. Should we withdraw our cruisers the Federal flag would soon resume on the ocean the rank we have forced it to abdicate. We cannot expect the *Alabama* and *Florida* always to avoid the pursuit of the enemy, and we should be prepared to supply their loss; I fear that the *Rappahannock* will prove to be as unfit for that service as the *Georgia*, and will not make more than one cruise.

"In deciding, however, the question of the disposition to be made, a new difficulty presents itself which applies alike to both classes. It has been found extremely difficult to obtain engineers for the *Georgia* and *Rappahannock*, two small vessels, and with the increased vigilance of the English authorities it will hereafter be found almost impracticable to man several large vessels. On the other hand, a few months may produce great changes in our favor. I know that the emperor's feelings are as friendly as ever, and a new ministry in England may enable him to indulge them. The chapter of accidents is always, in the long run, fruitful of great and unexpected results. Perhaps it may be better to go on and complete the ships. There is no reason to apprehend any interruption in the work, and there is no danger whatever of losing them by any proceeding similar to those pending in England, as there is no municipal law prohibiting the fitting-out of ships-of-war for the belligerent powers with whom France is at peace.

"I have given Captain Maury verbal explanations respecting the ships in England which I have thought it not prudent to commit to paper even with so safe a messenger.

"I have the honor to be, with great respect,
"JOHN SLIDELL."

To this letter Mr. Secretary Benjamin, who already realized that the scaffolding on which they had built their hopes was giving away, sent the following reply:

BENJAMIN TO SLIDELL.

"DEPARTMENT OF STATE,
RICHMOND, *April* 16, 1864.

"Hon. JOHN SLIDELL, etc., Paris, France:—

"*Sir*,—Your last despatch received is No. 56 of the 16th of February, which came to hand on the 4th instant. The interval of two months is longer than has occurred for more than a year past, and is regretted the more, as matters of great interest to us were pending, and numerous reports calculated to excite solicitude as to the present attitude of the Imperial government reach us from the Northern journals. I will not conceal from you that the President is greatly disappointed at the information contained in your No. 56. Grave doubt even is entertained of the *good faith* of the *high personage* by whose sanction and advice we *engaged* in an *undertaking* which *promised* results of the greatest importance. A *severe blow* has been *dealt* us from a *quarter* whence it was least expected, and a corresponding *revulsion* of *feeling* towards that *personage* has resulted.

"Mr. *Mallory* has written to the *officers charged* with these matters, that we have concluded against the propriety *of selling any* of the *vessels* in *progress* of *construction*. I hope that his instructions will arrive in time to prevent *the sale*. Our conclusion is, of course, based on the supposition that according to French law there is *no risk* of the *loss* or *confiscation* of these *vessels*, and that the only *hazard involved* in *keeping* them is, that they will *not* be allowed to go *to sea*. We prefer in such case taking our chances of some change of circumstances or policy. The length of *time required* for the *construction of iron-clads* in particular is so great that we would be inexcusable in *abandoning* all the *chances* of *future contingencies* of getting back the *money* already *expended*, or avoiding the further *expense of finishing* them. It is deemed by the President much more prudent to have *the vessels* promptly *completed* and *ready for service* at any moment, should the *adverse influences* which now *prevail* give *place* to other counsels.

"You will receive herewith a treasury draft for five hundred pounds sterling from the fund at the disposal of the department for secret service, of which no account is to be rendered to the treasury. Where you can properly take vouchers, they should accompany the account you will render to this department of the expenditure; for items not susceptible of being vouched, you will render a certificate on honor, of the payment.

"I have just heard of the arrival at City Point (about forty miles, I believe, below Richmond) of a French war steamer and two merchantmen, which come, doubtless, for the purpose of taking the tobacco belonging to the Imperial government, and which will be delivered in accordance with our promise.

"*April* 18.

"Your No. 57 of 5th of March has just come to hand. It is the duplicate, the original not yet received. The change of tone indicated by you as having marked your interview with M. Drouyn de Lhuys, together with the tenor of the remarks attributed to Lord Palmerston, seem to be of some significance, but we cannot attribute to them the same importance as would have been attached to such utterances at an early period of the war. It has been, perhaps, fortunate for us, notwithstanding the awful price paid in the blood of our best and bravest, that European powers have remained so inconceivably blind to their own interests in this great struggle. The end is now seen to be approaching, and we shall enter the family of nations with a consciousness that we have achieved our own success, not simply unaided by sympathy, but in spite of the unfriendly, and in some cases hostile, attitude of the great powers of Europe. We shall have no favor to reciprocate, but many wrongs to forget—some perhaps for which to exact redress. I never felt a more thorough conviction than I now entertain that the year 1864 will witness our honorable welcome into the family of nations, won by the conclusive demonstration of the inability of the North to continue a contest in which its resources, both of men and money, will have been exhausted in vain."

Whether Captain Bullock signed the contract for the iron-clads without the authority or approval of Mr. Slidell is a question which I will leave to be settled by those whom it may concern. I can, however, make a slight contribution towards its settlement. On the 20th of April, 1863, Slidell addressed a note to Benjamin in which the following passage occurred:

"I send you a copy of the memorandum I prepared for submission to the emperor. Captain Bullock has signed provisional contract for building four steamers of the *Alabama* class on a large scale. Contract to take effect when assurances satisfactory to me are given that the ships will be allowed to leave French ports armed and equipped. Contractors confident that these assurances will be given. I shall probably know the result in time to inform you by the same conveyance as I employ for this despatch."

On the 18th of June following, and before Slidell had the expected interview with, or any even conditional assurances from the emperor, he approved of the contract which Bullock and Arman had made, in the following words: "*In consequence of the ministerial* authorization which you have shown me *and which* I *deemed sufficient*, the contract of the 15th of April becomes binding." Nothing is here said about Imperial engagements to let the ships go out. The ministerial authorization is deemed sufficient. If he had never sanctioned the contract for the iron-clads, it seems not a little strange that the fact had not cropped out before in any of his correspondence; and that he should have berated the Imperial government in such vindictive terms for preventing their sailing under the Confederate flag.

Chapter XV.

Slidell Advises against any more Attempts to Fit out a Navy in Europe.—Concludes that "the Weak have no Rights; the Strong no Obligations."—Gwin on his Way to Mexico with an Autograph Letter from the Emperor to the French Commander.—Secretary Benjamin Reviews the Conduct of the French Government.—Slidell Directed to Maintain "a Reserved Demeanor."

WITH one more letter from Mr. Slidell and one more letter from Mr. Benjamin I close the documentary history of their connection with the naval operations of the Confederate States in France.

Both had gone out to shear, and came home shorn. Both wished to beguile France into the trap they had set, that should bring on a war and compel the emperor to fight their battle for them, and both found themselves and not the emperor in the trap. Of course they felt that they had been brutally wronged and were very indignant, as people always are who have been hoist by their own petard.

SLIDELL TO BENJAMIN.

"PARIS, *June* 2, 1864.
"Hon. J. P. BENJAMIN, Secretary of State:—

"*Sir*,—I am still without later despatches from you than your No. 34, of March 28, although we have Nassau dates up to 9th ultimo. Since my last, the 21st ultimo, the two corvettes of Bordeaux have been sold to the Prussian government, which has also become the purchaser of the second ram, building at the same place. The original owners of all these vessels will be reimbursed for all moneys expended on them, with interest, and a small percentage of profit. They were induced to take this course by a conviction of the impossibility of employing the ships in the manner first intended.

"The builders of the two remaining corvettes persist in saying that they will deliver them to us at sea, but I have been so grievously deceived and disappointed heretofore that I am far from placing implicit reliance on their assurances.

"I am quite satisfied that no further attempts to fit out ships-of-war in Europe should be made at present, but I am every day more and more fully convinced that when the war has ceased one of our earliest cares should be to lay the foundation of a respectable navy.

"We must indulge in no Arcadian dreams of following undisturbed the peaceful pursuits of agriculture. Instead of the millennium, which the peace philosophers pronounced some ten years ago to have arrived, there has been a series of bloody wars culminating in the most terrific struggle which the world has ever witnessed. The condition of national existence now is the capacity reached to defend itself and to inflict injuries on others. The weak have no rights; the strong no obligations. The much-vaunted reign of public opinion throughout the world is powerless to save Denmark from the most lawless spoliation, although her integrity was guaranteed by all the great powers of Europe. The justice of our cause, the heroism of our troops, the devotion of our people, while they excite the sympathy and command the admiration of Europe, not only have failed to secure us any friendly support from abroad, but even a fair neutrality.

"The two strongest powers submit to the insolent demands of the Lincoln government that their commerce may be safe on the ocean, and Mexico and Canada unmolested. And why? Because they have formed an exaggerated estimate of its capacity to do mischief.

"Ex-Senator Gwin is on his way to Mexico. His object is to colonize Sonora with persons of southern birth or proclivities residing in California. He bears an autograph letter from Louis Napoleon to the French commander-in-chief warmly recommending his enterprise.

"His scheme has been fully examined and approved, and offers, as I believe, fair chances of success. If carried out, its consequences will be most beneficial.

* * * * * * *

"I have the honor to be, with the greatest respect,
"Your obedient servant, JOHN SLIDELL."

BENJAMIN TO SLIDELL.

"DEPARTMENT OF STATE,
RICHMOND, *September* 20, 1864.
"Hon. JOHN SLIDELL, etc., etc., Paris:—

"*Sir*,—I have made no answer to your several despatches posterior to No. 63, because each mail led us to hope that the next would bring some definite solution to the affair of the *Rappahannock*, and thus enable the President to express his views of the action of the French government in this matter. The uncertainty is now at an end, and I have to acknowledge receipt of your Nos. 64 to 68 inclusive, the Nos. 67 and 68 having reached us on the 1st instant.

"A review of the conduct of the French government since the commencement of our national career exhibits the most marked contrast between friendly professions and injurious acts. It may not be without utility here to place on record a series of instances in which that government and its officers have interposed effectively to aid our enemies, while profuse in professions of sympathy for us.

"1st. France united with Great Britain in agreeing to respect a paper blockade of our entire coast, with a full knowledge of its invalidity, as since conceded to you on more than one occasion.

"2d. France joined Great Britain in closing all its ports to the entry of prizes made by us, thus guaranteeing, as far as was possible without open hostility, the vessels of our enemies from becoming prizes to our cruisers, and forcing us to destroy on the high seas, and thus lose the value of all vessels captured from our enemies.

"3d. France has entertained during the entire war the closest amicable relations with our enemies as an independent nation. It has, at the same time, violated the Treaty of February 6, 1778, the 11th article of which guaranteed to the states of Virginia, North Carolina, South Carolina, and Georgia, 'their liberty, sovereignty, and independence, absolute and unlimited,' by persistent refusal to treat these states as independent, and by countenancing the claim to sovereignty over them set up by the remaining states that were parties to that treaty.

"4th. This government succeeded in introducing into the roadstead of the Brassos Santiago cargoes of arms destined to pass through the neutral port of Matamoras into the Confederacy. The French naval officers seized these arms as being intended for the use of the Mexicans, in spite of the most conclusive evidence that they were destined for our defence against invasion. The people of Texas being thus deprived of arms, the town of Brownville and the Rio Grande frontier fell defenceless into the hands of the enemy.

"5th. The agents of the French government, after obtaining permission for the export of their tobacco, under license to pass the blockade, entered into a convention with our enemy, so objectionable in its character and so derogatory to our rights as an independent power that we have been forced to withdraw the permission.

"6th. This government was indirectly approached by the Emperor Maximilian with proposals for the establishment of friendly relations. The Emperor of the French is well understood to have interfered to prevent this result, and to induce the new emperor to seek favor from our enemies by avoiding intercourse with us.

"7th. The French government has taken pains to intimate to us that hospitalities to our vessels of war, entering their harbors, was accorded with reluctance; and by the delays interposed in the grant of permission to the *Alabama* to enter dock for necessary repairs, placed her commander in a situation which prevented him from declining without dishonor a combat in which his vessel was lost, chiefly by reason of her need of refitting and repair.

"8th. The Emperor of the French, after having himself suggested and promised acquiescence in the attempt of this government to obtain vessels-of-war by purchase or contract in France, after encouraging us in the loss of invaluable time and of the service of some of our best naval officers, as well as in the expenditure of large sums obtained at painful sacrifice, has broken his faith, has deprived us of our vessels when on the eve of completion, and has thus inflicted on us an injury and rendered to our enemies a service which establish his claim to any concessions that he may desire from them. This last act of the French government, professedly dictated by the obligation of preserving neutrality, is marked still more distinctly as unfriendly to the Confederacy by the fact that some of the vessels have been transferred to a European power engaged in war to which France is no party and in which she professes the same neutrality as in the contest on this side of the Atlantic.

"The detention of the *Rappahannock* is the last and least defensible of the acts of the French government, and it is in its nature totally irreconcilable with neutral obligations. A Confederate vessel, unarmed, sought and obtained asylum in the port of Calais. She was allowed to complete her repairs and to incur all the cost and expense necessary to enable her to go to sea. She was notified of the desire of the French government that she should leave the harbor, and, while engaged in coaling for that purpose and still unarmed, the French government, on the demand of our enemies, ordered her to be detained in port on the unintelligible pretext that she had not obtained her coal in advance. Six months have elapsed and the *Rappahannock* is still in a French port. In violation of the right of asylum we have been deprived of the services of this vessel, while, by the use of a system alternating between a studied silence and evasive statements, our representations have been eluded and our remonstrances rendered unavailing. After thus delaying the departure of the vessel until our enemies had had time to perfect arrangements for her capture, a reluctant consent to her departure was finally extorted, but coupled with conditions which would almost insure her falling into the hands of the enemy. The vessel, therefore, remains in the French port; its use during the war practically confiscated by the government for the benefit of our adversary, under circumstances as inconsistent with neutral obligations as they are injurious to our rights and offensive to our flag.

"It is impossible for the President, in view of such action on the part of a foreign government, to credit its professions of amity, nor can he escape the painful conviction that the Emperor of the French, knowing that the utmost efforts of this people are engrossed in the defence of their homes against an atrocious warfare waged by greatly superior numbers, has thought the occasion opportune for promoting his own purposes at no greater cost than a violation of his faith and duty towards us.

"It is unfortunately but too true that this government is not now in a position to resist such aggressions, and France is not the only nation which has unworthily availed itself of this fact, as the messages of the President have on more than one occasion demonstrated to the world. There is one contrast, however, between the conduct of the English and French governments that does not redound to the credit of the latter. The English government has scarcely disguised its hostility. From the commencement of the struggle it has professed a newly-invented neutrality which it had frankly defined as meaning a course of conduct more favorable to the stronger belligerents. The Emperor of the French professed an earnest sympathy for us and a desire to serve us, which, however sincere at the time, have yielded to the first suggestion of advantage to be gained by rendering assistance to our enemies. We are compelled by present circumstances to submit in silence to these aggressions, but we are not compelled, nor is it compatible with a proper sense of self-respect, to affect towards the Emperor of the French a continuance of the same regard and confidence to which the President formerly felt justified in giving public expression. Nor need we forego the hope, which it is, however, unnecessary to proclaim, that the day is not nearly so distant as is supposed by those who take themselves unworthy advantages, when the Confederacy will be able to impress on all nations the conviction of her ability to repel outrages from whatever quarter they may be offered.

"From the correspondence of the naval officers abroad with the Secretary of the Navy it appears that the French government was not satisfied with preventing our use during the war of the vessels built in French ports with the consent of that government, but refused permission to finish the vessels for delivery to us after the restoration of peace, and actually forced the builders to sell them to third parties. From the reports of Captain Bullock, it would seem that the arrangements to prevent the vessels from ever reaching our hands were so complete and carried out with such disregard of good faith and of contract on the part of the contractors and public officials that he was compelled to esteem himself fortunate in saving this government from the loss of the money invested. He represents the conduct of all parties to be such as should render the government ever most cautious in its dealings with France, and it is probable that the lesson will be well remembered.

"You will of course understand that in the foregoing observation it is far from the intention of the President to suggest that you should obtrude on the French government any manifestation of an indignation which, however deeply felt, can be followed by no action which could afford us redress. We believe that you will not find it difficult to maintain a reserved demeanor which will readily suggest the inference that the conduct of the emperor's government is regarded by the President as unfriendly, without giving any occasion for a rupture, which would add to the weight of the difficulties attendant on our struggle, and which is, therefore, carefully to be avoided. Any complaints which we may have to make against European powers must of necessity be deferred for a more favorable occasion, and all that we can do at present is to avoid any course of conduct that should fairly be construed into condonations of injuries that remain unredressed.

* * * * * * *

"I have the honor to be, very respectfully,
"Your very obedient servant,
"J. P. BENJAMIN,
"Secretary of State."

It is apparent from this correspondence, without reference to other confirmatory evidence, that Louis Napoleon was quite willing to secure to his friend Arman a good contract; that he was disposed to protract the war in America at least until Maximilian's supremacy in Mexico was assured, and for that purpose was prepared to render the Confederates any assistance in his power that would not compromise his relations with the United States. He had hoped, no doubt, that the ships building at Bordeaux and Nantes should get to sea and accomplish the work for which they were designed. He, no doubt, had been encouraged to believe, and hoped, that before the vessels were ready for sea the Confederate armies might have achieved a substantial victory like that of the Revolutionary army at Saratoga in 1777, when he would have been emboldened to follow the example of Louis XVI., and openly enter into an offensive and defensive alliance with the Confederates. No such victory, however, was won; the secret of the ships was divulged, and there was no course left for him but to fall back upon the literal terms of his engagement with Slidell, and to disclaim all responsibility for the consequences. The Confederates were not dealing at home with an infatuated sovereign like George III., and they were not represented at Paris by Benjamin Franklin, but by John Slidell. It is not surprising that such a difference in conditions was attended with a corresponding difference in results. Had a John Slidell been sent to Paris in 1776, instead of Benjamin Franklin, who would be bold enough to predict that the present United States would not still be a dependance of Great Britain?

CHAPTER XVI.

The Washington Government Charged with Bribery and Employing Spies.—Letters of Slidell and Benjamin.—Mason's Offer to Corrupt the Telegraph Company.—Edwin de Leon's Mission to "Enlighten Public Opinion in Europe" and Rig the Press. — Slidell's Effort to Tempt the Emperor with a Bribe of $7,000,000.—Mason and Slidell Bull the Confederate Cotton Loan in the London Market at an Expense of over $6,000,000 in a Single Month.

IN the letter of Captain Bullock to the Secretary of the Confederate Navy, dated November 23, 1863, reciting the circumstances which resulted in the exposure and explosion of the scheme for getting his rams out of France, Captain Bullock allows himself to say: "The extent to which the system of bribery and spying has been and continues to be practised by the agents of the United States is scarcely credible. The servants of gentlemen supposed to have Southern sympathies are tampered with; confidential clerks and even the messengers from telegraph offices are bribed to betray their trust," etc. These allegations, which doubtless originated with Slidell and Mason, I cannot allow to pass into history unchallenged. It is not strange that Captain Bullock should have supposed the cities of Europe were swarming with Federal spies, first because they have been used in war by the more civilized nations longer than artillery or gunpowder, and will be used by them long after the present arms of precision are only to be seen in museums; secondly, because he did not know how else to account for the difficulty they had in keeping any secrets. Captain Bullock does not seem to be aware of what his own experience should have taught him, that a criminal secret is almost as much of an absurdity and as near to an impossibility as a universal solvent, and for the same reason that no vessel can hold it. While I should as soon think of apologizing for the use of muskets as of spies against a public enemy, it will not be out of place here, following Captain Bullock's example, to give my testimony upon this subject, upon which, so far as France is concerned, I am as well informed as any one. Though holding positions in that empire during the war which would devolve upon me as much at least as upon any one else the duty of employing spies, I never had a spy in my employ during my official residence in France, nor did I ever pay any one nor authorize any one to be paid a penny for any secret information, procured at my instance for a mercenary consideration. Of course I should have employed spies had I needed them, but I did not need them. My relations with the all-knowing press, with the officials about the palace and departments, and, above all, with the representatives of foreign governments, who are always glad of an opportunity of placing a colleague under obligation, and who, with the exception of the English, Spanish, and Austrian representatives, were all in cordial sympathy with us, supplied me, at no expense, with all the information we required, and of a far more trustworthy character than can ordinarily be obtained through spies. The case of Mr. X constitutes no exception. I did not employ him. He brought his information to me, put me in possession of it without fee or reward, and only stipulated that if I used it in any official way he should be compensated. He was never employed by me, nor did he serve me in any other matter. What I have said for myself, I can say with scarcely less confidence of Mr. Dayton, who preceded me at the legation, and of Mr. Nicolay, who succeeded me at the consulate. Though it is among the possibilities, it is not among the probabilities that either ever spent a penny for the procurement of secret information without my being aware of it, and I certainly never had a suspicion of such a thing. What may have been spent on spies in Belgium and England I am unable to speak of with any positive knowledge, but I have no doubt the charge of Mr. Bullock could be made with as much if not with more propriety against any first-class newspaper in London or New York than against any Federal official in Europe during the war.

But as Captain Bullock has the pretension to have occupied with his colleagues a higher moral plane than that upon which war had theretofore been conducted, it may be useful to him, in case he has occasion to write anything more on this subject, to understand, better than he seems to have done, the very vitreous character of the edifice from which he and they discharge their missiles. But that the captain's tirade may not lose the benefit of any extenuating circumstances, I will here give the probable sources of his impressions of the wickedness of the Federal officers in Europe whom he so recklessly arraigns.

In a letter to Secretary of State Benjamin, dated November 19, 1863, and shortly after our knowledge of his ship-building operations was communicated to the Imperial government, Mr. Slidell wrote as follows:

"The agents and emissaries of the Washington government, not satisfied with the establishment of a vast organized system of espionage and the subornation of perjured informers, now unblushingly have recourse to theft and forgery to attain their ends. Mr. Dayton asserts that he has in his possession letters and other documents showing that certain vessels now being constructed at Bordeaux and Nantes belong to the Confederate States. A confidential clerk of the builders at Nantes has absconded, carrying off documents of which he was the custodian, and which in some respects correspond with the papers of which Mr. Dayton has deposited with the Minister of Foreign Affairs, what he asserts to be the true copies of originals. If he, in truth, have any such originals, he knows by whom and how they were stolen, and was doubtless an accessory as well before as after the fact.

"The faithless clerk must have been heavily bribed, for he abandoned an eligible situation which was his only means of support. He is an intelligent, well-educated man, having, it is said, always borne a good character, and is now a fugitive from justice for a crime which would consign him, if arrested, to the galleys.

"The builders say that the pretended copies of papers stolen from them and deposited with the Minister of Foreign Affairs contain interpolated matter, thus adding forgery to theft.

"Mr. Dayton has also furnished copies of letters and other

papers which were stolen from Captain F. Maury. A letter which I addressed to Captain Sinclair at Glasgow, that was never received by him, must have been intercepted by Federal emissaries. The post-office in France is, I think, above suspicion, and the theft must have been perpetrated on the other side of the Channel."

In reply to the foregoing Mr. Benjamin discharges the phials of his wrath upon his loyal countrymen in terms beside which Mr. Slidell's sound moderate if not weak.

BENJAMIN TO SLIDELL.

"RICHMOND, *January* 8, 1864.

"I am not at all surprised at the accounts you give of the action of the Northern emissaries in suborning perjury, committing thefts, and forging documents, for the furtherance of their objects. No crime is too revolting for this race, which disgraces civilization and causes one to blush for our common humanity. You have been removed from the scene of their outrages, and are evidently startled at conduct on their part which we look for as quite naturally to be expected. A people who have been engaged for the last three years in forging our treasury notes, cheating in the exchange of prisoners of war, exciting slaves to the murder of their masters, plundering private property without a semblance of scruple, burning dwellings, breaking up and destroying agricultural implements, violating female honor, and murdering prisoners in cold blood, not to speak of Greek fire, stone fleets, and other similar expedients of warfare, would scarcely excite your indignation. *I entertain no doubt whatever that hundreds of thousands of people at the North would be frantic with fiendish delight if informed of the universal massacre of the Southern people, including women and children, in one night.* They would then only have to exterminate the blacks (which they are fast doing), and they would become owners of the property which they covet, and for which they are fighting."

A few months later, and on the 15th of September of the same year, Mr. Benjamin sets himself down to explain the psychological distinctions, or, as he expresses it, "the radical difference as exhibited in the war between the people of the two Confederations."

"The vaunting and braggart spirit of the North," he says, "finds vent on the most trifling occasion, and magnifies the result of a successful skirmish into a grand victory that has broken the back of the rebellion. The cool and practical Southerner, looking reality in the face, is supposed to depreciate the importance of the most signal success, and to regard a grand victory as shorn of its value if any portion of the enemy's army escape destruction. Is this to be attributed on each side to the innate consciousness of the superiority of the Southern race? Is the North elated because any success is unexpected against our brave soldiers? Is the South dissatisfied because no success seems adequate to what should be effected by the marked superiority of our troops over those of the enemy? I am unable to solve the question."

What fustian this, to put into a diplomatic instruction!

It is evident that Captain Bullock had read, or otherwise been put in possession of the contents of these papers, and allowed himself to accept these official statements without making due allowance for the disappointment, vexation, and rage which dictated them.

Now let us see just how elevated was the plane upon which the Confederate officials in Europe carried on war, how far their example lent authority to their judgments of their Federal colleagues, and in what degree they qualified themselves to cast the first stone.

We will begin with the last charge in Mr. Slidell's letter, to the effect that his despatch had been stolen from Captain Maury and necessarily by "Federal emissaries."

"The post-office in France," he adds, "is, I think, above suspicion, and the theft must have been perpetrated on the other side of the Channel."

This letter was written in January, 1864.

In a letter to Benjamin, dated April 20, 1863, Slidell writes:

"On the 14th inst. I received from M. Mocquard, *chef du Cabinet* of the emperor, a note in which he said that he hastened to send me a paper which he thought could not fail to be of interest *to me*.

"It was a copy of a telegraphic despatch from Mr. Adams, of London, to Mr. Dayton, advising him that the *Japan*, alias *Virginia* (a Confederate cruiser), would probably enter a French port near St. Malo. On the following day I saw M. Mocquard, who told me he had been directed by the emperor to send me the despatch as soon as received.

"*All despatches go first through the Ministry of the Interior. If they have any political interest they are transmitted to the Tuileries by wires. Thus, I have no doubt, I was in possession of the paper as soon as Mr. Dayton.* I thanked M. Mocquard for his note, and said that I had called to ask his counsel as to the course I should pursue in relation to it. He asked me what I desired should be done in the matter. I said that, of course, I wished that every needful facility should be afforded by the government for the repair of the steamer. He advised me to prepare a note to that effect, which he would present to the emperor, and to feel assured that all would be right."

This was Slidell's notion of a post-office above

suspicion. As long as he supposed his own correspondence safe, it was no crime to tamper with the correspondence of a Federal minister.

The measure of respect which Bullock's official superiors thought due to the correspondence of Federal officials is further illustrated by the following telegram to Mr. Mason, who at that time represented the Confederate government with indifferent success at the court of St. James:

April 29.

"*Dear Sir*,—Offer $10,000 for the two authentic notes of Seward and Lincoln. Charge the Ruyters * to secure the letters of Corwin,† who quits Vera Cruz on leave of absence the 20th of May. Dayton is deceived by Drouyn de Lhuys. I send you the proofs, which you will return by the first post.

"MASON."

Now in regard to the use of money for purposes of corruption, let us look a little further and see with what kind of hands Captain Bullock and his diplomatic colleagues come before the tribunals of history. In April, 1862, Secretary Benjamin sent Edwin de Leon, of Virginia, to Europe as an agent of the Confederate government, and equipped him with a credit for £25,000 "to be used by him in the manner he might deem most judicious both in Great Britain and on the Continent, for the special purpose of enlightening public opinion in Europe through the press."

How was that £25,000 to be used, except in publications calculated to prejudice the Federal cause,

---

* The leading European telegraph agency.

† Thomas Corwin, Minister of the United States to Mexico.

to which the press would not extend its hospitality without some pecuniary inducement?

On the same day that Mr. Benjamin invested this large sum in the enlightenment of public opinion in Europe, he authorized Mr. Slidell to offer the Emperor of France $7,000,000 worth of cotton—more if necessary—to indemnify him for any expenses he might incur in sending an expeditionary fleet to the relief of the Confederates. Can Captain Bullock refer us to any similar attempt on the part of Federal officials to sell out their own government, or the Confederate government, and make either a dependancy of any foreign power?

In the same month of the same year Messrs. Mason and Slidell authorized Messrs. Erlanger to sustain the market for Confederate cotton bonds, so as to prevent subscribers who were losing confidence in the Confederacy from forfeiting the fifteen per cent. they had paid in, rather than pay the second instalment that was to fall due in a few weeks. Within a month the Messrs. Erlanger, upon this weak or wicked pretext, managed to invest for them over $6,000,000 in "bulling" the London market.

This and the next preceding statement are of such extraordinary character, and refer to events the knowledge of which has hitherto been confined to so few, that the public is entitled to the authority upon which I make them.

In reference to the first, in which a foreign power is invited to invade our shores, I cite the following letter from the Confederate Secretary of State. In this letter will be found the "proposals" which

Slidell was instructed to make to the emperor and to which reference is made on pp. 120-123 and 145.*

BENJAMIN TO SLIDELL.

"(*Confidential.*)   "DEPARTMENT OF STATE,
RICHMOND, *April* 12, 1862.

"Hon. JOHN S. SLIDELL, etc., Paris:—

"*Sir*,—A reference to the despatches of my predecessor suggested a doubt whether they are quite so definite on one or two points as may be desirable in order to place you fully in possession of the President's views.

"It is of course quite impossible at this distance and with communication so imperfect, to ascertain precisely the extent to which the government of the emperor may be committed by the understanding reported to exist between France and England on the subject of our affairs. There are, however, certain points on which the interests of the two countries are so distinct, if not conflicting, that the President can scarcely suppose his imperial majesty so far to have relinquished his right of independent action as to be entirely precluded from entering into any commercial conventions whatever. If, therefore, the impression of the President be not ill-founded, you may be able to effect negotiations on the basis of certain commercial advantages to be accorded to the French people. On this hypothesis, I proceed to lay before you the views of this government. As a general rule it is undoubtedly desirable that our relations with all countries should be placed on the same common footing; that our commercial intercourse should be as free as is compatible with the necessity of raising revenue from moderate duties and imposts. But in the exceptional position which we now occupy, struggling for existence against an enemy whose vastly superior resources for obtaining the material of war place us at great disadvantage, it becomes of primary importance to neglect no means of opening our ports, and thereby obtaining the articles most needed for the supply of the army. If, therefore, by a convention, conceding to the French emperor the right of introducing French products into this country free of duty for a certain defined period,

---

* Copies from the Confederate archives, in the possession of our government at Washington.

it were possible to induce his abandonment of the policy hitherto pursued, of acquiescence in the interdiction placed by the Northern government on commerce with these states, the President would approve of your action in making a treaty on such a basis. With your enlarged experience of public affairs, and thorough acquaintance with the resources and commercial necessities of the South, the President does not deem it necessary to enter into any detailed instructions in relation to the terms of such a treaty.

"There is, however, one contingency to be foreseen on which you might not feel at liberty to commit this government, and which it is therefore proper to anticipate. It is well understood that there exists at present a temporary embarrassment in the finances of France, which might have the effect of deterring that government from initiating a policy likely to superinduce the necessity for naval expeditions. If under these circumstances you should, after cautious inquiry, be able to satisfy yourself that the grant of a subsidy for defraying the expenses of such expeditions would suffice for removing any obstacle to an arrangement or understanding with the emperor, you are at liberty to enter into engagements to that effect. In such event the agreement would take the form most advantageous to this country, by a stipulation to deliver on this side a certain number of bales of cotton to be received by the merchant vessels of France at certain designated ports. In this manner one hundred thousand bales of cotton of five hundred pounds each would represent a grant to France of not less than $12,500,000, costing this government but $4,500,000, or frs. 63,000,000. If cotton be worth, as we suppose, not less than twenty cents per pound in Europe, such a sum would maintain afloat a considerable fleet for a length of time quite sufficient to open the Atlantic and Gulf ports to the commerce of France. I do not state this sum as the limit to which you would be authorized to go in making a negotiation on the subject, but to place clearly before you the advantage which would result in stipulating for payment in cotton.

"Again, vessels sent from France under convoy to receive the cotton granted as a subsidy would of course be sent with cargoes of such merchandise as is needed in the Confederacy. Now the prices of foreign goods are at the very lowest price, and in many articles four or five fold the cost in Europe. It is difficult to approximate the amount of profit that would accrue from such a shipment, but it ought at least to equal that on cotton taken back; so that the proceeds of the cotton granted as a subsidy, and the profits on the cargoes of the vessels sent to receive it, would scarcely fall short of frs. 100,000,000. On this basis you will readily perceive the extent to which the finances of France might find immediate and permanent relief if the subsidy were doubled; and the enormous advantages that would accrue to that government if by their opening one or more of the Southern ports to its own commerce the interchange of commodities should absorb half a million or a million of bales. If it should be your good-fortune to succeed in this delicate and difficult negotiation you might well consider that practically our struggle would have been brought to a successful termination, for you would, of course, not fail to make provision for the necessary supply of small arms and powder to enable us to confront our foes triumphantly.

"I have arrived at the conclusion that a sufficient sum of secret service money has not hitherto been placed at the disposal of our diplomatic agents abroad. With enemies so active, so unscrupulous, and with a system of deception so thoroughly organized as that now established by them abroad, it becomes absolutely essential that no means be spared for the dissemination of truth, and for a fair exposition of our condition and policy before foreign nations. It is not wise to neglect public opinion, nor prudent to leave to the voluntary interposition of friends, often indiscreet, the duty of vindicating our country and its cause before the tribunal of civilized man. The President, sharing these views, has authorized me to place at your disposal —— thousand dollars, which you will find to your credit with Messrs. Fraser, Trenholm, &c., of Liverpool, and which you will use for the service of your country in such way as you may deem most judicious, with special view, however, to the necessity of the enlightenment of public opinion in Europe through the press.

* * * * * * *

"I am, sir, very respectfully, etc.,
"J. P. BENJAMIN, Secretary of State.

"P.S.—Since closing this despatch it has occurred to the President that it would be more advisable to have a confidential agent in Europe for the purpose of carrying out the views above expressed in relation to the public press. He has therefore appointed Edwin de Leon, Esq., formerly United States Consul at Alexandria, in whose ability, discretion, and entire devotion to our cause he has entire confidence, and has supplied him with twenty-five thousand dollars, as a secret service fund to be used by him for the special purpose of obtaining the insertion in the public journals of Great Britain and the Continent such articles as may be useful in enlightening public opinion in relation to this country. Mr. de Leon will bear you this despatch, and I trust you will give him on all occasions the benefit of your counsels, and impart to him all information you may deem it expedient to make public, so as to facilitate him in obtaining such position and influence among leading journals and men of letters as will enable him most effectually to serve our cause in the special sphere assigned to him.

"J. P. BENJAMIN, Secretary of State."

The expenditure of over $6,000,000 under the direction of, and by the authority of, Mason, Slidell, and Benjamin to sustain the Confederate cotton bonds in the London cotton market is made upon the authority of the two following letters from Mason to Benjamin:*

J. M. MASON TO BENJAMIN.

"COMMISSIONER OF THE CONFEDERATE STATES,
No. 24 UPPER SEYMOUR STREET,
PORTMAN SQUARE, LONDON, *April* 9, 1863.

"Hon. J. P. BENJAMIN, Secretary of State:—

"*Sir*,—In my No. 32 of March ultimo, I gave the history of the Confederate loan up to that date, when it stood with apparent firmness at from 1¾ to 2 per cent. premium, and with every prospect, as I was assured by the bankers, that it was then sufficiently strong in the market not to fall below par.

"Subsequently, however, and within a few days afterwards, it fluctuated from day to day with a depressing tendency, until in a

---

* Copied from the Confederate archives in the possession of the government at Washington.

single day it fell from 2 to 2½ per cent., closing on that day at 4 to 4½ *discount*. The Easter holidays then intervened, when the exchange was closed for one or two days. At this time, the Erlangers with their advisers in London came to me and represented that it was very manifest that agents of the Federal government here, and those connected with them by sympathy and interest, were making concerted movements covertly to discredit the loan, by large purchases at low rates, and, succeeding to some extent, had thus invited the formation of a '*bear*' party, whose operations, if unchecked by an exhibition of confidence strongly displayed, might, and probably would, bring down the stock before settlement day (24th April) to such low rates as would alarm holders, and might, in the end, lead a large portion of them to abandon their subscriptions by a forfeiture of the instalments (15 per cent.) so far paid. They said that they with their friends, with a view to sustain the market, had purchased as far as they could go; but unless a strong and determined power was interposed they could not be responsible for the panic that might arise, and they advised that I should give them authority to purchase on government account, if necessary, to the extent of one million (sterling), at such times as might appear judicious, and until par was obtained. I represented the condition of things to Mr. Slidell, and asked his counsels in the matter. He agreed with me, that if necessary to prevent such serious consequences as might ensue to the government credit, the proposed interposition should be made. I further requested Mr. Spence (who was kept fully cognizant of the condition of things) to confer with the depositaries (Trenholm & Co.), at Liverpool, as to the projected measures, and to come up to London. He did so; and under these joint counsels, including Erlanger & Co., it was determined that if the market opened after the Easter recess under the same depression, that the government should buy, through Erlanger & Co., but of course without disclosing the real party in the market, in the manner indicated. I enclose herewith a copy of the Article of Agreement entered into with Erlanger & Co., to effect this end, dated the 7th instant. The next day (the 9th) was the first business day after the holidays. The loan opened under great depression, and with declining tendencies. In the course of the day purchases were made for our account, at from 4 to 3 and 2½ discount, to the amount of

£100,000. This had the effect of bringing the rates at the close of the day to the point last named (2¼ discount). The following day (yesterday) (to use the language of the stock exchange) the '*bears*' again made a rush, but were met with so decided a front that at the close of the day the stock stood at a half per cent. premium, and it was said by our bankers (who report to me every morning) that there were strong manifestations of the bears creeping in at the close of the day, to cover themselves as well as they could, at rates ranging from ⅛ to ½ premium. Yesterday the amount purchased under the arrangement is reported at about £300,000, and our bankers believe that our work is substantially done, and that the stock will now gradually rise to a healthy condition, and a premium. Of course no purchase will be made above par. The operations of yesterday were chiefly at par. All this thing is of course done in confidence and in silence. Should the market admit, or when it admits, sales will be made (never under par) until what the government may have bought shall be again placed. At worst, should it be found necessary to purchase to the extent proposed of £1,000,000, the effect will only be to reduce the loan by that amount.

"It is believed that after the adjustments ensuing at settlement day, and the payment of the next instalment of 10 per cent. on the 1st of May, matters will become sufficiently permanent, not only to dispense with further purchases, but to enable us gradually to sell out. I hope you will see the necessity which called on me to exercise this responsibility, and that what I have done will have the approval of the government. I confess I was, at first impression, exceedingly averse to it, and so expressed myself to Mr. Slidell; but each day since I am better satisfied with what has been done.

"*April* 10.— The market closed yesterday firm at from ¾ to 1 per cent. premium, an improvement on the day before. I understand there were large dealings, but only £30,000 purchased for government account, that, for the most part, at par.

"*April* 11 (Saturday).— The market closed to-day still upward, the rates at close ¾ to 2¼ premium.

"I have the honor to be, very respectfully,

"Your obedient servant,

"J. M. MASON."

"Articles of Agreement entered into this seventh day of April, in the year of our Lord one thousand eight hundred and sixty-three, between the Hon. J. M. Mason, special commissioner of the government of the Confederate States of America to England, acting with the advice of the financial agent of the Confederate government in England, of the first part; Messrs. Emile Erlanger & Co., bankers, Paris, of the second part:

"*Whereas*, Messrs. Emile Erlanger & Co. have contracted with the said government to issue in Europe a loan of three million pounds sterling, nominal amount ; and,

"*Whereas*, the said loan was fully subscribed for and issued to the public, and a deposit of fifteen per cent. has been paid upon it by the allotters; and,

"*Whereas*, it is believed that various parties have set themselves to depress the loan in the market by circulating rumors, by selling large amounts for future delivery, and by other machinations, in order to alarm the holders and, if possible, to drive them to abandon the loan; and,

"*Whereas*, these measures have been successful in depreciating the price to a discount, and thus tending to injure the estimation of the loan in public opinion, and if unresisted may have a disastrous effect on the interests of the government and the bondholders;

"*Therefore*, in order to meet these attempts and for the protection of the stockholders and that of the interest of the said government, it is hereby agreed,

"That Messrs. Erlanger & Co. shall, and are hereby authorized to, buy for account of the Confederate government in the market up to the amount of one million sterling, nominal capital, or any smaller amount, as may appear sufficient to restore the value of the said bonds to the position they ought to hold, as well in reference to the credit of the government as in view of the interest of the bondholders.

"Due notice of the amount so acquired shall be from time to time notified to the Hon. J. M. Mason and to the financial agent of the Confederate government; but it shall be in the power of Messrs. Erlanger & Co. to resell to the public the amount of stock, or any part of the amount, so acquired at a price not lower than the price of issue, say ninety per cent., subject, however, to the control of the said Hon. J. M. Mason, and any profits on these transactions shall inure to the benefit of the Confederate government. Should circumstances, however, require that the bonds be resold at a price below price of issue, such resale shall be effected only under the sanction of the Hon. J. M. Mason.

"The operations herein referred to will be conducted by Messieurs Emile Erlanger & Co. free of all commissions and charges (except the actual brokerage paid) to the government.

"LONDON, *April* 7, 1863.
"J. M. MASON, Special Com., etc., etc.
"EMILE ERLANGER & Co., H. Hamberrer.

"Witnesses to the signatures.
"J. W. SCHROEDER."

MASON TO ERLANGER & Co.

"Messrs. EMILE ERLANGER & Co., Paris:—

"*Gentlemen*,—In pursuance of the conversation we have had together, I hereby authorize you to buy in the market a further amount of the script of the seven per cent. cotton loan, not exceeding five hundred thousand pounds stock (£500,000), for account of the government of the Confederate States of America, on precisely the same terms and conditions as stipulated in the former agreement executed between us, and bearing date 7th instant, for the purchase of £1,000,000 stock, of which this is, in fact, an extension.

"I am, gentlemen, your obedient servant,
"J. M. MASON, Special Commissioner, etc."

The Creoles of Hayti have a proverb to the effect that one should never stoop down to tie his shoestrings in a melon-patch. If there is any wisdom in that caution it would have been wiser for Erlanger not to have acted as the broker of Mr. Mason to sustain the market for securities of which he and his clients were probably among the largest holders, nor for Mr. Slidell to act as Mason's counsellor in this transaction, with a daughter betrothed to one of Erlanger's sons. Mr. Erlanger did not, however, indulge in any such vulgar considerations of Creole prudence. On the contrary, he sustained the market as vigorously as if the Confederate bonds were his own, as we shall see by the following report of Mason to Benjamin. I know of nothing much more *naif* in all literature than this letter from the unsophisticated, narrow-minded, and pragmatical old Virginian:

"CONFEDERATE STATES COMMISSION,
LONDON, *April* 27, 1863.

"Hon. J. P BENJAMIN, Secretary of State:—

"*Sir*,—On the 7th of April instant I wrote you at some length on the condition and prospects of the loan, on which I am now to make a further report.

"The record here would show that this letter was numbered 34 as a despatch. Should this be so, *I suggest that it be treated as unofficial, and marked accordingly; it, perhaps, should not go on the official files to give it publicity.*

"I have now to report that, by means of the purchase upon government account therein referred to, the stock continued to stand from day to day at about therein noted on the 11th of April, say from 1½ to 2 per cent. premium. To maintain this strength, however, so large purchases were made that, on the 24th instant, they were found to exceed one million sterling; when, again, under the advice of Mr. Spence, I enlarged the power of the brokers to purchase to the additional extent of five hundred thousand of pounds if necessary.

"Settlement day was the 25th, and this new authority was deemed indispensable to prevent the stock again lapsing to a discount. Mr. Spence again reports that, on the 25th, the account between buyers and sellers was fully adjusted, and under circumstances leading to the belief that the bears were sufficiently punished to make them cautious of future like attacks.

"Mr. Spence,* under whose advice and guidance I acted in

---

* The Mr. Spence to whose advice and guidance Mr. Mason professes to have been so much indebted in his arduous efforts to

this matter, remained in London during the operation, and was each day in the City during business hours, attending to it in person. Both he and the bankers entertain strong hope, as the great mass of the stock is now in certain hands, that it will sustain itself on a level at least at par, or free from fluctuations caused by its adversaries, and that it will have the benefit of an upward tendency by accounts favorable to the success of the Confederate arms as they successively reach here.

"I shall not close this despatch for some days, and will have it in my power to note what effect may have been produced by the great and gratifying intelligence received yesterday of the signal repulse of the iron-clads at Charleston, the abandonment of the attack on Vicksburg, and the dangerous position of the enemy's forces at Washington, N. C.

"The very large purchases that were required to sustain the stock afford the best evidence that without them it would have fallen so low below par as to have brought it into great discredit, very possibly producing a panic so great as to induce holders

---

keep the eyes of English capitalists open to the merits of the Confederate bonds was a Liverpool merchant, who espoused the cause of the Confederates at an early stage, and did not a little with his pen to popularize it in England. He was so well informed about the state of public opinion there, and so ignorant of the sentiments of his clients, as to pledge them to abolish slavery as soon as their independence was established. To this no exception was taken until he asked to be officially recognized as an agent of the Confederacy. This Mr. Benjamin declined to do on the ground that, on the vital question of slavery, he did not reflect the sentiments or purposes of the Confederacy correctly. The disaffection came to a head when Erlanger was appointed the agent for effecting the cotton loan. I was told, by a person in a position to be well informed upon the subject, that he resented this treatment, and threatened to sell the Confederate bonds at 50, and break the market, in consequence of which they bought him off by giving him £6000. He subsequently sent in a bill for £15,000 for his services to the Confederate government. After threatening and wrangling for a while the difference was compromised by his receiving the same pay as the highest class Confederate commissioner, $12,000 in gold a year.

even to abandon the instalment paid, of 15 per cent., rather than incur risk of greater loss; and the more I have thought on the subject the better I am satisfied of the correctness of our judgment in going into the market to sustain it. The next instalment is due on the 1st of May, which, when paid, will amount to 25 per cent. After that both the bankers and Mr. Spence are sanguine that, under favorable accounts from the South, the stock will so rapidly improve as to enable them gradually to replace what was bought in, by sales from time to time as the market would bear.

"It is difficult satisfactorily to determine why the stock fell so rapidly to 4 or 5 per cent. discount after having for the first few days stood at a premium equal to the same amount, and under apparent avidity to obtain it, which prompted the overflowing subscription of nearly sixteen millions.

"I am not sufficiently conversant with the stock market or its tendencies to solve the question. My advisers ascribe it to the determined effort of Federal agencies here to throw the loan into discredit; and Mr. Spence thinks, among other causes, that it was placed too high (at ninety) upon the market. Be this as it may, I was satisfied that any risk should be taken to prevent the loan from falling through, and acted accordingly. Should we be unable to resell, it will, of course, much disturb all arrangements that have been made based upon the estimated receipts from the loan. I believe, however, that no loss will be sustained because of our purchases, and have even a confident hope that it will turn out a money-making operation. At worst, should we be obliged to hold the stock, there is little doubt it can be used to meet existing engagements of the government here.

"*May* 2.—I enclose an account that may interest you, showing the purchases made from day to day on government account, with the price affixed. The sales at the close of the account show only twenty-six thousand pounds (£26,000). It is thought now, however, that the market will daily grow stronger, and admit of sales more freely. On the day before yesterday (the 30th of April) twenty thousand pounds additional were sold at 1⅜ per cent. premium; yesterday was *dies non* at the stock exchange, a holiday.

"No intelligence yet of Mr. McCrea. I have the honor to be,
"Very respectfully, your obedient servant.

"Bought by order and for account of the government of the Confederate States of America:

April 7.—£75,000 at 3 Dis.	April 10.—	£5,000 at $1\frac{3}{8}$ Pm.
15,000 " $2\frac{1}{4}$ "		3,000 " $1\frac{9}{16}$ "
15,000 " $2\frac{1}{3}$ "		17,000 " $1\frac{5}{8}$ "
10,000 " $2\frac{1}{2}$ "		10,000 " $1\frac{1}{2}$ "
10,000 " $1\frac{1}{4}$ "	April 11.—	19,500 " $1\frac{1}{2}$ "
5,000 " 1 "		25,000 " $1\frac{5}{8}$ "
April 8.— 4,000 " $1\frac{1}{2}$ "	April 13.—	15,000 " $1\frac{1}{2}$ "
8,000 " $1\frac{1}{4}$ "		22,000 " $1\frac{5}{8}$ "
3,000 " $1\frac{1}{8}$ "	April 14.—	25,000 " $1\frac{1}{2}$ "
37,000 " 1 "	April 15.—	26,000 " $1\frac{3}{8}$ "
32,000 " $\frac{3}{4}$ "	April 16.—	45,000 " 1 "
3,000 " $\frac{7}{8}$ "	April 17.—	1,000 " $\frac{7}{8}$ "
3,000 " $\frac{5}{8}$ "	April 18.—	21,500 " 1 "
23,000 " $\frac{1}{2}$ "	April 20.—	67,500 " 1 "
47,000 " $\frac{1}{2}$ "	April 21.—	44,000 " 1 "
1,000 " $\frac{1}{8}$ "	April 23.—	5,000 " 1 "
110,000 " par.		35,000 " $1\frac{1}{4}$ "
April 9.— 10,000 " $\frac{1}{4}$ Pm.		65,000 " $1\frac{3}{8}$ "
1,000 " $\frac{3}{8}$ "		128,000 " $1\frac{1}{2}$ "
25,500 " $\frac{1}{2}$ "	April 24.—	5,000 " $1\frac{3}{8}$ "
5,000 " $\frac{5}{8}$ "		160,900 " $1\frac{1}{2}$ "
April 10.—51,000 " 1 "		5,000 " $1\frac{9}{16}$ "
13,000 " $1\frac{1}{4}$ "		100,000 " $1\frac{1}{4}$ "
17,000 " $1\frac{1}{2}$ "		14,600 " 1 "

Confed. 7% cotton, £1,388,500

Sold:
April 8.—£6,000 at $\frac{1}{2}$ Dis.
        5,000 " $\frac{1}{4}$ "
April 9.— 5,000 " par.
        5,000 " $\frac{1}{4}$ Pm.
April 10.— 5,000 " $1\frac{3}{8}$ "

£26,000

£1,362,500

E. & O. E.
LONDON, *April* 28, 1863."

This, we presume, was another of Mr. Benjamin's methods, and a pretty costly one, too, of "enlightening public opinion in Europe." Subtracting this $6,000,000 wasted in "rigging" the English market, and some $5,000,000 more, wasted upon ships which were never delivered, the balance realized from the $15,000,000 cotton loan by the Confederate government does not speak very highly for the morals or the financiering of the Confederate agents in Europe. Neither does the fraud, so deliberately planned and executed by Mr. Mason and his colleagues, appear any more venial because it was specially designed to mislead and defraud their special friends and foreign allies, who alone were stupid enough to buy their securities.

It would not be surprising if the people of this world should some day be just wicked enough to ask the first person they think likely to know, whether all the gentlemen concerned in sustaining the market with Confederate funds had as many of those but-too-much-coddled securities when they stopped "sustaining" the market as they had when they began.

I take it for granted that when Captain Bullock indited his complaints against the agents of the Federal government in Europe he could not have been aware of the disgraceful transactions of his colleagues which are disclosed in these letters of Mason.

But Mr. Benjamin's efforts "to enlighten public opinion in Europe" are not yet all told. In April of the following year, 1864, Mr. Benjamin sent Jacob Thompson of Mississippi and Clement C. Clay of Alabama with well-filled pockets, " on secret service, in the hope of aiding the disruption between the Eastern and Western States in the approaching election at the North." "It is supposed," wrote Mr. Benjamin to these gentlemen, "that much good can be done by the purchase of some of the principal presses, especially in the North and East."

This admission throws a lunar light upon the character of the work expected of Mr. de Leon with his $25,000.

If Captain Bullock was aware of all, or, indeed, of any one of the facts above recited, his imputations against the Federal officers, whether well or ill founded, come from him with an ill grace. He may be one of those short-sighted Sadduceans who supposed there was to be no resurrection of the diplomatic intrigues of such high-toned officials as those from whom he took his orders. If so, it is only an aggravation of his offence; for when he penned and printed his strictures, a peace of twenty years' duration had deprived him of every pretext for representations or misrepresentations which only a state of flagrant war could have palliated.

Chapter XVII.

Further Communications from M. X.—Message from General Prim.—His Proposal to Sell Cuba for $3,000,000.—The Infant of Spain in the Intrigue.

Before taking my final leave of this subject, I desire to give one brief chapter more of my experience with M. X, who played such an important if inconspicuous part in the destruction of the Confederate navy. I had proved too liberal a client to be neglected, and upon one pretext or another I was kept informed from time to time of his whereabouts and operations, his letters usually concluding with some intimation obviously intended to provoke my curiosity and to deepen my impression of his importance. Curiously enough, however, he never presented himself in person.

Of one of his communications, however, received long after the transactions we had together in regard to the Confederate steamers, I must make a note, for it proved to have a strange significance, and constitutes one of the links in a chain of events of which history may one day, possibly, recover the links that are missing. It reached me on the 25th of October, 1866, at Biarritz, where the court was then residing.

(Translation.)

"VILLA PLANTES DU GRAND BUREAU,
AT CARONAGE, NEAR GENEVA, SWITZERLAND.

"*Dear Sir*,—A secret agreement is negotiating at this moment between a European power and General Prim.

"These are the conditions:

"The general will receive three and a half millions to continue the insurrection in Spain, and some supplies of arms, powder, and material of war.

"On his side the general engages that, as soon as he succeeds, he will abandon all the Spanish Antilles.

"I wrote you the 4th of October last on this subject. Your silence leads me to think your government is not disposed to occupy itself with this matter. However, if it is, write me and I will repair to Paris.

"General Miramon has informed me of his departure for Mexico.

"Accept, dear sir, the assurance of my perfect respect."

This note evidently required a reply.

I had no doubt of the substantial truth of his statements, partly because men of his profession cannot afford to deceive their clients or those whom they wish to make such, but more because of a conversation I had held only a few days before receiving this note with the Infante of Spain, whom I met at Biarritz, and who seemed anxious to be recognized as the leader of a revolutionary party in his country. I will here quote from my notes, made at the time, the substance of what this brother of the then queen said to me, and the substance of which was often the theme of his conversation with me during the following winter in Paris:

"BIARRITZ, *October* 1, 1866.

"A long talk this morning with the Infante of Spain, who proposed darkly to make Cuba the price to us of such assistance as the United States might render to the Spanish *Emigrès* to overthrow the government. I asked him if he had broached this matter to Mr. Hale.* He said that Mrs. Perry, wife of the Secretary of Legation, is a Spanish woman, and long served as a spy of the Spanish government—that it was not, therefore, safe to speak to Mr. Hale. I told him I would see him in Paris. He thinks the revolution is ready to break out any moment; all that is wanting is a little money. He avowed that his business here (at Biarritz) was to intrigue for the movement and to counteract the intrigues of France for the extermination of the Bourbon race."

The Infante allowed me to receive the impression that he hoped I was inclined to put full faith in X's statements, and seemed not to doubt that he was authorized directly or indirectly by Prim to propose to me the abandonment of the Antilles by Spain for three and a half millions of dollars; that sum being enough to give him, as he supposed, and no doubt correctly, the control of the government. But I did not like X's making such a proposal to me in writing instead of seeking a personal interview. Nor did I care to put it into the power of men engaged in such an intrigue as X's note disclosed, to say and be able to prove that they were in correspondence with me upon the subject. Feeling, besides, that, next to a civil war, one of the greatest calamities that could befall the United States would be the acquisition of the Spanish Antilles, I briefly replied to him that I had no instructions from my government which authorized me to negotiate for the dismemberment of the ter-

---

* John P. Hale, then our Minister at Madrid.

ritory of any friendly power. This terminated my correspondence with Mr. X, and I have never heard from him since. Prim, who, in consequence of his abortive rebellion against O'Donnell's government in January preceding the epoch of the above-cited correspondence, was in exile fomenting disturbances and organizing rebellion in Spain, finally succeeded, and in 1868, in conjunction with Serrano, Topete, and others, brought about the revolution which compelled Isabella to abdicate, and which made him President of the Council, Minister of War, and Commander-in-Chief with the rank of Marshal. After several ineffectual efforts to find a foreign prince eligible to the throne of Spain, Prim fixed at last, on the 2d of July, 1870, upon Prince Leopold, of Hohenzollern, a choice which precipitated if it did not provoke the Franco-German war. Obliged to abandon his first choice, he finally prevailed upon the Italian Prince Amadeus to accept the crown, but he himself was assassinated on the very day that Amadeus landed in Spain, the 28th December, 1870. With Prim's death vanished probably the only chance that has ever yet occurred when the United States might have acquired any of the Spanish-American islands by purchase and without a war.

Chapter XVIII.

Conclusion.

Thus finally terminated the naval operations of the Confederacy in France. They proved abortive; but very inconsiderable changes in the course of events might have given to our civil war a far more tragical conclusion. Had Arman's ships been ready for sea a year sooner, as by his contract they should have been, when Mr. Lincoln's cabinet was rent by dissension, and a presidential election was pending, it is not probable that any amount of remonstrance on the part of our diplomatic agents would have prevented their being allowed to embark upon the predatory career for which they were designed.

They would not only have opened every Confederate port to the commerce of the world, but they might have laid every important city on our seaboard under contribution, the most probable result of which would have been a humiliating peace on the basis of a separation of the Confederate States from the Union, or worse, a rupture between the North Atlantic States and the States of the Northwest.

Had the war continued but a month longer, the *Stonewall* would have had possession of Port Royal, and if two months longer, the city of New York would probably have lain at her mercy. One more defeat, or one less victory of the Union arms, would certainly have given the Confederates one, and probably four vessels, each more formidable than anything which floated the Union Jack. The French government intended these vessels should in some way be placed at the disposal of the Confederate government. They only waited for it to show strength enough, or the Union weakness enough, to establish a reasonable presumption that these vessels could decide the contest.

Happily the Confederate victories and Union defeats did not come; the arm was palsied which was to wield the blade the emperor had been tempering for it, and he found it necessary to desert the Confederates as he deserted Maximilian, or find himself occupying a hostile attitude towards a nation once more at peace within its own borders, and with a million of veteran soldiers at its disposal. It required no prophet to inform him that to allow such a crisis to mature would bankrupt his government and cost him his crown, and probably his life. It was fear of us, not respect for his obligations either as a neutral or a friend, which made him abandon Arman and his associates. His course towards us from the beginning to the end of this plot was deliberately and systematically treacherous, and his ministers allowed themselves to be made his pliant instruments.

It is difficult to conceive of the interests and fortunes of a great historic state like France being left for one moment, in this nineteenth century, at the mercy of a group of men so utterly indifferent to the commonest obligations of honesty and justice.

We do not comprehend such apparent eccentricities of Providence, until we reflect that the great crises in the history of our race, in which we take the most pride, and to which we are under the greatest obligations, have been usually, if not always, preceded by events of which we are most ashamed; that, as it was not until the Hebrews were required to make bricks without straw that Moses came, so France would, in all human probability, be still writhing under a dynastic government but for the Bonapartes.

APPENDIX.

APPENDIX A.

No. 1.
MÉMOIRE À CONSULTER.*

VERS le *commencement de l'année* 1861, *une insurrection contre le gouvernement des États-Unis d'Amérique* éclata dans le Sud. Avant la fin de cette année les insurgés s'etaient organisés *sous le titre d'États Confédérés d'Amérique*, avaient adopté une constitution, et avaient levé une armée considérable avec laquelle ils ont poursuivi la guerre. Mais toutes communications leur étant interdictes avec la mer par *un blocus* que le *gouvernement français a toujours considéré comme effectif*, les confédérés ont cherché à se procurer des navires de guerre soit en Angleterre, soit en France.

Le 15 Avril, 1863, une *convention* était signée "entre M. J. Lucien Arman, constructeur maritime à Bordeaux, Député au Corps Législatif, d'une part et JAMES DUNWADY BULLOCK, agissant d'ordre et pour compte de mandats dont il a produit les pouvoirs en règle, élisant de son côté domicile pour le présent traité chez M. Erlanger d'autre part," par lequel le dit Arman s'engageait à *construire* 4 *bateaux vapeur*, d'une grande vitesse avec machine de 400 chevaux de force et disposés à recevoir un armement *de* 10 *ou* 12 *canons* et autant que possible à répondre aux conditions d'une corvette de la marine française.

Le but de ces vaisseaux *y* est constaté d'être a *établir une communication régulière par navires à vapeur entre Shanghai-Bocca, Jeddo, et San Francisco* passant par *le détroit de San Dieman* et aussi afin qu'ils soient propres si le cas se présente à être *vendus soit à l'Empire Chinois soit à celui du Japon.*

---

* The words printed in italics were underscored with pencil by M. Berryer.

Par l'article premier de cette convention M. Arman s'engage à construire pour son compte dans ses *chantiers* à Bordeaux deux des *navires* et à confier à M. VORUZ, *aussi Député au Corps Législatif,* l'éxecution de deux autres navires qui seront construits simultanément dans les *chantiers de Nantes,* sans entraîner d'autre intervention ou *garantie de la part de M. Arman* que le transmission à M. Bullock des *engagements* que M. Voruz et les constructeurs Nantais *prendront dans* les mêmes termes que M. Arman lui-même pour les navires qu'il construiré à Bordeaux. La vitesse du navire en eau morte devra être à la vapeur de 13 nœuds aumoins.

Le prix de chacun des navires construits et livrés était fixé à la somme de 1,800,000.

M. Bullock s'engage à faire connaître au constructeur la maison de banque qui serait chargée d'effectuer les paiements à Paris et qui accepterait les clauses financières du traité.

LETTRE DE M. ARMAN AU MINISTRE DE LA MARINE DEMANDANT L'AUTORISATION DE MUNIR LES 4 NAVIRES D'UN ARMEMENT.

"*Juin* 4, 1863.

"Le 4 Juin suivant le même M. Arman, constructeur maritime de Bordeaux, adressa a son Excellence le Ministre de la Marine une lettre dans laquelle il le priait de *lui accorder l'autorisation de munir d'un armemente de 12 à 14 canons de 30 quatre navires à vapeur* en bois et fer qui se construisent en ce moment.

"2 dans ses chantiers de Bordeaux.

"1 *chez M. Jollet Babin à Nantes.*

"1 *chez M. Dubigeon à Nantes.*

"Ces navires ajoute-t-il sont destinés par un armateur étranger à faire le service des mers de Chine et du Pacifique, entre la Chine, le Japon, et San Francisco. Leur *armement spécial* a en outre pour but d'en permettre éventuellement la vente *aux gouvernements* de Chine et de *Japon.* Les canons seront exécutés par les soins de *M. Voruz, ainé, de Nantes,* et les pièces accessoires de leur armement seront préparées à sa convenance soit à Bordeaux soit à Nantes. L'exportation de ces armes aura lieu, enfin dans le délai qui est nécessaire à la construction des navires qui sont *consignés à M. A. Eymond et Delphin* Henry armateurs à *Bordeaux* pour lesquels j'ai déjà envoyé en 1859 dans ces contrées sous pavillon anglais le vapeur le Cosmopolite.

"Les constructions étant déjà entreprises depuis *le 15 Avril dernier.* "Je prie votre Excellence de vouloir accorder le plus tôt possible à M. Voruz l'autorisation, etc."

Le 6 Juin, deux jours après l'envoi de cette lettre, *le Ministre de la Marine accorda* l'autorisation demandée.

Le même jour *M. Voruz, ainé, fondeur de canons à Nantes,* que M. Arman avait indiqué, adressa à *M. Blakeley, fondeur de canons à Londres,* la lettre suivante:

Copie de la lettre adressée à M. Blakeley.

."*Juin* 6, 1863.

"*Monsieur le Capitaine,*—Sur votre demande je *m'engage à vous livrer d'ici au 10 du mois de Juillet prochain* la quantité *de cinq mille obus dits de* 30 en tout semblables à ceux que j'ai livrés à l'artillerie impériale sauf l'alaisement du trou de la fusée qui aura 33 m. m. au lieu de 24 et le pas de vis qui sera fait pour les fusées dont vous me fournirez le modèle. Ces obus vous seront vendus au prix de *quarante francs les cent kilogrammes livrés sous vergues à Nantes.* Je me chargerai à vos frais et au mieux de vos intérêts du fret et de l'assurance jusqu'au port que vous désignerez en Angleterre. Ces obus seront payables à Paris sur l'avis du connaissement et par le banquier que vous désignerez ou bien je ferai traite sur vous à dix jours de vue et vous envoyant l'avis du connaissement.

"Recevez, Monsieur, etc.

"Voruz."

Deux jours après *M. Henri Arnous de Rivière* qui doit avoir une commission sur ces divers contrats adressa la lettre suivante à M. Voruz, ainé:

"Paris, *Juin* 8, 1863.

"M. Voruz, ainé, à Nantes:—

"*Monsieur,*—La complication financière survenue aujourd'hui dans l'affaire dont le contrat a été signé *le 14 Avril* dernier entre M. Arman, vous, *le Capitaine Bullock* motive la proposition que je viens vous soumettre.

"D'après nos calculs approximatif les deux machines sont représentées dans les 3,600,000 frs. diminués des 136,800 frs. de la commission Erlanger par un chiffre de 1,220,800 frs. et les coques des deux bateaux équipés pour une somme de 2,242,400 frs. Cette dernière somme devant être reçue par les constructeurs, je ne veux pas diminuer la commission de 3% qu'elle comporte à mon profit (soit 67,272 frs.).

"Mais comme il se peut faire que dans cette opération vous ayez à supporter seul le poids de la commission Erlanger je viens vous offrir de laisser en suspens la somme de 36,624 frs. qui me serait due sur les 1,220,800 frs. des machines jusqu'à ce que vous soyez assuré de votre revenu dans l'affaire.

"Au cas où notre bénéfice sur les machines serait moindre de 187,000 frs. je consens à supporter le déficit sur cette somme dans la proportion de 37 à 150 (à savoir 37 pour ma part et 150 pour la vôtre).

"Veuillez agréez l'assurance, etc.

"H. ARNOUS DE RIVIÈRE."

Le 15 Juillet suivant, M. Voruz, ainé, s'adressait au *Ministre de la Marine* dans les termes suivants:

"*Monsieur le Ministre*,—Par votre lettre en date du 6 Juin dernier vous avez bien voulu m'autoriser à éxécuter dans mes usines à Nantes les canons nécessaires à l'armement de quatre navires dont deux sont en construction à Bordeaux dans les chantiers de M. Arman et deux dans les chantiers de Nantes."

Il demande ensuite la permission de visiter l'établissement du gouvernement à Rueil pour voir les améliorations effectuées dans l'outillage et dont il pourrait profiter.

Cette autorisation lui fut accordée par une lettre du *Ministre de la Marine du 9 Août.*

Le 10 Juin M. Arman adressa la lettre suivante à M. Voruz:

"BORDEAUX, *Juin* 10, 1863.

"*Cher Monsieur Voruz*,—*Je vous accuse réception* de votre lettre chargée du 9, et *du mandat de Bullock,* frs. 720,000.00 qui était inclus.

"Je m'empresse de vous donner *d'écharge* ainsi que vous le désirez des pièces que vous avez signées aux mains de *M. Bullock* pour le premier paiement des deux navires de 400 chevaux que je construis *pour le compte des États Confédérés* simultanément avec *ceux qui* vous sont *confiés* et que vous faites construire par *Messieurs Jollet* et *Babin et Dubigeon.*

"Je vous remets ci-joint un plan de ce navire et je fais éxécuter en ce moment celui des emménagements.

"Il reste enfin à règulariser entre nous les frais de consignation, de surveillance, d'expédition par la maison A. Eymond et Delphin Henry à Bordeaux et par le capitaine Feneira.

"Comme vous le savez ces frais s'élèveront de 32 à 35 mille francs dont la moitié doit vous incomber. Vous vondrez bien m'autoriser à m'en couvrir sur vous au fur et a mesure de leur paiement.

"Enfin cher monsieur et ami nous allons faire ensemble de notre mieux pour que cette fourniture importante soit aussi bien faite que possible et en vous remerciant de votre intervention ces jours derniers, je vous prie de faire en sorte *d'obtenir de M. Bullock la promesse de nous* rembourser en fin de compte des escomptes de garantie que nous payons à *M. Erlanger.*

"Je serai très probablement Lundi à Paris afin d'encaisser moi-même le mandat que vous m'avez envoyé.

"Recevez, etc.   H. ARMAN.

"P.S.—Le plan ne peut que demain, faut-il l'expédier à Paris ou à Nantes?"

Il est évident que les vaisseaux dont il est question dans cette lettre sont les mêmes que ceux pour lesquels la semaine précédente une autorisation avant été demandée par un armateur étranger et sous le prétexte de faire la course des mers de Chine et du Pacifique. Ils sont construits sur les mêmes chantiers et sont *consignés à la même maison.* La seule différence digne de remarque est celle que cette lettre nous révèle, à savoir que *l'armateur* étranger n'est *autre que les États Confédérés* pour le compte desquels M. Arman dit expressément les construire. Dans cette même lettre M. Arman accuse réception de 720,000 frs. payés par Bullock à titre de 1er à compte sur 2 des navires qu'il construit dans les chantiers de Bordeaux.

Ce M. Bullock ici mentionné agissait en qualité d'agent en Europe pour les États Confédérés depuis le commencement de la rebellion. Il était spécialement chargé des achats et de la construction des vaisseaux destinés à faire la guerre contre le commerce et le gouvernement des États-Unis.

On voit par cette lettre que M. Arman indique *M. Erlanger* comme le banquier *qui garantit* le marché contracté par *M. Bullock* au nom du gouvernement confédéré. *Le même jour* que cette lettre était écrite M. Arman télégraphiait de Bordeaux à M. VORUZ alors à Paris, le message suivant:

"GRAND HÔTEL, PARIS.

"VORUZ,—J'ai signé sans modifications la lettre à Erlanger. Elle est au courrier.   ARMAN."

La lettre dont il est question dans ce télégram contenait exactement les engagements aux quels se reporte la lettre suivante envoyée par M. Erlanger *à M. Voruz:*

"*Monsieur,*—Voici les lettres d'engagements, le contrat et la copie. Comme vous habitez sous le même toit que le CAPITAINE BULLOCK, vous aurez peut-être l'obligeance de lui faire certifier la copie du contrat.

"J'ai écrit directement à M. Arman.

"Recevez, monsieur, etc.

"EMILE ERLANGER.

"PARIS, *Juin* 9, 1863.
"M. VORUZ, ainé, de Nantes, Grand Hôtel (Paris)."

Le même jour, 10 Juin, ce qui n'avait été jusque là qu'une *simple convention* verbale devenait un engagement écrit comme le prouve la lettre de *Messrs. Jollet et Babin à Messrs. Dubigeon et fils* tous les deux constructeurs de navires à Nantes auxquels nous avons déjà vu que M. Arman confiait simultanément la construction des vaisseaux pour le compte des confédérés.

"PARIS, *Juin* 10, 1863.

"*Mon cher Voruz,*—Après avoir près connaissance des conditions financières qui vous ont été faites par la maison Erlanger ainsi que les lettres intervenues entre vous et M. Slidell et Bullock nous venons vous rappeler nos conventions verbales afin de bien préciser nos positions respectives dans cette affaire. Dans le prix total de 1,800,000 frs. la machine et ses accessoires énumérés dans la lettre du 7 Mai, 1863, de M. Mazeline à M. Arman seront comptés à raison de 1607 frs. par cheval soit 642,800 frs. Le coque nous sera payé 1,157,200 frs. dont les versements nous seront faits au fur et à mesure de la rentrée des termes.

"Il est entendu que chacun de nous reste responsable de l'entière exécution du contrat en ce qui le concerne et que toutes les commissions et frais imprévus seront payés par chacun au prorata de la somme qui lui est attribuée.

"Dans le cas où *M. Mazeline* refuserait de garantir *seul la* vitesse de 13 nœuds portée au contrat, il est entendu que cette garantie sera commune entre nous et que les dommages et intérêts qui pourraient être réclamés si la vitesse n'etait pas atteinte seraient partagés par moitié, nous référant à cet égard aux conditions intervenues entre Messrs. Gourn et Mazeline pour la construction de la frégate Italienne, Castelfidardo.

"Agréez, etc.

"G. D. JOLLET ET BABIN,
"J. DUBIGEON ET FILS."

Il ressort de cette lettre que chacun de ces constructeurs s'engage à livrer un de ces navires moyennant certains arrangements financiers conclus avec M. Erlanger et après lecture d'une correspondance échangée entre Messrs. Arman, Slidell, et Bullock. M. Slidell est l'agent actuel de États Confédérés.

M. Mazeline indiqué au dernier paragraphe est le chef de la maison Mazeline et Cie. du Hâvre qui doit construire les machines pour les 4 navires en question.

La complicité de *cette maison* dans ce qu'elle appelle le marché Bullock est nettement reconnue dans la lettre suivante du 23 Juin adressée à M. Voruz:

"LE HÂVRE, *Juin* 23, 1863.
"M. I. VORUZ, ainé, Constructeur à Nantes:—

"*Monsieur,*—En paraphant il y a quelques jours le *marché Bullock* nous avons omis vous et nous de redresser une erreur de dimension des machines.

"La première specification portait que le diamètre intérieur de chaque cylindre serait de 1 m. 50 cm.; la course des pistons de 1 m.; le nombre de tours de 56.

"Vous devez vous rappeler, Monsieur que sur nos observations et pour avoir des hélices dont le pas et le nombre de tours soient en harmonie avec le maître couple immergé et la vitesse demandée, il a été admis qu'il fallait des cylindres ayant 1 m. 40 cm., diamètre intérieur de pistons ayant 0 m. 95 cm. de course, et une quantité de révolutions de 68 par minute.

"Nous ne mettons pas endoute que nous soyions d'accord mais pour la bonne règle, nous vous prions de nous écrire que *ces dernièrer* mesures qui *sont en construction* sont bien-celles convenues entre nous.

"Dans l'attente de votre réponse nous avons l'honneur, etc.

"MAZELINE ET CIE."

Lettre de M. Voruz *au Ministre de la Guerre* pour une autorisation à faire faire des canons 48 et des munitions pour les 4 navires.

Le 29 *Juillet*, 1863, *M. Voruz* demanda au *Ministre de la Guerre* l'autorisation de construire dans ses usines à Nantes, 48 canons de 30 par M. Arman dans sa lettre du 4 Juin. Chaque canon devant être muni de 200 obus cylindre-coniques avec les accessoires nécessaires. Cette autorisation fut accordée par une lettre du ministère datée *le 9 Août.* Trois lettres de M. Voruz et de son fils datées des 14, 15, et 17 Juillet expliquent suffisamment le caractère de ce marché:

"Paris, *Juillet* 14, 1863.

"*Mon cher Anthony*,—Le Capitaine Bullock et Arman sont partis hier pour Bordeaux ainsi que M. Erlanger. Je crains bien qu'ils soient dans l'obligation *de traiter* avec Arman pour les *navires blindés.* Peut-être peut-on craindre qu'Arman ne fasse des propositions à M. Erlanger pour sa petite chaloupe.

"Mais ne t'arrête pas à mes inquiétudes. Continuez à faire des plans bien faits et ayant bonne mine et comme il pourrait se faire que Bullock et Arman se rendent à Nantes en revenant de Bordeaux, tenez-vous prêts à les recevoir et si je suis prévenu à temps de leur arrivée à Nantes je partirai pour vous aider à les recevoir. Ainsi donc ne m'envoyez pas ces dessins avant que je ne les demande.

"Comme je l'ai annoncé par dépêche l'affaire *avec Blakeley* est faite et très-bonne surtout avec la fourniture des 200 boulets par pièces. Le marché est ferme pour 48 pièces, mais le marché est fait d'une manière qui nous assure la fourniture exclusive de tout ce qui pourra être exécuté en France.

"Le courrier me presse et je suis obligé de m'arrêter.

"Voici le prix de base de l'atelier:

La fonte................	700 frs.	la tonne.
Le fer forgé............	2000 "	"
L'acier.................	2000 "	"
Le bronze..............	5000 "	"

"Les 48 pièces de 30 sont vendues la pièce à Bullock, 7000 frs.

"Nous donnerons sur ce prix à Blakeley 10% sur ce chiffre soit 700 frs. Le reste c'est à dire la différence entre notre prix d'atelier et les 6300 frs. sera partagé moitié pour Blakeley et l'autre ½ des bénéfices se partagera entre Arnous et nous.

"*Les* boulets nous sont *toujours* payés 40 frs. les ⚹ k. et nous ne devrons rien à Blakeley.

"Tâche que Pétermann m'envoie surtout la pièce qui constate que l'affaire Perrier a été signifiée à Gâche. Si d'autres pièces sont prêtes qu'il me les envoie également.

"N. B.—Bien des choses à tout le monde et dis à ta mère que je me porte bien et annonce lui cette bonne affaire.

"Tout à toi, J. Voruz, ainé.

"P. S.—J'ai le plan de la machine a vanier les canons."

"Nantes, *Juillet* 15, 1863.

"*Mon cher père*,—J'ai reçu ta lettre de ce matin. Tous ces messieurs étant partis pour Bordeaux je crains bien que l'affaire batterie soit coulée. Il est possible que n'étant pas sur les lieux je vois de travers mais je pensais que cette affaire aurait pu se traiter comme la première. C'est à dire trouver ou écrire à Arman et lui dire nous partagerons par la moitié car enfin nos dessins étaient prêts hier et par conséquent nous étions dans l'affaire aux mêmes titres que Arman Dailleurs de toutes façons il est indispensable que Arman eût une portion de l'affaire 'pour les autorisations de sortie.'

"Maintenant s'il n'est enfin pas possible d'avoir une portion des bateaux il faut absolument que Arman te donne quelques machines. Je crois qu'en le chauffant il peut difficilement s'y refuser. Quand nous serons là nous avons tous les éléments pour faire notre prix de revient bien exact.

"Maintenant je crois qu'il faut s'arranger avec Arnous pour que Bullock s'il ne vient pas à Nantes repasse par Paris en revenant de Bordeaux par ce qu'alors nous irons l'y trouver dessins en mains.

"Tu me dis dans ta lettre que tu as traité les canons mais as-tu traité aussi les affûts? Ensuite tu as traité les boulets mais quel est leur mode de paiement? Et puis ces bombes étant pour les canons des 4 bâtiments elles devront recevoir à Nantes leurs fusées, leurs ailettes. Est-ce que ce sera nous qui garnirons ainsi ces obus et y a-t-il un prix de convenu pour celà ou sera ce l'anglais qui nous fournira ailettes et fusées et alors dans ce cas combien nous paiera-t-on pour leur pose sur les obus?

"*L'anglais t'a-t-il donné l'adresse où expédier les* 5000 *projectiles faits* et la manière de tirez sur lui?

"Puis ces obus sont-elles en tout semblables aux 5000 déjà faites?

"Il faudrait qu'il signe le dessin de canon que tu as eu l'approuvant.

"Il faudrait qu'il nous donne ensuite les indications nécessaires qu'il nous avait promises à savoir: le diamètre exact du canon extérieurement et celui exact des rondelles (acier intérieur). Ces deux diamètres devant être fixés par l'inventeur par rapport à la retraite, ces cercles étant entrés à chaud.

"Ci inclus la liste des prix pour matériel chemins de fer pour l'Italie (affaire Lavaure).

"J'ai fait ta commission à Pétermann.

"Maintenant je vais te donner mon opinion sur l'affaire boulets et canons.

"1. L'affaire boulets a été arrangée avec Arnous telle qu'il partage avec nous le bénéfice en dessus de 27 frs., il n'y a donc rien à dire et cependant cela lui fait en définitive 16% de commission.

"En effet 40 frs. prix de vente 27 frs.=13 frs., $\frac{13}{2}$=6.5 commission pour Arnous et 6.5 de boni pour nous.

"Or le prix de vente étant 40 frs. on peut dire: $6.5 : 40 :: x : 100$.

"$x=16$ donc Arnous à 16% sur les obus ce qui est loin d'une commission de 3 ou 5%.

"2. L'affaire Arnous me fait à moi l'effet d'un gaspillage remarquable sur les deniers de l'acheteur, mais une chose frappe surtout c'est l'énormité des commissions des tiers, commissions qui égalent et surpassent non seulement la nôtre mais aussi notre gain comme constructeur et cependant c'est nous qui avons tout l'embarras et les responsabilités. Voilà pourquoi je trouve notre part insuffisante relativement aux autres ce qui n'empêche pas que c'est une bonne affaire pour nous.

"Voici quelques chiffres:

Prix d'atelier concédé.

Un canon se compose de { fonte.......2632 k. à 0.70......frs. 1842.40
acier....... 640 à 2.00...... 1280.00
fer......... 10 à 2.00...... 21.00

Prix d'atelier concédé pour un canon.......frs. 3143.40

"Or le prix de revient que nous en avions fait montait à 3160 frs. Tu vois donc que le prix d'atelier concédé est à très-peu de chose près le nôtre c'est, donc bon.

Or le prix vendu à Bullock est...............frs. 7000
Blackley prend d'abord 10% soit.............. 700

7000 — 700 =frs. 6300
6300 — 3143.40=frs. 3156.60

Prix d'atelier.

C'est cette différence de..................frs. 3156.60

Dont Blakeley prend la moitié soit....... 1578.30
Arnous ¼............................ 789.15
À nous l'autre ¼..................... 789.15
Ce qui nous fait en définitive une commission de..................789.15 × 48 = 37,879.20
Puis pour Arnous la même chose soit....... 37,879.20
Puis pour Blakeley......1578.30 × 700 × 48 = 109,358.40

"Ce sont les deux chiffres de Arnous et de Blakeley que je trouve formidables par rapport à nous constructeurs.

"Car en ramenant en centièmes Blakeley prend 32% et sur l'affaire qui nous reste après que Blakeley a enlevé ses 32% Arnous prend 16%. L'affaire est faite; il n'y a donc pas à revenir, seulement, c'est là l'effet que j'ai éprouvé.

"Il faudrait pendant que tu es à Paris te procurer un ciseleur pour un an pour toutes nos statues. Tu sais qu'il n'est pas besoin d'un ciseleur No. 1.

"Je te serre la main,   ANTHONY.

"Les pièces Gache sont encore à l'enregistrement nous te les enverrons demain si nous ne les avons que demain matin, mais peut-être les aurai-je ce soir; alors Perregault te les portera.

"Je t'envoie les prix pour matériel chemins de fer. Ces prix sont très bas: traite donc plus haut si c'est possible.

"Deplus ces prix ne comportent pas les droits d'entrée pour l'Italie que nous n'avons jamais pu savoir exactement. Ils seraient donc en plus.

"Le Drawback est tout déduit."

"PARIS, *Juillet* 17, 1863.

"*Mon cher Anthony*,—Je ne te parle plus de l'affaire canons et boulets, elle est faite. Cependant je te dirai que nous ne devons les boulets que comme les autres. Si nous faisons du travail nous demanderons paiement avant d'exécuter pour ce que nous devrons faire en dehors de ce que nous avons fait sur les 5000 que nous exécutions.

"Je me suis réservé la fourniture des affûts, si le prix nous convient et pour bien apprécier ce prix, M. Blakeley va nous envoyer un affût en nature.

"Le paiement de cette fourniture se fera la 1ère traite au 17 Octobre pour 6035 livres c'est à dire 150,875 frs. ce qui forme environ le tiers de la fourniture.

"Je vais m'entendre avec lui pour le 2ème tiers, le 3ème se fera en livrant.

"Les boulets que nous allons faire sont en tout semblables aux 5000 que nous venons d'exécuter, ne les fais pas commencer de suite.

"Nous allons tirer de suite à 6 semaines pour le montant des 5000 boulets qui doivent être dans ce moment-ci exécutés. Donne-moi par retour du courrier leur poids, si tout n'est pas encore terminé l'on peut malgré cela me donner un poids tellement apprécié que cela suffit.

"Si *M. Blakeley* est encore à Paris je lui ferai accepter les traites comme je vais le faire aujourd'hui pour les 150,875 frs. dont je te parle d'autre part. Il désire que nous gardions ces 5000 projectiles à Nantes jusqu'à nouvel ordre de sa part.

"Le dessin de canon est signé par lui.

"Il nous donnera plus tard les indications de détail.

"Je suis complètement de ton avis sur ce que tu appelle le gaspillage de commission mais il fallait commencer comme cela et en définitive l'affaire est excellente surtout lorsque l'on y comprend les 9600 boulets et je suis bien aise de te dire que je suis convaincu que cette affaire aura des suites qui nous seront profitables.

"Le prix des canons ne comporte que de canon seul mais complet avec lumière percée et mire.

"Je reçois aujourd'hui une lettre d'Arnous de Bordeaux qui me dit qu'Arman vient de signer le marché pour deux cannonières blindées de 300 chevaux de force pour deux millions chaque. Il me prie de l'attendre à Paris où il ne sera de retour que dimanche soir par la raison qu'il est allé à Rive de Gier chez Petin et Gaudet *avec Bullock.*

"Il faut donc m'envoyer les plans de Dubigeon et les instructions nécessaires pour ébaucher cette affaire. Il faut tâcher que Dubigeon fasse connaitre le prix qu'il demande pour *son navire.* Puis tu me donneras en même temps celui que tu suppose pour la machine.

"Il va sans dire que tu vas m'envoyer en même temps le plan du petit bateau Erlanger. (Il ne faut pas dire à Dubigeon qu'Arman a vendu 2,000,000 chaque cannonière.)

"Il faut que Dubigeon et toi vous vous teniez prêts a partir pour Paris aussitôt que je vous préviendrai.

"Il faut également me dire de suite quelle quantité nous pourrions traiter et si Jollet et Babin seraient décidés à en construire. Tâche de me dire cela par retour du courrier ou au plus tard pour dimanche puisque je dois causer avec Arnous dimanche soir.

"N'oublie pas de donner connaissance de ma lettre à ta mère car je lui avais annoncé mon arrivée pour cette semaine, tandis que je ne sais plus au juste quand je partirai de Paris.

"Soigne ton rhume et n'oublie pas de m'envoyer de suite les plans et les détails que je demande.

"Ci inclus une lettre d'Arnous qui indique l'avancement des 2 bateaux qu'Arman construit.

"Tout à toi, J. VORUZ, ainé."

Dans les lettres cidessus *M. Voruz parle* de négociations entre M. Arman et le Capitaine Bullock pour la construction de 2 cannonières blindées de 300 chevaux de force devant coûter 2,000,000 frs.

Or ces négociations ont pour objet une commande distincte de celle des 4 bateaux à vapeur qui font l'objet du contrat du 15 Avril.

Déjà M. Arman avait soumis les plans d'une batterie cannonière à *M. Maury "contre-amiral des États Confédérés d'Amérique,"* et dans la lettre où se trouvait cette offre il écrivait:

"Le bâtiment que je propose est enfin un navire complet et je m'engage dans le délai d'un mois après la signature du marché à vous fournir la preuve de l'autorisation de sortie de l'armement que vous aurez à mettre sous ce navire."

Pendant ces négociations, M. Arnous de Rivière adressa à M. Voruz le lettre suivante:

"LONDRES, *Juin* 28, 1863.

"*Mon cher M. Voruz*,—Après bien des démarches, des lettres, des dépêches, des voyages, et autres ennuis dont je vous épargne le détail j'ai fini par réunir à Londres. Blakeley, Bullock, et Husset, je crois que nous en viendrons à bonne fin de notre marché d'artillerie.

"Ce nouveau système de canon semble prendre faveur, et la Russie fait à Blakeley des offres considérables pour qu'il établisse une fonderie à St. Pétersbourg sous sa surveillance. Il cherchait un fondeur et j'ai saisi cette occasion. Il y a là une grosse affaire. Je vais vous l'amener à Nantes coûte que coûte et nous ne le laisserons partir sans traites.

"Je vous envoie maintenant les plans et spécifications de ces canons ainsi que le prix auquel ils sont manufacturés à Liverpool par la maison Foster et Cie. Je vous prie de livrer la chose à l'étude *sans retard*. J'attends aussi avec impatience les plans pour le petit bateau cannonière de 250,000 frs. et ceux plus importants de corvettes blindées de 1,500,000 frs. Les marchés pourraient se passer de suite. Je vous en prie faites que ces plans et projets soient prêts *sans retard* croyez bien que mes appréciations de temps sont justes et qu'il faut nous hâter d'obtenir ces commandes. La concurrence grossit chaque jour et les évènements qui se déroulent à l'avantage de nos clients les rendent de plus en plus exigeants et de moins en moins nécessiteux.

"Je serai à Paris mercredi je voudrais bien y trouver ces documents."

"LONDRES, *Juin* 9.

"J'ai interrompu cette lettre hier afin de la compléter aujourd'hui par des renseignements plus exacts. À Liverpool on fondé pour *Blakeley* ses canons à raison de 320 livres sterlings soit environ 8000 frs...frs. 8,000
Il les vend *aux confédérés* 480 livres sterlings soit...... 12,000

Reste par pièce un bénéfice de $\frac{50}{100}$ soit......frs. 4,000

"Son marché avec la maison Foster est celui-ci:

"Les fondeurs ont établi leur prix d'atelier à tant le k. pour la fonte, pour le fer forgé et pour l'acier. Ce prix leur étant après le bénéfice partage à savoir pour Blakeley $\frac{10}{100}$ prélevés d'abord et puis la ½ du reste, le reliquat au fondeur.

"Exemple un canon pesant 300 k. se décomposerait en:

fonte........1000 à	500 frs. la tonne........frs.	500
fer forgé.....1000 à 1250	"	....	1,250
acier........1000 à 3500	"	....	3,500
Pour le fondeur total prix alloué............frs.	5,250
Le canon se vend par exemple....frs. 8,000	
	5,250	
Bénéfice....frs. 2,750...	2,750
$\frac{10}{100}$ prélévés sur le bénéfice pour le brevet	
Blakeley soit.............................	275
Bénéfice comme reste....frs. 2,475	
Dont moitié pour le fondeur en dehors de son	
prix d'atelier soit........................frs.	12,375

"Votre prix devant être tel que vous puissiez fabriquer ce serait le bénéfice en dehors c-à-d. les 123,750 frs. que nous aurions à partager ensemble. Tous ces chiffres ne sont que des exemples pour vous donner une idée de l'affaire.

"J'ai insisté pour que dans cette opération nous ayons droit à la moitié du brevet en France pour ces canons afin d'éviter toute concurrence.

"Répondez-moi maintenant à *Paris* si vous êtes disposés à un marché de ce genre. Si votre présence était nécessaire je vous télégraphierais de Paris et vous auriez la bonté de venir. Préparez-vous aussi à vendre la Comtesse Lubo.

"Je suis prêt à conclure un avantageux marché. Tenez cependant la chose secrète surtout pour mon père qui n'en recevra pas moins sa part de bénéfices mais qui parle beaucoup trop.

"Au revoir prochainement mon cher M. Voruz et croyez-moi toujours votre très affectionné,

"HENRI ARNOUS RIVIÈRE.

"51 rue de la Pépinière, Paris."

Un contract pour deux navires à hélices fut signé le 16 Juillet suivant, un jour avant que la nouvelle n'en fut donnée par M. Voruz à son fils.

En voici les termes:

"ENTRE LES SOUSSIGNÉS.

"L. Arman, constructeur maritime à Bordeaux, Député au Corps Legislatif, quai de la Monnaie, No. 6, et nous James Dunwady Bullock *agissant d'ordre* et pour *compte de mandant* dont il a produit les pouvoirs en règle, élisant domicile pour ce présent traité chez *M. M. Emile Erlanger, rue de la Chaussée d'Antin*, 21, à Paris.

"Ont été arrêtées les conditions suivantes:

"Art. 1. M. Arman s'engage envers M. Bullock, qui l'accepte, à construire pour son compte, dans ses chantiers de Bordeaux deux batiments hélices à vapeur à coque bois et fer de 300 chevaux de force à 2 hélices avec deux Blockhaus *blindés* conformes au plan accepté par M. Bullock.

"Ces navires auront les dimensions principales suivantes:

		Pieds anglais.
Longueur de perpendiculaire à perpendiculaire..................	52.40 m...	171.10
Longueur au maitre hors menches....	9.00	.. 29.5
id. blindage........................	10.00	.. 32.8

"Creux sur quille à la ligne droit des bans:

		Pieds anglais.
Tirant d'eau du pont.................	9.20 m...	17.
id. au milieu......................	4.40	..14.4

"Vitesse minimum par mer calme douze nœuds.

"Art. 2. Ces navires recevront une nature goëlette à humiers.

"Les pièces de mâture seront en bois de choix et de pin rouge pour les pièces principales,

"Le gréement dormant sera en fil de fer et les manœuvres courantes seront en chanvre premier brin product mécanique.

"Les voiles seront en toile de lin de No. proportionné à l'importance des voiles.

"Les aussières et amarre seront en nombre et dimensions suffisantes.

"Les chaînes et les ancres seront de force et dimensions proportionnées au navire.

"Les ferrements seront exécutés avec le plus grand soin tant pour la coque que pour la mâture le greement et le pauliage. Ils comprendront en outre, les pitons et les crocs pour canons placés dans la muraille et le pont du navire.

"Les embarcations seront au nombre de quatre elles seront voilies et garnies de leurs accessoires.

"Art. 3. Chaque bâtiment sera livré dans les mêmes conditions que les corvettes clippers complètement muni de ces agrès apparaux et ustensiles de toutes sortes. Des spécifications comprendront l'énumération de tous les objets de détail qui sont nécessaires aux divers maîtres pour armement et rechange y compris la fourniture des objets réclamés pour la table et la literie de l'état-major.

"Resteront seuls à la charge de M. Bullock, les canons les armes, les projectiles, les poudres, les vitres, le combustible et enfin les salaires et les vivres de l'équipage.

"Les charbons, etc., pour les épreuves seront fournis par M. Arman.

"Art. 4. La charpente de la coque sera exécutée suivant les prescriptions d'un devis détaillé d'exécution.

"Elle sera lamée chevillée et doublée en cuivre rouge.

"Le matelas sous la cuirasse sera en bois de Peack de l'Inde.

"Les barrats, la casenigue et les vaigres seront exécutés en fer.

"Les enménagements de la cale et ceux de l'entre-pont seront établis conformément au plan de détail.

"Tous les matériaux seront égaux à ceux de même espèce entrant dans la marine française.

"Art. 5. *Les bâtiments seront munis d'une machine à vapeur de 300 chevaux de force, de 200 kilogramètres le cheval à condensation construite par M. Mazeline du Hâvre.*

"Une spécification fera connaître les dimensions des principales pièces de cette machine.

"Les hélices seront en bronze à 4 ailes.

"Les machines devront pouvoir mouvoir les 2 hélices à la fois ou une seule en avant et l'autre en arrière.

"Les chaudières auront leurs soupapes chacune de 1 k. 60 par centimètre carré et seront du systéme tubulaire, avec tubes en laiton elles seront sous la ligne de flottasion et conformes pour les dimensions des matériaux aux types de la marine Impériale française.

"Un appareil distillataire sera attaché aux chaudières de manière a être placé sous la surveillance du mécanicien.

"Art. 6. Les deux navires devront être admis et prêts à faire leurs essais dans un délai de 10 mois.

"La réception s'effectuera à Bordeaux et les navires seront conduis à la mer.

"Art. 7. La vitesse des navires à la vapeur par mer et en temps calme ne devra pas être moindre de 12 nœuds.

"La calaison maximum à l'arrière ne devra par dépasser 4 m. 60.

"Les sautes devront être d'une capacité de 280 lb. de charbon elles en recevront 200 aumoins pour le chargement normal par rapport au tirant d'eau.

"Le poids réservé à l'artillerie et ses accessoires dans le calcul général des poids d'armement est de 60.

"Art. 8. Les plaques de fer composant la cuirasse seront de 12, 11, 10, 9 cent. d'épaisseur disposés conformément aux indications.

"Elles seront fabriquées par Messrs. Petin Gaudet de Rive de Gier et soumises à des épreuves équivalent à celles de la machine Impériale.

"Art. 9. Le prix de chacun de ces navires construits et livrés dans les conditions qui précedent est fixé à la somme de 2 millions de francs qui sera payée à Paris

  $\frac{1}{5}$ comptant,
  $\frac{1}{5}$ lorsque le navire sera monté en trois bads,
  $\frac{1}{5}$ lorsque les barrots du pont serait en place,
  $\frac{1}{5}$ à la mise à l'eau,
  $\frac{1}{5}$ à la livraison.

"Art. 10. Il pourra être apperçu en sus le prix des navires une retenue de mille francs par chaque jour de retard au delà du delai fixé pour la livraison.

"Art. 11. M. Bullock a désigné la maison E. Erlanger et Cie. comme étant chargée d'effectuer les paiéments à Paris et devant acceptes les clauses financières du present traité.

"Art. 12. Les navires et les machines seront pendant leur construction assurés contre l'incendie pour une valeur aumoins égale aux sommes reçues en à compte.

"Fait double à Bordeaux le 16 Juillet, 1863.
       "ARMAN et JAMES D. BULLOCK."

Dans les lettres des 14 et 17 Juillet *M. Voruz* parle aussi d'une convention passée entre lui et Blakeley *pour* 48 *canons et* 200 *boulets* par pièce. La lettre suivante donne la commande finale:

"Paris, *Juillet* 14, 1863.

"*Mon cher monsieur*,—Votre lettre d'aujourd'hui donne l'explication dont j'avais besoin sur notre convention avec lettres des 11, 12, et 13 courant. Elle met notre affaire sur un bon pied. En conséquence je vous prie de faire faire tout de suite 48 *canons de* 30 *et* 9600 *obus suivant les dessins que je vous ai donnés. Demain nous nous mettrons d'accord sur les essais et les prix.*

"Je suis, monsieur, etc. J. M. Blakeley.

"À M. Voauz, ainé, de Nantes."

Plus tard M. Voruz reçut de M. Bullock une lettre de laquelle il résulte qu'ils traitaient pour un plus grand nombre de canons. Voici la copie de la lettre:

"Liverpool, *Août* 12, 1863.

"J'ai reçu M. Voruz votre lettre du 4 ct. avec les indications de prix du canon de 30 et de ses accessoires. Il ne m'est pas possible de dire si je vous donnerai un ordre positif et direct pour de semblables canons avant d'avoir appris du Capitaine Blakeley comment l'affaire de son propre modèle de canon cerclé a été comprise. Je serais cependant charmé de traiter une affaire avec vous, si nous pouvons nous accorder sur les conditions; nous discuterons tout cela quand j'irai à Nantes. Il est dans mes intentions de confier mes affaires à aussi peu de mains que possible et j'espère que nous tomberons d'accord sur tous les points essentiels de telle sorte que *nos relations pourront prendre une plus grande extension même en cas de paix, notre gouvernement aura besoin, sans doute pendant un certain temps de s'adresser en France pour la construction de ses vaisseaux et machines* et pour ce qui me concerne personellement, je serai, enchanté que les rapports que j'ai eu avec vous vous amenassent pour l'avenir à des commandes plus considérables encore.

"Veuillez S. V. P. m'informer si les corvettes avancent et me dire quand les seconds paiements seront dus.

"Je vous écrirai une semaine avant mon arrivée à Nantes.

"Bullock."

De l'exposé qui vient d'être fait et des documents qui l'accompagnent il résulte:

1. Que *M. Arman* de Bordeaux construit actuellement dans ses chantiers *deux steamers* de guerre et deux steamers-béliers pour la marine des soi-disants États Confederés d'Amérique.

2. Que Messrs. Jollet et Babin et Messrs. Dubigeon et fils de Nantes construisent deux autres steamers de guerre sur le même modèle et sous les mêmes conditions et pour le même objet que M. Arman.

3. Que Messrs. Mazeline et Compagnie du Hâvre construisent des machines soit pour plusieurs de ces vaisseaux soit pour tous.

4. Que M. Voruz de Nantes fabrique pour ces vaisseaux 58 canons et des munitions en grande quantité.

5. Que M. Erlanger est l'agent financier par l'intermédiaire duquel l'argent des États Confédérés est versé entre les mains de ceux qui se chargent de ces navires et que c'est lui qui garantit le parfait paiement.

6. Que Bullock est l'agent qui fournit les modèles des navires et qui signe les contrats pour le compte des États Confédérés.

7. Enfin que M. Blakeley de Londres donne les modèles de canons et de leurs munitions et partage le profit résultant du contrat pour la fourniture des munitions aux dits navires.

Ces faits étant établis donnent lieu aux questions suivantes:

1. Ceux qui y ont participé, ont-ils violé les lois françaises et peuvent-ils être poursuivis judiciairement?

2. S'ils ont violé les lois françaises de quel crime se sont-ils rendus coupables et quelles peines ont-ils encourues?

3. Quelle marché convient-il de suivre pour déférer ces faits coupables à la Justice?

No. 2.

CONSULTATION DE M. BERRYER.

L'ANCIEN avocat soussigné,

Vu le mémoire à consulter présenté au nom du gouvernement des États-Unis d'Amérique, ensemble les pièces justificatives qui y sont jointes,

Délibérant sur les questions qui lui sont soumises,

EST D'AVIS DES RÉSOLUTIONS SUIVANTES:

De l'exposé contenu dans le mémoire à consulter, et des documents qui l'accompagnent, résulte la preuve complète des faits qu'il importe d'abord de résumer.

En 1861, au mois de Février plusieurs États du Sud de l'Amérique septentrionale, régie alors par la *Constitution fédérale des États-Unis*, résolurent de se séparer des États du Nord, et se réunirent en un Congrès pour constituer le *gouvernement des États Confédérés d'Amérique*. La guerre entre les confédérés et le gouvernement fédéral éclata dans le mois d'Avril.

Au 10 Juin de la même année, parut dans la partie officielle du *Moniteur* une déclaration soumise par le Ministre des Affaires Étrangères à l'Empereur des Français et revêtue de son approbation.

Par cet acte solennel, l'Empereur prenant en considération l'état de paix qui existe entre la France et les *États-Unis d'Amérique* résolut de maintenir une stricte neutralité dans la lutte engagée entre le gouvernement de l'*Union* et les États qui prétendent former une confédération particulière,

Déclare entre autres dispositions:

" ... 3. Il est interdit à tout Français de prendre commission de l'une des deux parties pour armer des vaisseaux de guerre ... ou de concourir d'une manière quelconque à l'équipement ou l'armement d'un navire de guerre ou corsaire de l'une des parties.

" .... 5. Les Français résidant en France ou à l'étranger devront également s'abstenir de tout fait qui, commis en violation des lois de l'Empire ou du droit des gens, pourrait être considéré comme un acte hostile à l'une des deux parties et contraire à la neutralité que nous avons résolu d'adopter."

La déclaration impériale se termine en ces termes:

"Les contrevenants aux défenses et recommandations contenues dans la présente déclaration seront poursuivis, s'il y a lieu, conformément aux dispositions de la loi du 10 Avril, 1825, et aux articles 84 et 85 du Code pénal, sans préjudice de l'application qu'il pourrait y avoir lieu de faire auxdits contrevenants des dispositions de l'article 21 du Code Napoléon, et des articles 65 et suivants du décret du 24 Mars, 1852, sur la marine marchande, 313 et suivants du Codé pénal pour l'armée de mer."

Malgré cette déclaration publique de la neutralité de la France, malgré les prohibitions formelles qu'elle prononce conformément aux règles du droit des gens et aux dispositions spéciales des lois françaises, une convention a été conclue le 15 Avril, 1863, entre M. Lucien Arman, constructeur maritime à Bordeaux, et le capitaine James Dunwady Bullock, Américain, agent du gouvernement des États Confédérés du Sud, stipulant dans cet acte *d'ordre et pour compte des mandats* qu'il ne fait pas connaître, et dont, est-il dit, *il a produit les pouvoirs en règle*. Pour l'exécution du traité, M. Bullock élit domicile chez M. Erlanger, banquier, à Paris.

Par ce traité, M. Arman "s'engage à construire quatre bateaux à vapeur de quatre cent chevaux de force et disposés à recevoir un armement de dix à douze canons."

Il est stipulé que M. Arman construira dans ses chantiers à Bordeaux deux de ces navires, et *confiera à M. Voruz l'exécution des deux autres navires, qui seront construits simultanément dans les chantiers de Nantes.*

Pour déguiser la destination de ces quatre navires, il est écrit dans l'acte qu'ils doivent être consacrés à " établir une communication régulière entre Shang-haï, Yeddo, et San Francisco, passant par le détroit de Van-Diémen, et aussi qu'ils doivent être propres, si le cas se présente, à être vendus soit à l'empire chinois, soit à l'empire du Japon."

"Enfin M. Bullock s'engage à faire connaître aux constructeurs la maison de banque qui sera chargée d'effectuer à Paris le payement du prix de chacun de ces navires, fixé à la somme 1,800,000 frs.

Le 1 Juin suivant, M. Arman, pour se conformer à l'ordonnance royale du 12 Juillet, 1847, adressa à M. le Ministre de la Marine la demande d'une autorisation de munir d'un armement de douze à quatorze canons, de 30, quatre navires à vapeur en bois et fer, en construction, *deux dans ses chantiers à Bordeaux, un chez Messrs. Jollet et Babin à Nantes, un chez M. Dubigeon à Nantes.*

" Ces navires, est-il dit dans la lettre adressée au ministre, sont destinés *par un armateur étranger* à faire le service des mers de Chine et du Pacifique entre la Chine, le Japon, et San Francisco.

Leur armement spécial a en outre pour but d'en permettre éventuellement la vente aux gouvernements de Chine et du Japon.

"Les canons seront exécutés par les soins de M. Voruz, aîné, de Nantes."

La lettre de M. Arman se termine en ces mots:

"... Les constructions étant déjà entreprises depuis le 15 Avril dernier, je prie Votre Excellence de vouloir bien accorder le plus tôt possible à M. Voruz l'autorisation que je sollicite et que prescrit l'ordonnance royale du 12 Juillet, 1847."

Sur cet exposé et pour la destination supposée des quatre navires, l'autorisation fut accordée par M. le Ministre de la Marine, dès le 6 Juin, ainsi qu'elle était demandée par M. Arman.

Le même jour, 6 Juin, 1863, M. Slidell, autre agent du gouvernement des États Confédérés, adressait à M. Arman la lettre suivante:

"En conséquence de l'autorisation ministérielle que vous m'avez montrée et que je juge suffisante, le traité du 15 Avril devient obligatoire."

Trois jours après, le 9 Juin, M. Erlanger, banquier à Paris, chez qui M. Bullock avait pris domicile dans le traité du 15 Avril, et qui devait garantir les payements aux constructeurs, écrivait à M. Erlanger:

"Je m'engage à vous garantir les deux premiers payements des navires que vous construisez pour les Confédérés, moyennant une commission, etc."

Les conditions financières proposées par M. Erlanger furent acceptées par M. Arman, qui, le même jour, le 9 Juin, adressa à M. Voruz, à Nantes, le télégramme suivant:

"À M. Voruz, Grand Hôtel, Paris.

"J'ai signé, sans modification la lettre à Erlanger; elle est au courrier. ARMAN."

De son côté, M. Erlanger écrivait, sous la même date, à M. Voruz, à Nantes:

"Voici les lettres d'engagements, le contrat et la copie. Comme vous habitez *sous le même toit que le capitaine Bullock*, vous aurez peut-être l'obligeance de lui faire signer la copie du contrat. J'ai écrit directement à M. Arman. Recevez, etc."

Le lendemain 10 Juin, M. Arman adressait à M. Voruz une lettre ainsi conçue:

"*Cher M. Voruz*,—Je vous accuse réception de votre lettre chargée du 9 et du mandat de Bullock de 720,000 frs. qui était inclus. Je m'empresse de vous donner décharge; ainsi que vous le désirez, des pièces que vous avez signées aux mains de M. Bullock pour le *premier payement des deux navires de* 400 *chevaux que je construis pour le compte des Confédérés*, simultanément avec ceux que vous faites construire par Messrs. Jollet et Babin, et Dubigeon. . . .

"Je vous prie de faire en sorte d'obtenir de M. Bullock la promesse de nous rembourser en fin de compte des escomptes de garantie que nous payons à M. Erlanger.

"Recevez, etc."

D'autre part, Messrs. Jollet et Babin, et Dubigeon fils, chargés de la construction, dans leurs chantiers, à Nantes, de deux des quatre navires, ainsi qu'il est dit dans la lettre adressée le 1 Juin par M. Arman à M. le Ministre de la Marine, écrivaient le 10 du même mois à M. Voruz:

"*Mon cher Voruz*,—Après avoir pris connaissance des conditions financières qui vous ont été faites par la maison Erlanger, *ainsi que des lettres intervenues entre vous et Messrs. Slidell et Bullock*, nous venons vous rappeler nos conventions verbales, afin de bien préciser nos positions respectives dans cette affaire."

D'autres personnes, avec entière connaissance de la véritable destination de ces constructions et de ces armements maritimes, devaient prendre une part notable dans les bénéfices de l'opération et supporter proportionnellement les escomptes de garantie stipulés en faveur de M. Erlanger. C'est pour s'entendre sur ce dernier objet que M. Henri Arnous Rivière, négociant à Nantes, écrivait dès le 8 Juin à M. Voruz, ainé: "La complication financière survenue aujourd'hui dans l'affaire dont le *contrat a été signé le* 15 *Avril dernier* entre M. Arman vous et le capitaine Bullock, motive la proposition que je viens vous soumettre."

Messrs. Mazeline et Cie., du Havre, étaient chargés de la confection des machines à vapeur pour les quatre navires à hélice dont les coques se construisaient dans les chantiers de Bordeaux et de Nantes. Mais ignoraient-ils la véritable destination de ces bâtiments de guerre lorsqu'ils écrivaient à M. Voruz, ainé, le 23 Juin, 1863:

"Monsieur, *en paraphant,* il y a quelques jours, *le marché Bullock,* etc., nous avons omis, vous et nous, de redresser une erreur de dimension des machines, etc.—Nous vous prions de nous écrire que ces dernières mesures, *qui sont en construction,* sont bien celles convenues entre nous."

Tout était donc parfaitement concerté entre les divers participants, pour l'exécution du traité passé le 15 Avril, 1863, entre M. Arman, constructeur français, et M. le capitaine Bullock. Ce traité a été expressément ratifié par M. Slidell, agent diplomatique des États Confédérés, suivant sa lettre adressée à M. Arman, le 6 Juin, 1863.

Les autorisations ministérielles exigées par la loi française pour la construction et l'armement des bâtiments de guerre, ont été accordées; l'administration ayant sans doute été abusée par la prétendue destination qu'un *armateur étranger* devait donner à ces navires de guerre dans les mers de Chine et du Pacifique, et par la condition *éventuelle* de les vendre aux gouvernements de Chine ou du Japon. Mais leur destination véritable pour le service des États belligérants du Sud est parfaitement connue de tous les intéressés. Les constructions des vaisseaux, de leurs machines, de leurs armements sont en pleine activité. Les payements, garantis aux constructeurs par une maison de banque puissante, sont en partie effectués.

Une seconde opération doit avoir lieu. Le 14 Juillet, 1863, M. Voruz, ainé, écrivant de Paris à son fils M. Anthony, lui annonce que le capitaine Bullock et M. Arman sont partis la veille pour Bordeaux ainsi que M. Erlanger, banquier, et qu'il s'agit d'un traité pour des *navires blindés.* En même temps il lui dit qu'une affaire est faite avec un sieur Blakeley, fondeur anglais; pour la fourniture de 48 pièces de canon avec 200 boulets par pièce. Le marché dit-il, est fait d'une manière qui nous assure la fourniture exclusive de tout ce qui *pourra être exécuté* en France.

Le 15 Juillet, le même M. Voruz, en rappelant à M. le Ministre de la Marine que, par sa lettre en date du 6 Juin, il a bien voulu l'autoriser à exécuter dans ses usines, à Nantes, les canons nécessaires à l'armement de quatre navires, *dont deux sont en construction à Bordeaux, dans les chantiers de M. Arman, et deux dans les chantiers de Nantes*, demande au ministre "la permission de visiter l'établissement du gouvernement à Ruelle, pour avoir les améliorations effectuées dans l'outillage, etc." Cette permission fut accordée le 9 Août.

Une nouvelle convention est signée double à Bordeaux le 16 Juillet, 1863.

"Entre M. Arman, constructeur maritime à Bordeaux, député au Corps Législatif, quai de la Monnaie, 6, et M. James Dunwady Bullock, agissant d'ordre et pour compte de mandants dont il a produit le pouvoirs en règle, élisant domicile chez M. Emile Erlanger, rue de la Chaussée d'Antin, 21, à Paris:

"Ont été arrêtées les conventions suivantes:

"Art. 1. M. Arman s'engage envers M. Bullock, qui l'accepte, à construire pour son compte, dans ses chantiers de Bordeaux, deux bâtiments hélices à vapeur, à coque bois et fer, de 300 chevaux de force, à deux hélices, avec deux *blockhaus blindés*, conformes au plan accepté par M. Bullock.

"Art. 3. Resteront seuls à la charge de M. Bullock les canons, les armes, les projectiles, les poudres, le combustible et enfin les salaires et les vivres de l'équipage.

"Art. 5. Les bâtiments seront munis d'une machine à vapeur de 300 chevaux de force de 200 kilogramètres le cheval, à condensation, construite par M. Mazeline du Hâvre.

"Art. 6. Les deux navires devront être admis et prêts à faire leurs essais dans un délai de dix mois.

"Art. 9. Le prix de chacun de ces navires est fixé à la somme de 2 millions de francs qui sera payée à Paris un cinquième comptant.

"Art. 11. M. Bullock a désigné la maison E. Erlanger et Cie., comme étant chargée d'effectuer les payements à Paris et devant accepter les clauses financières du présent traité."

Le 17 Juillet, M. Voruz, ainé, écrit:

"Je reçois aujourd'hui une lettre d'Arnous, de Bordeaux, qui me dit qu'Arman vient de signer le marché pour 2 canonnières blindées de 300 chevaux de force, pour deux millions chaque."

Enfin, le 12 Août, M. Bullock, resté chargé par l'article 3 du traité du 16 Juillet ci-dessus, des canons, des armes, des projectiles, etc., pour les deux canonnières blindées, adressait à M. Voruz la lettre suivante :

"Liverpool, *Août* 12, 1863.

"J'ai reçu, M. Voruz, votre lettre du 4 courant, avec les indications de prix du canon de 30 et de ses accessoires. Il ne m'est pas possible de dire si je vous donnerai un ordre positif et direct pour de semblables canons avant d'avoir appris du capitaine Blakeley comment l'affaire de son propre modèle de canon cerclé a été comprise. Je serais cependant charmé de traiter une affaire avec vous, si nous pouvons nous accorder sur les conditions. Nous discuterons tout cela quand j'irai à Nantes.

"Il est dans mes intentions de confier mes affaires à aussi peu de mains que possible, et j'espère que nous tomberons d'accord sur tous les points essentiels, de telle sorte que *nos relations pourront prendre une plus grande extension même en cas de paix. Notre gouvernement aura besoin, sans doute, pendant un certain temps de s'adresser en France pour la construction de ses vaisseaux et machines*, et, pour ce qui me concerne personnellement, je serais enchanté que les rapports que j'ai eus avec vous vous amenassent pour l'avenir à des commandes plus considérables encore.

"Veuillez, s'il vous plaît, m'informer si les corvettes avancent et me dire quand les seconds payements seront dus.

"Je vous écrirai une semaine avant mon arrivée à Nantes.

"Bullock."

Les termes de cette lettre s'appliquent évidemment au projet d'armement des deux *canonnières blindées* dont la construction a été l'objet du traité passé à Bordeaux, le 16 Juillet, entre Messrs. Arman et Bullock. Ce dernier, capitaine au service de la confédération des États du Sud, a agi d'ordre et pour compte de *son gouvernement*. Il n'est pas possible de méconnaître que ces deux canonnières sont, ainsi que les quatre navires pour lesquels avait été conclu le marché du 15 Avril précédent, destinées au service des États Confédérés du Sud dans la guerre qu'ils soutiennent contre les États fédéraux de l'Amérique du Nord.

La preuve matérielle de ces faits résulte trop évidemment des conventions passées entre les diverses personnes qui ont participé à leur réalisation, et de la correspondance échangée entre elles pour le réglément de leurs intérêts particuliers. Les faits sont de la plus haute gravité. Expressément interdits à tous les Français par la déclaration impériale du 10 Juin, 1861, ils constituent de flagrantes violations des principes du *droit des gens* et des devoirs imposés aux sujets de toute puissance neutre, devoirs dont l'accomplissement loyal est la première garantie du respect dû à la liberté des États neutres et à la dignité de leurs pavillons. Ce sont là des actes de manifeste hostilité contre l'une des deux parties belligérantes à l'égard desquelles le gouvernement français a *résolu de maintenir une stricte neutralité*.

"Il faut éviter, dit Vatel, livre 3, chapitre VII, de confondre ce qui est permis à une nation libre de tout engagement, avec ce qu'elle peut faire si elle prétend être traitée comme parfaitement neutre dans une guerre. Tant qu'un peuple neutre veut jouir sûrement de cet état, il doit montrer, en toutes choses, une exacte impartialité entre ceux qui se font la guerre, car *s'il favorise l'un au préjudice de l'autre*, il ne pourra pas se plaindre quand celui-ci le traitera comme adhérent et associé de son ennemi. La neutralité serait une *neutralité frauduleuse* dont personne ne veut être la dupe.

"Cette impartialité, ajoute Vatel, qu'un peuple neutre doit garder, comprend deux choses: 1, ne point donner de secours, ne fournir librement ni troupes, ni armes, ni munitions, ni rien de ce qui sert directement à la guerre."

Ce sont là des actes d'hostilité qui, réprouvés par le droit des gens, sont caractérisés crimes et délits par les lois françaises qui en prononcent la répression pénale.

L'article 84 du Code pénal est ainsi conçu:

"Quiconque aura, par des actions hostiles, non approuvées par le gouvernement, exposé l'État à une déclaration de guerre, sera puni du bannissement, et, si la guerre s'en est suivie, **de la déportation**."

Cette disposition de la loi est, dans l'opinion du soussigné, évidemment applicable aux auteurs et complices des faits qui sont résumés plus haut. Quels que soient les motifs et quel que soit le caractère de la lutte si déplorablement engagé au sein de l'union américaine, soit qu'on la considère comme une guerre civile, même comme une insurrection d'une partie de la nation américaine contre le gouvernement établi, soit que l'on envisage la séparation qui veut s'opérer les armes à la main, comme une division de la nation en deux corps distincts, en deux peuples différents. *La guerre entre ces deux parties,* nous dit encore Vatel, *retombe à tous égards dans le cas d'une guerre publique entre deux nations différentes.* Les peuples qui ne veulent point être entraînés à prendre part à cette guerre doivent se renfermer dans les stricts devoirs de la neutralité qu'ils proclament.

Au milieu du déchirement intérieur de la nation américaine, dans l'état de paix où est la France avec le gouvernement des États-Unis, dans l'état des relations d'amitié et de commerce qui lient les deux pays, il n'est pas d'action hostile qui puisse provoquer plus d'irritation et faire soulever contre la France de plus justes griefs que le secours et la fourniture d'armements maritimes donnés par des Français à l'ennemi du gouvernement de Washington, au moyen des traités conclus avec les confédérés, et de construction de navires et de fabrication d'armes de guerre opérées publiquement dans les ports, sur les chantiers et dans les usines de la France.

L'action des entrepreneurs de ces armements est d'autant plus compromettante et expose d'autant plus notre pays à être considéré comme ennemi et à voir faire contre lui une déclaration de guerre, que les armements dont il s'agit se font avec des autorisations régulièrement données par l'administration française. Ce n'est plus ici le cas d'appliquer les principes qui règlent d'ordinaire, à l'égard des nations neutres, les conséquences des expéditions de *contrebandes de guerre* quoique naviguant sous pavillon neutre. Les expéditeurs de ces marchandises, telles que les armes, les munitions, toutes les matières préparées pour la guerre, sont seuls responsables: ils peuvent être saisis et déclarés de bonne prise, leur pavillon ne les couvre pas; mais il n'en résulte aucune responsabilité à la charge du gouvernement auquel ces expéditeurs et armateurs appartiennent.

Dans les traités et dans l'exécution des traités intervenus entre les constructeurs français et les agents des États Confédérés, le nom et l'autorité du gouvernement français ont été compromis par les autorisations accordées. Les faits se présentent donc avec le caractère d'une action hostile de la part de notre gouvernement contre le gouvernement américain. Avec ce caractère, les faits pourraient donc exposer la France à une déclaration de guerre.

Mais il est vrai de dire que cette apparente compromission du gouvernement français n'est que le résultat du dol pratiqué par les constructeurs et participants du traité du 15 Avril, qui, à l'aide d'une fausse indication de la destination des navires, ont trompé les Ministres de la Marine et de la Guerre. Que des explications loyalement données de gouvernement à gouvernement, que le retrait des autorisations accordées à Messrs. Arman et Voruz, fassent tomber toute plainte et récrimination de la part du gouvernement des États-Unis, le caractère criminel des faits dont ces messieurs et leurs coopérateurs se sont rendus coupables n'en sera pas modifié, et ils n'en auront pas moins fait *des actions hostiles* qui exposaient la France à une déclaration de guerre; ils sont donc dans le cas textuellement prévu par l'art. 84 du Code pénal. Ils n'ont pas le droit d'alléguer qu'ils ont été légalement autorisés par le gouvernement. La fraude dont ils ont use, viciant dans leur essence même les actes dont ils pértendaient se prévaloir, leur culpabilité est aggravée aux yeux de la justice française.

Il est d'autres de nos lois dont les contractants et participants des marchés des 15 Avril et 18 Juillet, 1863, ont frauduleusement éludé les dispositions.

La loi du 24 Mai, 1834, porte, art. 3: "Tout individu qui, sans y être légalement autorisé, aura fabriqué ou confectionné des armes de guerre, des cartouches et autres munitions de guerre, ... sera puni d'un emprisonnement d'un mois à deux ans et d'une amende de 16 frs. à 1000 frs.

"Art. 4. Les infractions prévues par les articles précédents seront jugées par les tribunaux de police correctionnelle. Les armes et munitions fabriquées sans autorisation *seront confisquées.*"

Dans l'intérêt du développement de la fabrication française et de notre commerce extérieur, une ordonnance royale, du 12 Juillet, 1847, a réglé l'application de cette loi de 1834 et les formalités administratives qui doivent être remplies par les fabricants d'armes.

On lit dans l'article 1er de l'ordonnance du 12 Juillet:

"Conformément à l'article 3 de la loi du 24 Mai, 1834, tout individu qui voudra fabriquer ou confectionner des armes de guerre pour l'usage des navires de commerce, devra obtenir préalablement l'autorisation de notre ministre Secrétaire d'État au Département de la Guerre, et de notre ministre Secrétaire d'État au Département de la Marine et des Colonies, quant aux bouches à feu et aux munitions."

Dans la pratique, ces dispositions de l'ordonnance, qui semblaient n'être applicables qu'à l'armement de nos navires de commerce, ont été étendues à la fabrication et à la livraison des armes de guerre au commerce étranger.

Pour obtenir les autorisations toujours requises en pareil cas, et pour pouvoir livrer aux confédérés les armements de guerre qu'ils s'étaient engagés à leur fournir, Messrs. Arman et Voruz ont adressé leurs demandes à Messrs. les Ministres de la Marine et de la Guerre. Les autorisations leur ont été accordées, même ils ont obtenu la permission de visiter les établissements de l'État pour profiter des améliorations apportées à l'outillage.

C'est à la vue de ces autorisations, qu'il a dit lui paraître suffisantes, que l'agent diplomatique des confédérés a ratifié, le 6 Juin, 1863, le traité passé le 15 Avril précédent entre Messrs. Arman et Bullock. Mais, comme on l'a vu dans la lettre adressée par M. Arman à M. le Ministre de la Marine le 1er Juin, ce n'est qu'en trompant sciemment le ministre sur la destination des armements dont ils voulaient munir le quatre navires construits à Bordeaux et à Nantes, que ces messieurs se sont fait accorder les autorisations qu'ils sollicitaient indûment.

De telles autorisations subrepticement obtenues doivent donc être considérées comme nulles et de nul effet. Messrs. Arman, Voruz, et leurs complices, sont donc dans un cas de violation de la loi du 24 Mai, 1834, et sous le coup des peines correctionnelles qu'elle prononce.

Le crime et le délit, résultant de la violation de l'article 84 du Code penal et de la loi de 1834, constituent Messrs. Arman et Voruz et leurs co-intéressés *contrevenants aux défenses et recommandations contenues dans la déclaration impériale du 10 Juin* et doivent être, ainsi qu'il est dit dans cette déclaration, poursuivis conformément aux dispositions de la loi.

Les faits qui doivent donner lieu à ces poursuites légales ont été commis au préjudice et contre la sécurité du gouvernement des États-Unis. Il est hors de doute que ce gouvernement est en droit, comme tout étranger, de se pourvoir devant les tribunaux français pour réclamer la répression et la réparation de faits accomplis en France qui lui sont dommageables. Ici, le dommage est incontestable, parce que, indépendamment de la livraison des navires et de leurs armements de guerre, le fait notoire de la construction et de l'armement en France, sous l'apparente autorisation du gouvernement français, de navires de guerre destinés aux confédérés, était en lui-même pour ceux-ci un puissant encouragement à soutenir la lutte, et portait ainsi un incalculable préjudice au gouvernement fédéral.

Il reste au soussigné à indiquer au gouvernement des États-Unis quelles voies judiciaires il peut suivre pour faire prononcer contre les coupables les réparations qui lui sont dues et quelles doivent être ces réparations.

Le gouvernement des États-Unis peut rendre plainte devant les tribunaux français pour raison des faits dont la criminalité vient d'être établie, et notamment quant au crime prévu par l'article 84 du Code pénal. Cette plainte devra être remise soit à la diligence d'un agent spécialement autorisé; soit sur la poursuite de l'envoyé extraordinaire et plénipotentiaire des États-Unis en France, aux procureur impérial.

Conformément aux dispositions des articles 63 et 64 du Code d'instruction criminelle la plainte peut être portée ou devant le magistrat du lieu où le crime et le délit ont été commis, ou devant celui de la résidence de l'inculpé. Comme il y a plusieurs complices et agents des faits incriminés, le juge du domicile de l'un d'eux est compétent pour recevoir la plainte, et tous les complices seront appelés devant lui en raison de la connexité des faits dénoncés.

Messrs. Bullock et Slidell, agents des confédérés, sont, quoique étrangers, justiciables des tribunaux français pour raison des faits coupables qu'ils ont provoqués ou auxquels ils ont participé sur le territoire français. La plainte devra énoncer les faits inculpés et être appuyée des pièces justificatives.

Pour faire prononcer les réparations qu'il se propose de demander, le gouvernement américain devra par son agent spécial déclarer qu'il entend se constituer partie civile, c'est-à-dire qu'il entend soutenir la poursuite à fin de réparation, concurremment avec le ministère public. En se constituant partie civile, le gouvernement des États-Unis doit être averti qu'il pourra être tenu de donner caution *judicatum solvi*, aux termes de l'article 166 du Code de procédure civile, ainsi conçu:

"Tous étrangers demandeurs principaux ou intervenants seront tenus, si le défendeur le requiert, avant toute exception, de fournir caution, de payer les frais et dommages intérêts auxquels ils pourraient être condamnés."

Enfin il faut faire observer que l'une des personnes contre lesquelles la plainte devra être collectivement portée est membre du Corps Législatif, et qu'en raison de la qualité qui lui appartient, avant de donner suite à la plainte, le ministère public devra demander à l'assemblée l'autorisation de poursuivre, conformément à l'article 11 du décret organique de Février, 1852.

Dans le cas où l'on ne voudrait porter plainte que pour raison de la violation de la loi du 24 Mai, 1834, et de l'ordonnance de 1847, au lieu de soumettre la plainte au juge d'instruction ou de la remettre au procureur impérial, l'action devant être portée devant un tribunal correctionnel, le gouvernement américain pourrait procéder par voie de citation directe, et il porterait devant le juge correctionnel sa demande à fin de réparations civiles et de dommages et intérêts.

Dans le cas enfin où le gouvernement des États-Unis renoncerait à intenter, pour raison des faits dont il s'agit, soit une action au criminel par voie de plainte, soit une simple action correctionnelle, il peut séparer l'action civile de l'action publique, et intenter contre ceux qui lui ont fait préjudice une action devant les tribunaux civils, sauf au ministère public à exercer l'action publique en répression du crime et du délit s'il le juge à propos.

Devant le tribunal civil, le gouvernement des États-Unis n'aura à invoquer, en justifiant des actes dont il a souffert, que les dispositions de l'art. 1382 du Code civil, où il est écrit:

"Tout fait quelconque de l'homme, qui cause à autrui un dommage, oblige celui par la faute duquel il est arrivé à le réparer."

À fin de réparation du crime ou du délit commis envers lui, le gouvernement fédéral demandera, à titre d'indemnité, la confiscation des constructions et fabrications faites à son préjudice. Il pourra même, après avoir intenté le procès, demander, à titre de mesure conservatrice, d'être autorisé à saisir provisoirement et à ses risques et périls tous les objets construits et fabriqués, comme éléments des faits criminels dont la réparation peut être ainsi ordonnée sans que, devant les juridictions compétentes, les dispositions des lois pénales aient reçu leur application.

Délibéré à Paris, le 12 Novembre, 1863,

BERRYER,
ancien bâtonnier de l'Ordre des avocats de Paris.

APPENDIX B.

COURT-MARTIAL OF COMMODORE CRAVEN.

CHARGES AND SPECIFICATIONS.

CHARGE.—Failing to do his utmost to overtake and capture or destroy a vessel which it was his duty to encounter.

SPECIFICATION.—In this: that on or about the 24th day of March, 1865, the said Commodore Thomas T. Craven, commanding the U. S. S. *Niagara*, and having under his control the U. S. S. *Sacramento*, then lying off Corunna, on the coast of Spain, and a vessel of the enemy, known as the *Stonewall*, being at that time on its way out of the Bay of Corunna, as was plainly seen by and well known to him, did fail to use any exertions or make any effort whatever to overtake and capture or destroy the said vessel of the enemy, as it was his duty to have done; but did remain quietly at anchor for more than twenty-four hours after having seen said vessel on its way out of the Bay of Corunna; his pretext for this failure in duty being that "the odds in her (the *Stonewall's*) favor were too great and too certain to admit of the slightest hope of being able to inflict upon her even the most trifling injury;" and that, had he gone into an engagement, "the *Niagara* would most undoubtedly have been easily and promptly destroyed;" and, as subsequently stated by him in an official letter addressed "To the Hon. H. J. Perry, Chargé d'Affaires, Madrid," and dated March 25, 1865, "with feelings that no one can appreciate, I was obliged to undergo the deep humiliation of knowing that she (the *Stonewall*) was there—steaming back and forth—flaunting her flags and waiting for me to go out to the attack. I dared not do it. The condition of the sea was such that it would have been perfect madness for me to go out. We could not possibly have inflicted the slightest injury upon her,

and should have exposed ourselves to almost instant destruction—a one-sided combat, which I do not consider myself called upon to engage in." GIDEON WELLES,
Secretary of the Navy.

NAVY DEPARTMENT, *October* 20, 1865.
Upon this charge and specification, the court found:

"Specification of the charge proven, except in so far as the words 'as it was his duty to have done,' declare it to be the imperative duty of the accused to join battle with the *Stonewall* on the 24th day of March.

"The court, in considering these specifications as only proven in part, and the accused guilty in a less degree than charged, does not wish to deprive an officer of the discretionary powers due to his command, nor to establish the principle that it is always and under all circumstances imperative that two wooden vessels should attack an iron-clad; but the court intends to express its censure upon Commodore Craven's defective judgment on the 24th day of March, 1865, arising from his want of zeal and exertion in not making constant and personal observation of the rebel ram while at Ferrol, and thereby endeavoring to ascertain the truth or falsehood of the received reports of her character. The court intends, also, to reflect upon the conduct of the accused in remaining quietly at anchor in the Bay of Corunna, while his enemy was parading about in neutral waters, flaunting his flags, etc., when, in the judgment of this court, it was his duty to have gone out with his two vessels in the same neutral waters, and there to have made observations of her qualities as to speed, rapidity of turning, etc., as well as to have made close inspection of all her vulnerable points. He would then, also, have been ready to avail himself of any opportunity that might have offered, had his enemy been disposed to have given him battle in the open sea. At all events, he could have kept her in sight and been satisfied as to her whereabouts. Neither does the court find it in evidence that he had formed with his consort any plan of attack should an action have occurred.

"And, therefore, the court doth adjudge him guilty in a degree of a charge preferred, and doth find him guilty of the charge in a less degree than charged.

"And the court doth award the following sentence, viz.: that the accused, Commodore Thomas T. Craven, be suspended from duty on leave pay for two years.

> "Vice-Admiral D. G. FARRAGUT, President.
> H. PAULDING, Rear-Admiral.
> C. H. DAVIS, Rear-Admiral.
> J. A. DAHLGREN, Rear-Admiral.
> T. TURNER, Commodore.
> JAS. S. PALMER, Commodore.
> JNO. A. WINSLOW, Commodore.
> S. P. LEE, Captain.
> MELANCTHON SMITH, Captain."

This record was returned by the Secretary of the Navy to the court for revision, on the ground that it was in conflict with law, and if approved would tend to render the provisions of law which the accused is charged with violating a "dead letter;" and, further, would leave it discretionary with courts to depart from the law in another respect by assuming, in fact, the power to mitigate punishments.

Thereupon the court revised its decision, and found "these specifications of the charge proven, except the words 'as it was his duty to have done,' and doth find the accused, Commodore Thomas T. Craven, of the charge guilty. And doth award the following punishment: That the accused, Commodore Thomas T. Craven, be suspended from duty for two years on leave pay."

The secretary was no better satisfied with this finding than the previous one, and he ordered the proceedings of the court set aside and the Commodore released from arrest. In assigning his reasons for this order, he said:

"The offence for which Commodore Craven was tried is one which the law, with a view no doubt to the protection of the public interests and national character in time of war, has included among those to which the penalty of death is attached.

"The same law has enjoined it upon courts-martial, 'in all cases of conviction, to adjudge a punishment adequate to the character and nature of the offence committed.' It leaves it discretionary with the court-martial to recommend the person convicted to clemency; this clemency, however, to be exercised, not by the court, but by the revising power or the President of the United States, who are expressly clothed with the power to mitigate or remit punishment.

"In all these provisions the law is clear, precise, and free from ambiguity. It can hardly require argument to make it plain that a punishment that would be deemed too mild for a trivial offence or misdemeanor—a nominal punishment—cannot be adequate punishment for an offence to which the law has attached the penalty of death.

"Yet the court, in this case of conviction of a capital offence, has adjudged a punishment which is obviously nothing more than a nominal punishment, if it be even as much. 'Suspension from duty for two years on leave pay' is, in itself, nothing more than leave of absence for the same period; and nothing is added to it to give it a semblance of real punishment, not even as much as a reprimand, severe or otherwise, public or private. Such punishment as this no officer could obtain from the department as a favor.

"The final proceedings of the court are inexplicable to the department. If, after finding the accused guilty of a capital offence, they had stated mitigating circumstances as a justification for awarding a light punishment, the department, while considering their course as erroneous and in violation of law, might still have perceived some indication of sufficient motive and consistent action. But instead of pointing to mitigating circumstances, they have prepared and left on record a statement that aggravated the circumstances.

"In this statement they censure the accused for 'his want of zeal and exertion in not making constant and personal observation of the rebel ram while at Ferrol, and thereby endeavoring to ascertain the truth or falsehood of the received reports of her character.'

"They reflect also upon 'the conduct of the accused in the Bay of Corunna while his enemy was parading about in neutral waters, flaunting his flag,' etc.

"And they say: 'Neither does the court find it in evidence that he had formed with his consort any plan of attack should an action have occurred.'

"Any one of the derelictions of duty here specified would deserve some greater punishment than a leave of absence for two years.

"If it was the duty of the accused to have encountered the *Stonewall*, and, through negligence or any other cause, he failed in any one particular to do his duty, then he did not do his utmost to capture or destroy the vessel, and is guilty of the charge preferred against him. The court have found him guilty of it; and, from the facts which they find proved, it appears that the accused, instead of failing merely in a single particular, failed in many respects—instead of doing his utmost, in fact did nothing—and was wholly and inexcusably derelict. He was therefore not only guilty of the charge, but guilty in the broadest sense, and such guilt called for adequate punishment.

"Such is the necessary inference from what the court finds proved. But this inference is destroyed, and the finding of guilty contradicted by what the court find not proved.

"They say they find the specifications of the charge proven, except the words 'as it was his duty to have done.' This exception destroys and annihilates the gravamen of the charge. The charge against the accused was, as required by law, specific. It was founded solely upon the assumption that it was the duty of the accused to encounter the *Stonewall* at the time and place specified. If, as the court state, it is not proved that it was his duty to encounter that vessel, then he is not proved guilty of the charge preferred against him, and the court have committed a grave error in finding him guilty of it.

"It is therefore impossible for the department to gather from the action of the court whether the accused is guilty or not. Their finding on the charge declares him guilty, but their finding on the specification, and the nominal punishment awarded, imply that they considered him not guilty. The incongruous whole has the aspect of an unsuccessful attempt at compromise between those members of the court who believed the accused guilty and others who believed him not guilty.

"The whole action of the court unfortunately suggests to officers of the navy an inference which the department, in behalf of the court, must strenuously disclaim, as not intended for them, or, at least, as not maturely considered. This inference is, that the general rule with a commanding officer of the navy should be: 'Do not fight if there is a chance of defeat,' rather than the converse rule: 'fight if there is a chance of victory.'

"The principle uniformly inculcated as a rule of naval action has been, that it is the first duty of a commander in war to take great risks for the accomplishment of great ends.

"The proceedings of the court are set aside, and Commodore Thomas T. Craven is hereby relieved from arrest."

GIDEON WELLES,
Secretary of the Navy.

APPENDIX C.

THE MINISTER OF JUSTICE TO THE AMERICAN MINISTER.

"Paris, *le 27 Juin*, 1887.

"*Monsieur*,—Par un office en date du 23 Mai dernier, vous avez bien voulu me faire savoir que M. John Bigelow, ancien Ministre des États-Unis désirerait, dans un intérêt purement historique, obtenir copie du dossier des poursuites qui auraient été tentées devant le tribunal de Nantes contre un Sr. Petermann, à l'occasion de la soustraction par celui-ci chez M. Voruz, constructeur, de diverses pièces rélatives à la commande de navires de guerre, pour le compte des Confédérés Américains.

"En réponse à cette communication, jai l'honneur de vous adresser sous ce pli une note émanant de M. le Ministre de la Justice et d'où il résulte, comme vous le verrez, qu'aucune poursuite n'a été intentée à Nantes et qu'aucune information n'a été ouverte par le parquet de cette ville contre le Sr. Petermann.

"Agréez les assurances de la haute considération avec laquelle jai l'honneur d'être Monsieur,

"Votre très humble et très obeissant servitem,

"Flourens.

"Monsieur MacLane,
"Minister des États-Unis, à Paris."

"Note.

"Il résulte des recherches faites par M. le Procureur-Général de Rennes qu'aucune poursuite n'a été intentée et qu'aucune information n'a été ouverte à Nantes contre le Sr. Petermann à l'occasion de la soustraction par celui-ci chez M. Voruz, constructeur, de diverses pièces relatives à la commande de navires de guerre pour le compte des Confédérés Americains.

"Au moment de la guerre de sécession, M. Voruz avait reçu

des États du Sud la commande de deux navires de guerre. Petermann qui etait employé de ce constructeur se laissa corrompre. Il détourna les traités passés entre les États du Sud et M. Voruz et les livra à prix d'argent.

"Le *Phare de la Loire*, publia ces traités, M. de Chasseloup-Loubat, alors Ministre de la Marine avertit M. Voruz que la livraison des navires entrainerait des difficultés. Un croiseur des États-Unis gardait en effet la sortie du port de Saint Nazaire.

"Les Confédérés du Sud prierent alors M. Voruz de vendre les navires, même à perte, pour regagner une partie de leurs avances. M. Voruz fût assez heureux pour les céder au Perou, et les navires furent livrés sans difficulté au gouvernment du Perou.

"Petermann n'a été poursuivi, M. Voruz n'a dailleurs pas porté plainte contre lui."

INDEX.

"ALABAMA," the commander of, prevented from declining with honor a combat in which his vessel was lost, 154.

Appendix A, No. 1. Memoire à Consulter, 199; No. 2. Consultation de M. Berryer, 217; B. Court-martial of Commodore Craven, 232; C. Letter from the Minister of Justice to the Hon. Robert M. McLane, 238.

Arman, ship-builder at Bordeaux, constructs vessels of war for Confederate States, 5; his amendment to emperor's address, 31; pretends to have sold the Confederate ships to foreign governments, 34, 49, 50; his amendment dropped *sub silentio*, 36; interviewed by Gueroult, 37; receives positive instructions from the emperor to sell the ships *bonâ fide*, 52; pretended sale of the *Stonewall* to Denmark, 65; his balance sheet, 102, 103, 195, 199, 211, 213, 223.

Armstrong, Sir W., to supply ordnance stores for Confederate ships, 15.

Arnous de Rivière, 210, 211.

Augerville, residence of Berryer, 20.

BALANCE SHEET, 102, 103.

Benjamin, J. P., doubts the good faith of "a high personage," 155; decides against selling any of the vessels in process of construction; sends treasury draft of £500 to Slidell for secret service, 156; reviews the conduct of the French government, accuses it of aiding the enemies of the Confederacy while profuse in expressions of sympathy for it, 161; contrasts the conduct of the English and French governments, 165; recommends a "reserved demeanor" towards the emperor, 165; letter to Slidell, 171; his indictment of the people of the Northern States; thinks that the universal massacre of the Southern people would make hundreds and thousands of the Northern people frantic with fiendish delight, 171; authorizes Slidell to bribe the emperor, 175–177; sends Jacob Thompson and Clement C. Clay on secret service, 188.

Berryer, Antoine Pierre, eminent barrister, 19; quotation from his address, 92; visited at Augerville, 20; his last appearance at the bar, 92, 93; death, 101; Consultation de, 217.

Biarritz, 191.

Bigelow, John, visit from Mr. X. and his disclosures, 1; letter to Seward, 39; verifies sale of Confederate steamers, 57; announces the escape of the *Stonewall* to the Minister of Foreign Affairs, 61; invites Minister of Foreign Affairs to instruct French ambassador at Madrid to detain the *Stonewall*, 62; requests Mr. Perry to urge Spanish government to detain the *Stonewall*, 70; letter to Commodore Craven, 72; notifies Minister of Foreign Affairs that the crew of the Confederate steamer *Florida* had been transferred to the *Stonewall*, 76; complains of the Franco-Austrian intervention in Mexico, 91; institutes suit in the French courts against Arman and others, 97.

Blakeley, Captain, a London manufacturer of ordnance, 6, 199, 201, 209 et seq.

Boudet, Minister of the Interior, interviews Gueroult *in re* publication of Berryer's consultation, 39.

Brassos, Santiago, cargoes of arms at, for the Confederacy seized by the French naval officers, 162.

Bullock, Captain J. D., agent of the navy department of the Confederate government in Europe, contracts for vessels of war with Arman and Voruz, 5; letter to Voruz, 6; denounces diplomatic agents of the United States government; contracts for ships in France at the instigation of the Imperial government, 43, 119; "secret service of the Confederate States," 14; agrees with Arman for a fictitious sale of vessels to Danish government, 49, 50; reports departure of *Stonewall* from Lisbon, 79; Commodore Craven's neglect to pursue the *Stonewall* "a good deal criticised," 80; his plans for dispersing the blockading fleet, 84; vessels seized by English government, 85; denounces the emperor for a breach of faith in refusing his ships exit under Confederate flag, 107; a short-sighted Sadducean, 189, 199, 201, 202, 205, 209, 213, 223 et seq.

Chasseloup-Loubat, letter to Minister of Foreign Affairs about escape of *Stonewall*, 67.

Clay, Clement C., sent on secret service, 188.

Cobden, Richard, letter to Mr. Bigelow, 33.

Confederate cotton loan, the market of, sustained, 187.

Confederate States of America, 2; naval operations terminated, 194.

Confederate war-ships, emperor informs Slidell that the destination of the vessels must be concealed, 137; two corvettes sold to the Prussian government, 159; Slidell advises against fitting out more ships of war in Europe, 160.

Cowley, Lord, declared his government had no official knowledge of the emperor's views on the subject of recognition, 111.

Craven, Commodore, 70; letter from Bigelow advising against lawless violence, 72; letter to Perry, 74; tempted to run the *Stonewall* down, 75; did not consider his force sufficient to justify the pursuit of the *Stonewall*; arrives at Corunna, 76, 77; his failure to fight the *Stonewall* criticised, 80; letter to Secretary of Navy giving reasons for not pursuing the *Stonewall*, 82; court-martial ordered, found not to have failed in his duty in not attacking the *Stonewall*, 232; renewed evidences of his government's confidence in him, 88; remains in active service until retired by age, 88; his death, 89.

Cuba, proposal to sell, to the United States, 191.

Dayton, Mr., United States Minister at Paris, submits proofs of Confederate ship-building in France to **French** government, 17; remonstrates at its continuance, 26; enters formal protest against facilities given to Confederate ship-building, 34; death, 56; did not employ spies, 169.

Declaration of neutrality, 20.

Department of the Marine (France) sanctions clandestine ship-building to assist the Confederates, 2, Appendix A.

Drouyn de Lhuys, French Minister for Foreign Affairs, 10; evasive answer to American minister's remonstrance, 62; letter to Mr. Bigelow declining responsibility for the escape of the *Stonewall;* encloses letter from Minister of Marine, 64; letter to, from Minister of Marine, about escape of *Stonewall*, 67; notified that *Florida's* crew had been shipped on board the *Stonewall*, 76; appointed Minister of Foreign Affairs, 112; first interview of Slidell with, 142, 143, 144; courteous but non-committal, 145; Slidell's second interview with, 148; says France should not be forced into a war by indirection, 148.

Dubigeon fils, 5, 205, 213 *et seq.*, Appendix A.

EMPEROR, the, of the French, Slidell's first interview with, 116; surprised that the Confederate troops had no coffee, 118; regretted having respected the blockade, 118; occupies a small house at Vichy, 120; receives Slidell's proposal to hire his fleet, 120; says the policy of nations is controlled by their interests and not by their sentiments, 122; considered the idea of supplanting American with Indian cotton chimerical, 122; prefers an armistice of six months to mediation; shows a letter from the King of Belgium urging the great powers to treat the separation of the Union as final and to stop the war, 128; suggests building the Confederate steamers as for the Italian government, 130; shows a letter from a New-Yorker, 130; authorizes Slidell to assure the Austrian ambassador that he will recognize the Confederates if Spain would take the initiative, 136; prefers English Whigs to English Tories, 136; insists that the destination of the Confederate ships must be concealed, 137; prevents Confederates establishing friendly relations with Maximilian, 162; willing to secure Arman a good contract, 165; disposed to protract war in America until Maximilian's supremacy was insured; hoped Arman's ships would get to sea before their destination was discovered, 165.

Erlanger & Co. guarantee pay for Confederate ships, 5; permitted to advertise cotton loan in Paris, 152; authorised by Slidell and Mason to sustain the market for Confederate cotton bonds, 175, 179, 187; invest $6,000,000 in "bulling" the market, 182; Mason's agreement with, for sustaining the market, 182, 187, 180; letter from Mason, 183, 199 *et seq.*

Eymand and Delphin, proposed consignees for the Confederate ships, 8.

FAVRE, JULES, retained as counsel for the United States in place of Berryer, deceased, in the suit against Arman and others, 101; appointed Minister of Foreign Affairs, 101.

Ferrol, the *Stonewall* arrives at, 77; *Niagara* and *Sacramento* arrive at, 78.

Florida, Confederate steamer, crew of, shipped on board *Stonewall*, 76.

France, post-office above suspicion, 173.
Fuller, David, United States messenger at Paris consulate, 1.

GUEROULT, editor of the *Opinion Nationale*, forbidden to publish Berryer's opinion, 28; interview with Arman and Rouher, charges them with conspiracy, 37, 38.
Gwin goes to Mexico to colonize Sonora; bears autograph letter from Louis Napoleon to Bazaine.

HALE, JOHN P., 192.

INFANTE of Spain, intriguing for a revolution, 191.

JOLLET ET BABIN, ship-builders at Nantes, construct vessels-of-war for the Confederates, 5, 205.
Juarez, treaty with the United States to enable him to carry on the war against France, 124.

LEON, EDWIN DE, sent to Europe as agent of the Confederate government with £25,000 to enlighten public opinion, 174.
Leopold, King of the Belgians, assents to Maximilian's aspirations, 23; autograph letter to the King of France urging the interference of the great powers to put an end to the war; thinks the reconstruction of the American Union hopeless, 128; hopes for success of French arms in Mexico, 130.
Leopold, Prince, 193.
Lindsay, M.P., Letter to, from New York, 130.

MALLORY, Secretary of Confederate Navy, decides against selling the Confederate ships building in France, 156.
Marine, department of, M. Chasseloup-Loubat sanctions clandestine ship-building for Confederates, 2.
Mason, John M., Confederate agent in London, 7; offers $10,000 to secure notes of Seward and Lincoln, 174; directs letters of Corwin to be secured, 174; authorizes Erlanger to sustain the market for Confederate cotton bonds, 178, 179, 180–187; invests $6,000,000 in "bulling" the market, 187; letter detailing his plans and success in "bulling" the market, 187; letter to Erlanger, 183; letter to Benjamin, 184.
Maury, M., contre-amiral des États Confédérés d'Amerique, 211.
Maximilian, archduke, accepts the crown of Mexico, 23; proposes to enter into friendly relations with Confederate government, 162; shot, 95.
Mazaline et Cie., 205.
McClellan, his letter accepting Democratic nomination for the Presidency, 141; greatly disappoints the emperor's hopes of peace, 141.
McLane, United States Minister at Paris, letter to, from the Minister of Justice, 98.
Mercier thought an offer of mediation would create additional exasperation, 115; considered the re-establishment of the Union impossible, 115.
Memoire à Consultér, 199.

Mexico, military organization of, by Prince Maximilian of Austria, 90; Maximilian shot, 95.
Minister of Justice, letter to the United States Minister in Paris, in reference to the prosecution of Petermann, 98.
Mocquard, private secretary of the emperor, reports that the emperor found more difficulties than he had anticipated about the Confederates building ships-of-war in France, 133.
Moltke, Count, Danish Minister, denies purchase of the *Stoerkodder* from Arman, 59.
Moreau, Henri, counsel for the United States, associated with M. Berryer, 92–101.
Mysterious visitor calls at United States Paris consulate, reports ship-building in France for the Confederates, 1, 190–193.

NEUTRALITY, French declaration of, published in *Moniteur*, 21.
Niagara, frigate, 70; arrives at Corunna, 77; joined by United States ship *Sacramento*, Spanish authorities uneasy, 77; and *Sacramento* follow *Stonewall* to Lisbon; unfitness for a conflict, 86; went out twice to give the *Stonewall* battle, 87; sold at auction and burned, 89.
Nicolay, John C., did not employ spies, 169.

ORDNANCE stores, plans, specifications, etc., for Confederate ships, 14.
Opinion Nationale, French republican journal, 28; *Les Corsairs du Sud* accuses the Imperial government and Arman of conspiracy, 37, 38.

PAGE, THOS. J., captain of *Stonewall*, 71; leaves for Madrid and Paris, 72; returns to Ferrol, 78; arrived at Nassau, 80; at Havana learns of General Lee's surrender, 80; negotiates with Cuban authorities for surrender of *Stonewall*, 80.
Perry, Chargé d'Affaires at Madrid, telegram from, announcing arrival of *Stonewall* at Ferrol in Spain, 62; receives letter from Commodore Craven; believes *Stonewall* not in a seaworthy condition, 74.
Perry, Mrs., accused of being a spy, 192.
Persigny asks for Slidell an interview with the emperor, 112.
Petit, Gaudet, et Cie., armor-plate makers, 14, 210.
Phare et Loire, French journal in which the contracts for ship-building were published, 99.
Plans, specifications, and ordnance stores for Confederate ships, 14.
Petermann, Voruz's absconding clerk, no prosecution instituted, 98, 99, 238.
Port Royal, Bullock plans an attack on, 79, 194.
Prim, General, Minister of War, wishes to sell the Antilles, 191; provokes insurrection in Spain, 193; prevails upon Prince Amadeus to accept the crown, 193; death, 193.

"RAPPAHANNOCK," her detention a precedent for the detention of the *Stonewall*, 63; reported unfitness for service, 154; detention of, 163.
Rivière, Arnous de, letter to Voruz, 211, 199, 213 *et seq.*
Roebuck, letters to W. S. Lindsay, 138.
Rouher, Minister of State for France, interviewed by Gueroult, 37.

"SACRAMENTO," the United States ship, arrives at Corunna, 77; anchors at Ferrol, 78; the *Niagara* and, follow the *Stonewall* to Lisbon, 79; her unavailable condition, 87.

Seward, W. H., Secretary of State, issues instructions for Mr. Dayton's guidance, 30; submits further instructions to Mr. Dayton, 34.

Slidell, John, Confederate commissioner at Paris, 7; accuses agents of the Washington government of theft and forgery, 96; seeks to identify one Petermann, an absconding clerk of Voruz, 97; obtains through intervention of Persigny an audience of the emperor at Vichy, 110; letter to Benjamin, 110; question of veracity between Lord Cowley and Thouvenel, 111; his opinion of English statesmen, 112; interview with Thouvenel, 114; hands him letter demanding recognition for Confederate States with a memorandum on blockade, 115; account of his first interview with the emperor, 116; proposes to give a thousand bales of cotton for the assistance of French fleet, 120; born in New York city, 123; second interview with the emperor, 126; would accept emperor as umpire between the belligerents, 128; letters to Benjamin, interview with Mocquard, 133; third interview with the emperor, 135; authorized to offer to guarantee Cuba to Spain, 136; reads Roebuck's letter to the emperor, 136; asks an interview for Roebuck and Lindsay, 136; letter to Benjamin; meets the emperor at the races, thanks him for admitting his son at St. Cyr, 139; McClellan's letter accepting the Democratic nomination for president dissipated his hopes of peace, 141; first interview with Drouyn de Lhuys, 142; assigns reasons for expecting a formal recognition of Confederate government, 143; reads to Drouyn de Lhuys a letter from a visitor to Lord Palmerston, 144; advises him of the cotton subsidy proposition which had been submitted to the emperor, 145; second interview with Drouyn de Lhuys, 148; informs him that the plan of building ships-of-war in France originated with the emperor, 148; third interview with Drouyn de Lhuys, 150; recommended to confer with him through a friend, 150; receives assurance from Rouher that the Confederate ships should be permitted to go to sea, 151; obtains permission to advertise cotton loan in Paris papers, 151; letter to Benjamin, 152; the building of the war steamers interfered with, 153; evidence of their ownership in the hands of Mr. Dayton, 153; suggests the completion of the ships, 155; Benjamin's reply, 155; approves of the contract with Arman, 157; letter to Benjamin, 159; advises against further attempts to fit out ships-of-war in Europe, 160; letters stolen from Captain Maury, 171; post-office in France above suspicion, 171; tries to bribe the emperor, 175–177; authorizes Erlanger et Cie. to sustain the market for Confederate bonds, 175, 179, 180–187, 199, 205, 213 *et seq.*

Specifications, plans, and ordnance stores for Confederates, 14.

Spence, Mason acting under his advice, some account of, 184.

Stoerkodder, afterwards the *Stonewall*, ship built by Arman for the Confederates, 57.

Stonewall, statement of American Minister regarding her escape, 61; arrival at Ferrol, 62; alleged sale of, to Denmark, 65; letter from Minister of Marine to Minister of Foreign Affairs about her escape, 67; at Corunna in a leaky condition, 71; goes to Ferrol for repairs, 71; Craven tempted to run her down, 75; her subsequent career recited by Captain Bullock, 76; arrives at Havana, 80; is surrendered to the Captain-General of Cuba, 81; delivered up to the United States, 81; sold by United States government to government of Japan, 81.

THOMPSON, JACOB, sent on secret service, 188.

Thouvenel, E., Minister of Foreign Affairs (France), 22; Slidell's unsatisfactory interview with, 110; resigns portfolio of Foreign Affairs, 111; his surprise at Lord Cowley's assertion, 111.

VORUZ, ainé, iron-founder and machinist at Nantes, also member of the Corps Législatif, 6, 201, 206.

Voruz, Anthony, 207, 199, 209, 213 *et seq.*

X, Mr., mysterious visitor reports ships building for Confederates at Bordeaux and Nantes, 1, 169; proposes the sale of all the Spanish Antilles to the United States, 191.

THE END.

SOME BOOKS FOR THE LIBRARY

PUBLISHED BY

HARPER & BROTHERS, FRANKLIN SQUARE, N. Y.

☞ HARPER & BROTHERS *will send any of the following works by mail, postage prepaid, to any part of the United States or Canada, on receipt of the price.*

☞ *For a full list of* HISTORICAL WORKS *published by* HARPER & BROTHERS, *see their New and Enlarged Catalogue, which will be sent to any address on receipt of ten cents.*

MACAULAY'S ENGLAND. The History of England from the Accession of James II. By THOMAS BABINGTON MACAULAY. New and Elegant Library Edition, from New Electrotype Plates. 8vo, Cloth, Paper Labels, Uncut Edges and Gilt Tops, Five Volumes in a Box, $10 00 per set; Sheep, $12 50; Half Calf, $21 25; 12mo, Cloth, 5 vols., $2 50; Sheep, $5 00; 8vo, Paper, 5 vols., $1 00. (*Sold only in Sets.*) 8vo, Cloth, in 1 vol., $1 25.

MACAULAY'S MISCELLANEOUS WORKS. The Miscellaneous works of Lord Macaulay. In Five Volumes, 8vo, Cloth, with Paper Labels and Uncut Edges, in a Box, $10 00; Sheep, $12 50; Half Calf, $21 25. (*Sold only in Sets.*)

HUME'S ENGLAND. History of England, from the Invasion of Julius Cæsar to the Abdication of James II., 1688. By DAVID HUME. New and Elegant Library Edition, from New Electrotype Plates. Six Volumes in a Box, 8vo, Cloth, with Paper Labels, Uncut Edges and Gilt Tops, $12 00; Sheep, $15 00; Half Calf, $25 50. 6 vols., 12mo, Cloth, $3 00; Sheep, $6 00. (*Sold only in Sets.*)

HILDRETH'S UNITED STATES. The History of the United States. *First Series.*—From the First Settlement of the Country to the Adoption of the Federal Constitution. *Second Series.*—From the Adoption of the Federal Constitution to the End of the Sixteenth Congress. By RICHARD HILDRETH. 6 vols., 8vo, Cloth, with Paper Labels, Uncut Edges and Gilt Tops, $12 00; Sheep, $15 00; Half Calf, $25 50. (*Sold only in Sets.*)

TILDEN'S WRITINGS AND SPEECHES. The Writings and Speeches of Samuel J. Tilden. Edited by JOHN BIGELOW. 2 vols., 8vo, Cloth, Uncut Edges and Gilt Tops, $6 00.

GIBBON'S ROME. The History of the Decline and Fall of the Roman Empire. By EDWARD GIBBON. With Notes by Dean MILMAN, M. GUIZOT, and Dr. WILLIAM SMITH. New Edition, from New Electrotype Plates. Six Volumes in a Box, 8vo, Cloth, with Paper Labels, Uncut Edges and Gilt Tops, $12 00; Sheep, $15 00; Half Calf, $25 50. 6 vols., 12mo, Cloth, $3 00; Sheep, $6 00. (*Sold only in Sets.*)

MOTLEY'S DUTCH REPUBLIC. The Rise of the Dutch Republic. A History. By JOHN LOTHROP MOTLEY, LL.D., D.C.L. With a Portrait of William of Orange. Three Volumes in a Box, 8vo, Cloth, with Paper Labels, Uncut Edges and Gilt Tops, $6 00; Sheep, $7 50; Half Calf, $12 75. (*Sold only in Sets.*)

MOTLEY'S UNITED NETHERLANDS. History of the United Netherlands, from the Death of William the Silent to the Twelve Years' Truce. With a full View of the English-Dutch Struggle against Spain, and of the Origin and Destruction of the Spanish Armada. By JOHN LOTHROP MOTLEY, LL.D., D.C.L. With Portraits. Four Volumes in a Box, 8vo, Cloth, with Paper Labels, Uncut Edges and Gilt Tops, $8 00; Sheep, $10 00; Half Calf, $17 00. (*Sold only in Sets.*)

MOTLEY'S JOHN OF BARNEVELD. Life and Death of John of Barneveld, Advocate of Holland. With a View of the Primary Causes and Movements of the "Thirty Years' War." By JOHN LOTHROP MOTLEY, LL.D., D.C.L. Illustrated. Two Volumes in a Box, 8vo, Cloth, with Paper Labels, Uncut Edges and Gilt Tops, $4 00; Sheep, $5 00; Half Calf, $8 50. (*Sold only in Sets.*)

ZOGBAUM'S HORSE, FOOT, AND DRAGOONS. Horse, Foot, and Dragoons. Sketches of Army Life at Home and Abroad. By RUFUS FAIRCHILD ZOGBAUM. With Illustrations by the Author. Square 8vo, Ornamental Cloth, $2 00.

GENERAL BEAUREGARD'S MILITARY OPERATIONS. The Military Operations of General Beauregard in the War between the States, 1861 to 1865; including a brief Personal Sketch and a Narrative of his Services in the War with Mexico, 1846–8. By ALFRED ROMAN, formerly Colonel of the 18th Louisiana Volunteers, afterwards Aide-de-Camp and Inspector-General on the Staff of General Beauregard. With Portraits, etc. 2 vols., 8vo, Cloth, $3 50; Sheep, $4 50; Half Morocco, $5 50; Full Morocco, $7 50. (*Sold exclusively by Subscription.*)

Some Books for the Library.

CURTIS'S LIFE OF JAMES BUCHANAN. Life of James Buchanan, fifteenth President of the United States. By GEORGE TICKNOR CURTIS. 2 vols., 8vo, Cloth, Uncut Edges and Gilt Tops, $6 00.

MEMOIRS OF GENERAL DIX. Compiled by his Son, MORGAN DIX. With Five Steel-plate Portraits. 2 vols., 8vo, Cloth, Uncut Edges and Gilt Tops, $5 00.

SHIPS OF WAR. Modern Ships of War. By Sir EDWARD J. REED, M.P., Late Chief Constructor of the British Navy, and EDWARD SIMPSON, Rear-Admiral U. S. N., Late President U. S. Naval Advisory Board. With Supplementary Chapters and Notes by J. D. JERROLD KELLEY, Lieutenant U. S. N. Illustrated. Square 8vo, Ornamental Cloth, $2 50.

LODGE'S ENGLISH COLONIES IN AMERICA. English Colonies in America. A Short History of the English Colonies in America. By HENRY CABOT LODGE. 8vo, Half Leather, $3 00.

HARPER'S POPULAR CYCLOPÆDIA OF UNITED STATES HISTORY.
From the Aboriginal Period to 1876. Containing Brief Sketches of Important Events and Conspicuous Actors. By BENSON J. LOSSING. Illustrated by Two Steel-plate Portraits and over 1000 Engravings. 2 vols., Royal 8vo, Cloth, $10 00; Sheep, $12 00; Half Morocco, $15 00. (*Sold by Subscription only.*)

PICTORIAL FIELD-BOOK OF THE REVOLUTION; or, Illustrations by Pen and Pencil of the History, Biography, Scenery, Relics, and Traditions of the War for Independence. By BENSON J. LOSSING. 2 vols., 8vo, Cloth, $14 00; Sheep, $15 00; Half Calf, $18 00.

PICTORIAL FIELD-BOOK OF THE WAR OF 1812; or, Illustrations by Pen and Pencil of the History, Biography, Scenery, Relics, and Traditions of the last War for American Independence. By BENSON J. LOSSING. With 882 Illustrations, engraved on wood by Lossing & Barritt, chiefly from Original Sketches by the Author. Complete in One Volume, 1084 pages, large 8vo. Price in Cloth, $7 00; Sheep, $8 50; Full Roan, $9 00; Half Calf, or Half Morocco extra, $10 00.

KINGLAKE'S CRIMEAN WAR. The Invasion of the Crimea: its Origin, and an Account of its Progress down to the Death of Lord Raglan. By A. W. KINGLAKE. Maps and Plans. 6 vols., 12mo, Cloth, $2 00 per vol.; Half Calf, $3 75.

GREEN'S HISTORY OF THE ENGLISH PEOPLE. History of the English People. By JOHN RICHARD GREEN, M.A. With Maps. In Four Volumes. 8vo, Cloth, $10 00 per vol.; Sheep, $12 00; Half Calf, $19 00.

GREEN'S SHORT HISTORY OF THE ENGLISH PEOPLE. A Short History of the English People. By JOHN RICHARD GREEN. With Maps and Tables. New and enlarged Edition, from New Electrotype Plates. Crown 8vo, Cloth. (*Just Ready.*)

GREEN'S MAKING OF ENGLAND. The Making of England. By JOHN RICHARD GREEN. With Maps. 8vo, Cloth, $2 50; Sheep, $3 00; Half Calf, $4 75.

GREEN'S CONQUEST OF ENGLAND. The Conquest of England. By JOHN RICHARD GREEN, M.A., LL.D. With Portrait and Colored Maps. 8vo, Cloth, $2 50; Sheep, $3 00; Half Calf, $4 75.

M'CARTHY'S HISTORY OF ENGLAND. A History of Our Own Times, from the Accession of Queen Victoria to the General Election of 1880. By JUSTIN M'CARTHY. 2 vols., 12mo, Cloth, $2 50.

DRAPER'S AMERICAN CIVIL WAR. History of the American Civil War. By JOHN W. DRAPER, M.D., LL.D. In Three Volumes. 8vo, Cloth, $10 50; Sheep, $12 00; Half Calf, $17 25.

ABBOTT'S FREDERICK THE GREAT. The History of Frederick the Second, called Frederick the Great. By JOHN S. C. ABBOTT. Illustrated. 8vo, Cloth, $5 00; Sheep, $5 50; Half Calf, $7 25.

ABBOTT'S FRENCH REVOLUTION. The French Revolution of 1789, as Viewed in the Light of Republican Institutions. By JOHN S. C. ABBOTT. 100 Illustrations. 8vo, Cloth, $5 00; Sheep, $5 50; Half Calf, $7 25.

ABBOTT'S NAPOLEON BONAPARTE. The History of Napoleon Bonaparte. By JOHN S. C. ABBOTT. With Maps, Illustrations, and Portraits on Steel. 2 vols., 8vo, Cloth, $10 00; Sheep, $11 00; Half Calf, $14 50.

ABBOTT'S NAPOLEON AT ST. HELENA. Napoleon at St. Helena; or, Interesting Anecdotes and Remarkable Conversations of the Emperor during the Five and a Half Years of his Captivity. Collected from the Memorials of Las Casas, O'Meara, Montholon, Antommarchi, and others. By JOHN S. C. ABBOTT. Illustrated. 8vo, Cloth, $5 00; Sheep, $5 50; Half Calf, $7 25.

www.ingramcontent.com/pod-product-compliance
Lightning Source LLC
Chambersburg PA
CBHW032143230426
43672CB00011B/2434